THE TACIT MODE

SUNY Series in
Constructive Postmodern Thought
David Ray Griffin, editor

THE TACIT MODE

Michael Polanyi's Postmodern Philosophy

JERRY H. GILL

STATE UNIVERSITY OF NEW YORK PRESS

Published by
State University of New York Press, Albany

For information, address the State University of New York Press,
State University Plaza, Albany, NY 12246

Production by Marilyn P. Semerad
Marketing by Fran Keneston

Library of Congress Cataloging-in-Publication Data

Gill, Jerry H.
    The tacit mode : Michael Polanyi's postmodern philosophy / Jerry
H. Gill.
       p. cm. — (SUNY series in constructive postmodern thought)
    Includes bibliographical references and index.
    ISBN 0-7914-4429-5 (hc : alk. paper). — ISBN 0-7914-4430-9 (pb :
alk. paper)
    1. Polanyi, Michael, 1891– . I. Title. II. Series.
B945.P584G55   2000
192—dc21   99-24066
                                           CIP

10 9 8 7 6 5 4 3 2 1

for John Fife and Rick Ufford-Chase
amigos, compadres, maestros

CONTENTS

Introduction to SUNY Series in Constructive Postmodern Thought

The rapid spread of the term *postmodern* in recent years witnesses to a growing dissatisfaction with modernity and to an increasing sense that the modern age not only had a beginning but can have an end as well. Whereas the word *modern* was almost always used until quite recently as a word of praise and as a synonym for *contemporary,* a growing sense is now evidenced that we can and should leave modernity behind—in fact, that we must if we are to avoid destroying ourselves and most of the life on our planet.

Modernity, rather than being regarded as the norm for human society toward which all history has been aiming and into which all societies should be ushered—forcibly if necessary—is instead increasingly seen as an aberration. A new respect for the wisdom of traditional societies is growing as we realize that they have endured for thousands of years and that, by contrast, the existence of modern civilization for even another century seems doubtful. Likewise, *modernism,* as a worldview is less and less seen as the Final Truth, in comparison with which all divergent worldviews are automatically regarded as "superstitious." The modern worldview is increasingly relativized to the status of one among many, useful for some purposes, inadequate for others.

Although there have been antimodern movements before, beginning perhaps near the outset of the nineteenth century with the Romanticists and

---

The present version of this introduction is slightly different from the first version, which was contained in the volumes that appeared prior to 2000.

the Luddites, the rapidity with which the term *postmodern* has become widespread in our time suggests that the antimodern sentiment is more extensive and intense than before, and also that it includes the sense that modernity can be successfully overcome only by going beyond it, not by attempting to return to a premodern form of existence. Insofar as a common element is found in the various ways in which the term is used, *postmodernism* refers to a diffuse sentiment rather than to any common set of doctrines—the sentiment that humanity can and must go beyond the modern.

Beyond connoting this sentiment, the term *postmodern* is used in a confusing variety of ways, some of them contradictory to others. In artistic and literary circles, for example, postmodernism shares in this general sentiment but also involves a specific reaction against "modernism" in the narrow sense of a movement in artistic-literary circles in the late nineteenth and early twentieth centuries. Postmodern architecture is very different from postmodern literary criticism. In some circles, the term *postmodern* is used in reference to that potpourri of ideas and systems sometimes called *new age metaphysics,* although many of these ideas and systems are more premodern than postmodern. Even in philosophical and theological circles, the term *postmodern* refers to two quite different positions, one of which is reflected in this series. Each position seeks to transcend both *modernism,* in the sense of the world that has developed out of the seventeenth-century Galilean-Cartesian-Baconian-Newtonian science, and *modernity,* in the sense of the world order that both conditioned and was conditioned by this worldview. But the two positions seek to transcend the modern in different ways.

Closely related to literary-artistic postmodernism is a philosophical postmodernism inspired variously by physicalism, Ludwig Wittgenstein, Martin Heidegger, a cluster of French thinkers—including Jacques Derrida, Michel Foucault, Gilles Deleuze, and Julia Kristeva—and certain features of American pragmatism.* By the use of terms that arise out of particular segments of this movement, it can be called *deconstructive, relativistic,* or *eliminative* postmodernism. It overcomes the modern worldview through an antiworldview,

---

* The fact that the thinkers and movements named here are said to have inspired the deconstructive type of postmodernism should not be taken, of course, to imply that they have nothing in common with constructive postmodernists. For example, Wittgenstein, Heidegger, Derrida, and Deleuze share many points and concerns with Alfred North Whitehead, the chief inspiration behind the present series. Furthermore, the actual positions of the founders of pragmatism, especially William James and Charles Peirce, are much closer to Whitehead's philosophical position—see the volume in this series entitled *The Founders of Constructive Postmodern Philosophy: Peirce, James, Bergson, Whitehead, and Hartshorne*—than they are to Richard Rorty's so-called neopragmatism, which reflects many ideas from Rorty's explicitly physicalistic period.

deconstructing or even entirely eliminating various concepts that have generally been thought necessary for a worldview, such as self, purpose, meaning,
a real world, givenness, reason, truth as correspondence, universally valid
norms, and divinity. While motivated by ethical and emancipatory concerns,
this type of postmodern thought tends to issue in relativism. Indeed, it seems
to many thinkers to imply nihilism.* It could, paradoxically, also be called
ultramodernism, in that its eliminations result from carrying certain modern
premises—such as the sensationist doctrine of perception, the mechanistic
doctrine of nature, and the resulting denial of divine presence in the world—
to their logical conclusions. Some critics see its deconstructions or eliminations as leading to self-referential inconsistencies, such as "performative self-
contradictions" between what is said and what is presupposed in the saying.

The postmodernism of this series can, by contrast, by called *revisionary, constructive,* or—perhaps best—*reconstructive.* It seeks to overcome the
modern worldview not by eliminating the possibility of worldviews (or
"metanarratives") as such, but by constructing a postmodern worldview through
a revision of modern premises and traditional concepts in the light of ines-
capable presuppositions of our various modes of practice. That is, it agrees
with deconstructive postmodernists that a massive deconstruction of many
received concepts is needed. But its deconstructive moment, carried out for
the sake of the presuppositions of practice, does not result in self-referential
inconsistency. It also is not so totalizing as to prevent *re*construction. The
reconstruction carried out by this type of postmodernism involves a new unity
of scientific, ethical, aesthetic, and religious intuitions (whereas post-structur-
alists tend to reject all such unitive projects as "totalizing modern
metanarratives"). While critical of many ideas often associated with modern
science, it rejects not science as such but only that *scientism* in which the data
of the modern natural sciences alone are allowed to contribute to the construction of our public worldview.

The reconstructive activity of this type of postmodern thought is not
limited to a revised worldview. It is equally concerned with a postmodern
world that will both support and be supported by the new worldview. A

---

*Peter Dews says that, although Derrida's early work was "driven by profound ethical impulses,"
its insistence that no concepts were immune to deconstruction "drove its own ethical presuppositions into a penumbra of inarticulacy" (*The Limits of Disenchantment: Essays on Contemporary European Culture* [London: New York: Verso, 1995], 5). In his more recent thought, Derrida
has declared an "emancipatory promise" and an "idea of justice" to be "irreducible to any
deconstruction." Although this "ethical turn" in deconstruction implies its pulling back from a
completely disenchanted universe, it also, Dews points out (6–7), implies the need to renounce
"the unconditionality of its own earlier dismantling of the unconditional."

postmodern world will involve postmodern persons, with a postmodern spirituality, on the one hand, and a postmodern society, ultimately a postmodern global order, on the other. Going beyond the modern world will involve transcending its individualism, anthropocentrism, patriarchy, economism, consumerism, nationalism, and militarism. Reconstructive postmodern thought provides support for the ethnic, ecological, feminist, peace, and other emancipatory movements of our time, while stressing that the inclusive emancipation must be from the destructive features of modernity itself. However, the term *postmodern,* by contrast with *premodern,* is here meant to emphasize that the modern world has produced unparalleled advances, as Critical Theorists have emphasized, which must not be devalued in a general revulsion against modernity's negative features.

From the point of view of deconstructive postmodernists, this reconstructive postmodernism will seem hopelessly wedded to outdated concepts, because it wishes to salvage a positive meaning not only for the notions of selfhood, historical meaning, reason, and truth as correspondence, which were central to modernity, but also for notions of divinity, cosmic meaning, and an enchanted nature, which were central to premodern modes of thought. From the point of view of its advocates, however, this revisionary postmodernism is not only more adequate to our experience but also more genuinely postmodern. It does not simply carry the premises of modernity through to their logical conclusions, but criticizes and revises those premises. By virtue of its return to organicism and its acceptance of nonsensory perception, it opens itself to the recovery of truths and values from various forms of premodern thought and practice that had been dogmatically rejected, or at least restricted to "practice," by modern thought. This reconstructive postmodernism involves a creative synthesis of modern and premodern truths and values.

This series does not seek to create a movement so much as to help shape and support an already existing movement convinced that modernity can and must be transcended. But in light of the fact that those antimodern movements that arose in the past failed to deflect or even retard the onslaught of modernity, what reasons are there for expecting the current movement to be more successful? First, the previous antimodern movements were primarily calls to return to a premodern form of life and thought rather than calls to advance, and the human spirit does not rally to calls to turn back. Second, the previous antimodern movements either rejected modern science, reduced it to a description of mere appearances, or assumed its adequacy in principle. They could, therefore, base their calls only on the negative social and spiritual effects of modernity. The current movement draws on natural science itself as a witness against the adequacy of the modern worldview. In the third place, the present movement has even more evidence than did previous movements of the ways in which modernity and its worldview are socially and spiritually destructive. The fourth and probably most decisive difference is that the present movement is based on the awareness that *the continuation of modernity threatens the very survival of life on our planet*. This awareness, combined with the growing knowledge of the interdependence of the modern worldview with the militarism, nuclearism, patriarchy, global apartheid, and ecological devastation of the modern world, is providing an unprecedented impetus for people to see the evidence for a postmodern worldview and to envisage postmodern ways of relating to each other, the rest of nature, and the cosmos as a whole. For these reasons, the failure of the previous antimodern movements says little about the possible success of the current movement.

Advocates of this movement do not hold the naively utopian belief that the success of this movement would bring about a global society of universal and lasting peace, harmony and happiness, in which all spiritual problems, social conflicts, ecological destruction, and hard choices would vanish. There is, after all, surely a deep truth in the testimony of the world's religions to the presence of a transcultural proclivity to evil deep within the human heart, which no new paradigm, combined with a new economic order, new child-rearing practices, or any other social arrangements, will suddenly eliminate. Furthermore, it has correctly been said that "life is robbery": a strong element of competition is inherent within finite existence, which no social-political-economic-ecological order can overcome. These two truths, especially when contemplated together, should caution us against unrealistic hopes.

No such appeal to "universal constants," however, should reconcile us to the present order, as if it were thereby uniquely legitimated. The human proclivity to evil in general, and to conflictual competition and ecological destruction in particular, can be greatly exacerbated or greatly mitigated by a world order and its worldview. Modernity exacerbates it about as much as imaginable. We can therefore envision, without being naively utopian, a far better world order, with a far less dangerous trajectory, than the one we now have.

This series, making no pretense of neutrality, is dedicated to the success of this movement toward a postmodern world.

David Ray Griffin
Series Editor

Introduction
Deconstructing Modernism

Perhaps it is safe to say that the terms *postmodern* and *deconstruction* have become the most important "buzz words" in intellectual circles over the past two decades. It is interesting to note that Michael Polanyi introduced the term *postcritical,* in the subtitle of his *magnum opus Personal Knowledge,* over forty years ago. Thus, well before contemporary thinkers became obsessed with dismantling the world view put in place by the great minds of the modern era, Polanyi had addressed the same issues, albeit from a decidedly different angle of approach. It is the purpose of this book to present and explore the main features of this distinctive angle of approach as it is expressed in Polanyi's major works.

Although the terms *postmodern* and *postcritical* are not synonymous, they both seek to express a dissatisfaction with the consequences, and thus the presuppositions, of the world view construction in Western thought after the dissolution of the Middle Ages. Both deconstructionists and Polanyi aim at getting free of the limitations and arrogance of modernism without returning to the authoritarianism of medieval times. Nevertheless, Polanyi and deconstructionists offer quite different diagnoses of what they take to be the problems *and* prescriptions as to what should be done about modernism. This difference can be captured in the distinction between the terms *deconstruction* and *reconstruction.* The latter term best describes Polanyi's angle of approach and will be the focus of the following explorations.

The actual foundation of modern thought was laid by the major thinkers of the sixteenth and seventeenth centuries, namely Rene Descartes, David Hume, and Immanuel Kant. These thinkers will be taken up in chapter 1. What is needed at this juncture is a brief tracing of the character of modernism as it took shape during the nineteenth and twentieth centuries, together with a brief account of how deconstructionist thinkers have sought to understand and overcome this perspective that has come to define the way we in the West understand understanding. After this orientation, we shall turn our attention to Polanyi's understanding of the basis of modern thought and to his proposal for getting beyond its debilitating dilemmas.

The nineteenth century began with and was dominated by a basic belief in the notion of progress, couples with a deep confidence in the ability of human thought to comprehend the essential structure and meaning of human existence and reality itself. This perspective was focused in a propelled by the philosophy of Georg Hegel, a philosophy that saw reality as fundamentally a matter of mind and ideas, on the one hand, and knowledge as a function of strict rationality, on the other hand. In this sense, it is possible to represent Hegel's thought as the crowning glory of pinnacle of Western intellectual achievement, as the quintessence of modernism. In Hegel's words, "[W]hat is real is rational and what is rational is real." This way of construing reality and knowledge left little room for doubt concerning the basis and nature of human cognition as defined by Western standards.

In addition to the idealistic and rationalistic flavor of Hegel's philosophy, there was a commitment to the inevitability of evolutionary of "dialectical" progress in human history as the Ideal and Absolute Spirit guiding the development of the cosmos makes itself concrete in world affairs. This dialectical pattern was said to govern the ongoing struggle between the ideas arising throughout the course of history, a struggle that follows a "thesis-antithesis-synthesis" dynamic. In the intellectual realm, this dialectic was seen as guaranteeing the achievement of truth, and in the sociopolitical realm it was supposed to underwrite the establishment of Western culture as the final expression of ultimate reality. The confidence, if not arrogance, of this version of modernism should be quite obvious. It is probably no accident that it went hand-in-hand with the imperialism that Western Europe and the United States foisted on most of the rest of the world during the last two centuries.

In many ways, the roots of the postmodern rebellion are to be found in the thought of various thinkers who sought to do battle with the sweeping dominance of Hegelean philosophy. Friedrich Nietzsche, Søren Kierkegaard, and Karl Marx, each in his own way strove to undermine both the idealism and the rationalism of Hegel's thought. The real impact of these philosophers was not felt until well into the twentieth century, and only recently have they been claimed as the progenitors of the postmodernist movement by many contemporary thinkers. A quick sketch of these three diverse points of view will prove helpful.

Kierkegaard's rejection of Hegel's rationalistic idealism focused on two main issues. The first was the assumption that objective knowledge of reality is possible within human existence. He stressed the limited character of our cognitive capacities and the vital role that must be played by volitional commitment in all human knowing. For Kierkegaard, all knowing begins with a personal or "subjective" act of faith, and in religious matters knowledge that goes beyond faith is simply out of the question. Kierkegaard's second focus was in fact the subtle identification of religion and philosophy that had taken place, both within Hegel's thought and in the surrounding culture. As Kierkegaard put it, "When everyone is a Christian, no one is a Christian." Faith has everything to do with spirituality and nothing whatsoever to do with philosophical abstractions. In this way, he sought to undermine the arrogance and absolutism of modern Western thought and culture.

Marx's rejection of Hegel's "idealistic dialectic" began with a reversal of its fundamental premise, namely the substitution of a materialistic substructure for the idealistic one. For Marx, all of human experience and culture is determined by the dynamics of the socio-economic processes that underlie them. Thus, he said, "I have stood Hegel on his head." Marx did accept the dialectical character of these socio-economic processes, and he traced the various stages thereof from tribal life through capitalism to what he called the "classless society" of communism. Although he rejected the arrogance of Hegel's version of "modernism," it is quite clear that Marxism itself embodies a similar vision since it not only accepts the notion of 'inevitable progress' but insists that it is grounded in objective scientific fact.

Nietzsche's attack on modernism was more similar to that of Kierkegaard than Marx. He was highly critical of the confidence placed in "objective" knowledge by scientists and philosophers alike, while stressing the absolute importance of individual creativity over both conformity and tradition. At the same time, however, Nietzsche did embody a commitment to the confidence in progress inherent within the evolutionary ideology of his time. In this way, his form of rebellion against modernism clearly parts company wit that of Kierkegaard. Nietzsche debunked the traditional morality of his day, urging individuals to define and express their own values. In so doing, he believed, humanity can transcend itself by giving rise to what he called the "Overman," a truly higher form of existence. Thus, he was partly postmodernist and partly modernist in his philosophy.

Despite the powerful character of these three visionaries, whose insights only came to fruition in the twentieth century, the nineteenth century concluded with strong confidence in human cognition and social progress. The philosophies of Henri Bergson, on the one hand, and Auguste Comte, on the other hand, surely can be said to have carried the day at the turn of the century. Bergson's theory of creative evolution, focused in the notion of 'elan vital', gave fuel to the idea of progress, even though his critique of scientific knowledge had a decidedly postmodern ring. Comte's "positivist" approach to knowing, which gave rise to the social sciences, clearly embodied the modernist confidence in rationality and progress. The nineteenth century, then, was both modernist and postmodernist.

The first three-quarters of the twentieth century were essentially characterized by a fundamental dichotomy between those thinkers who sought to *refine* the insights of modern philosophy and those who sought to *overthrow* them. The former are generally designated by the terms logical *positivism, logical empiricism,* or *analytic philosophy* and are represented by the like of Bertrand Russell, the early Ludwig Wittgenstein, and Rudolf Carnap. The latter are usually called "existentialist" or "phenomenological" thinkers and are represented by Jean-Paul Sartre, Martin Heidegger, Edmund Husserl, and Albert Camus. The influence of the former has extended to the social sciences in the work of B. F. Skinner and Noam Chomsky, who strongly disagree with each other while sharing a common commitment to the modernist vision of human rationality. The influence of the latter has been felt primarily in the arts and religion in the work of W. H. Auden, Paul Tillich, Ingmar Bergman, James Joyce, T. S. Elliot, Pablo Picasso, and Ivan Stravinsky.

The concern to refine modern philosophy took the form of restricting the definition of knowledge to include only those ideas and claims that can be grounded in sensory experience and tested by empirical methods. Thus, the so-called verifiability criterion of meaning and truth became the order of the day, and all religious, ethical, and aesthetic values were set aside as "noncognitive" and subjective. The distinction between fact and value was made absolute, and the claims of science and logic were deemed the sole source of knowledge about the natural and social worlds. Even history and literature came to be dominated by this emphasis on objectivity, resulting in what is known as "historicism" and "new criticism," respectively. Both movements, in their efforts to interpret their respective materials, sought to bracket out any and all factors that could in any way be considered valuational and/ or subjective so as to fulfill the modernist definition of knowledge.

The twentieth-century concern to overthrow modern philosophy was focused in an effort to refashion the definition of knowledge altogether. What these thinkers and artists did was to emphasize the personal, subjective aspect of human experience, following the lead of Kierkegaard and Bergson. Their point was to set aside the positivist or analytic understanding of "meaningfulness," which was limited to a concern with linguistic meaning, in favor of a more existential understanding, one that stresses the psychological and valuational aspects of life. Even though this redefinitional effort provided the roots of the postmodernist movement, it still is the case that in itself it remains very much a part of modernism because it reinforces the fact-value dichotomy.

Thus, both forms of twentieth-century philosophy, the empiricist and the existential, actually operate on a common modernist foundation, the one in a positive fashion and the other in a negative fashion. The current status of modernism can best be understood as the final result of the philosophy of Immanuel Kant, which will be taken up in some detail in the next chapter. Suffice it to say at this juncture that Kant's way of setting the limits of knowledge and establishing an absolute demarcation between science and religion, between pure and practical reason, has become the benchmark of the modernist perspective.

It is only against this background that one can begin to understand the deconstructionist dimension of the postmodernist movement, which has received its primary impetus from the thought of Jacques Derrida and Michel Foucault. They begin with the observation that all interpretive efforts, including those that seek to set the limits and goals of proper interpretation, are based in certain assumptions about the nature of human experience and cognitivity. Even rationalist attempts to provide an ultimate foundation for knowledge, such as those of Descartes and Kant, themselves employ the very criteria and logical methods that they seek to justify. An awareness of this basic fact establishes the permanent possibility of skepticism with regard to all human efforts to gain any unassailable knowledge.

However, deconstructive postmodernists part company with traditional skepticism by construing this lack of an ultimate ground for any and all knowledge claims and interpretive activity as an opportunity for free and creative exploration of meaning in general, as well as of the meaning of specific factual and/or interpretive claims. What they see is a newfound freedom to *de*construct the interpretive frameworks and cognitive hegemony so carefully *con*structed and shaped by Western philosophy over the last twenty-five hundred years. Even as Nietzsche and Dostoyevsky said that if God is dead, everything is permitted, so these thinkers are saying that since knowledge is a human invention, humans are free to redefine it continuously.

Derrida has developed this perspective along both philosophical and literary lines, insisting that meaning is always a matter of interpretation, and the results one gets are always dictated by where one starts and the road one takes. On this basis, he encourages us to consider hitherto unexplored interpretive possibilities in regard to nearly all the standard texts comprising the entire corpus of Western culture. Moreover, we are now said to be free to play with language, both written and spoken, by way of discovering fresh and interesting meanings hidden within the traditional structures of grammar and connotation in our discourses. Derrida's works are replete with deconstructive analyses of the standard texts of our cultural heritage, including poets, philosophers, and scientists.

Foucault, for his part, has developed this perspective along a more sociopolitical angle, stressing the fact that each and every point of view arises within a given context and is posited by certain persons who have specific goals in mind. Thus, there is a definite spin or twist that comes with and largely directs any given value proposal or cognitive claim. As Marx would have pointed out, those in power are the ones who dictate what gets done and said in every aspect of human life. History is controlled as well as written by the "winners." Foucault's analysis of the development and role of prisons in Western culture, for example, provides an excellent demonstration of his deconstructive perspective. Even justice, like meaning and knowledge, is subject to the sociopolitical dynamics that govern its definition and implementation.

The crucial element that defines the deconstructionist perspective on postmodernism is its positive attitude toward the persistent challenges of skepticism. The standard posture struck by thinkers who argue against the possibility of any objective knowledge is one of total relativism and despair over the negative character of their conclusions. Even David Hume expressed deep frustration over the results of his skeptical analysis of the basis of causal inference, concluding that knowledge as it is generally defined is not achievable. However, deconstructionists read this situation not as a dead-end, but as an opportunity, even a license for open-ended, free-lance interpretive possibilities. Meaning and truth—and even justice—are now viewed as entirely in the mind and/or mouth of the speaker.

The positive results of this way of viewing things are said to be the liberation of intellectual activity from the cognitive "imperialism" of Western culture and the stimulation of fresh, innovating thought. Every domain of intellectual endeavor, from philosophy and science, through art and literature, to politics and religion, is now free to explore and invent modes of thought and speech without the need to conform to the methods and criteria of traditional Western epistemological "absolutism." In this way, it can be said that the traditional intellectual edifices of Western thought can and should be *deconstructed* so that "modernism," as such, may be replaced by a "postmodernism," which will allow for far greater cognitive freedom and creativity.

It cannot be denied that this approach to the issues involved in these epistemological discussions performs an extremely useful service in pointing out the difficulties inherent in traditional Western understandings of cognitivity. Nevertheless, as a solution to these difficulties and dilemmas, deconstructionism leaves a great deal to be desired for two fundamental reasons. The first of these pertains to the limited positive results that can be said to have followed from its application in various disciplines, while the second and more crucial reason pertains to its failure to acknowledge the vicious character of its own circular reasoning. Since addressing the first reasons would consume a great deal of space and time without really speaking to the issues with which Michael Polanyi was concerned, I shall forego this option. Some treatment of the second reason is in order, however, since it leads directly into a consideration of Polanyi's thought.

The central difficulty with the deconstructionist approach to understanding meaning and knowledge is that if it really is the case that each and any interpretation of a given statement, text, or mode of behavior, including that of its author, is as valid as any other, then not only do these notions themselves lose all meaning, but so does the statement that this is the case. Derrida even denies that the speaker's intentional meaning has any priority. The proposition that all knowledge claims are relative must, of course apply to itself. So must the claim that any utterance can be understood to mean anything the hearer takes it to mean. Such affirmations undercut themselves even as they are affirmed. Indeed, they undercut meaningfulness itself.

The irony of the deconstructionist approach to postmodernism was clearly demonstrated a few years ago at an international conference attended by Derrida himself. A noted American philosopher delivered a paper in which he explored the implications of deconstructionism for theology. At the conclusion of the paper, Derrida protested that he had never intended for his ideas to have theological implications. Whereupon the person who had presented the paper replied, "So what?" Thus, it became clear that what statements mean is not an open question but is rather a function of the speaker's intentions in conjunction with certain social and linguistic conventions. None of us, including Derrida, can have it both ways.

In short, there are two kinds of circularity, the one vicious and the other benign. For example, the circularity involved in statements such as "This sentence is being used as an example," "It is reasonable to expect people to act reasonably," and "I am now speaking in English" is quite benign because it is simply an instance of itself. However, the circularity involved in statements such as "No one can understand this statement," "I do not exist," and "Any statement, including this one, can mean anything the hearer want it to" is vicious because it is self-stultifying—if it is taken seriously, it cannot be taken seriously. Clearly, the deconstructionist perspective engages in this latter form of circularity, and because of this it is difficult to take it seriously. Modernism deserves a better critique than this.

It is precisely at this juncture that Polanyi's version of postmodernism can be seen to be so very relevant and valuable. What he termed his "post-critical" philosophy also offers a negative analyses of the presuppositions of modern thought, but rather than *de*construct the intellectual achievements of the Western worldview, he preferred to *re*construct them by means of a recon-sideration of their actual meaning and implications. Polanyi was prepared to acknowledge the necessity of the circular character of all cognitive endeavor, but he sought to develop a circularity that is not vicious but benign. In this way, he was able to avoid both the arrogance of traditional epistemologies and the skepticism and/or relativism of approaches like deconstructionism.

Another way to put all this is to speak in terms of what is often called "foundationalism." Most philosophers in the West have tried to ground knowl-edge in or on some sort of foundation or bedrock, that will provide a basis for our confidence in human cognitive activity. The rationalists spoke of "self-evident" truths and the empiricists spoke of "primary sense data," while others talked of "intuition" or the "principles of commonsense." Decon-structionists have, along with many other contemporary philosophies, pretty much rendered such efforts nonviable. They then go on to deny any perma-nent grounding for meaning and knowledge whatsoever. Polanyi, too, struck a nonfoundationalist posture, but he continued to maintain that there is a viable grounding, albeit of a different sort, for human cognitive activity.

The sort of grounding for knowledge offered by Polanyi is best under-stood in terms of what might best be called the "tacit mode." It will, of course, be the burden of this present book to spell out in considerable detail just what this notion means and what it implies for the sorts of issues dis-cussed on the foregoing pages. It is sufficient to state at this point that Polanyi's proposal involves reconsidering the essential character of our human cogni-tive capacities and redefining the meaning and structure of meaning and knowing in accordance with this reconsideration. In brief, Polanyi believed that throughout its history Western philosophy has defined knowledge far too narrowly, thereby overlooking both its deep nature and its broader significance; it has almost completely ignored the tacit dimension or mode of all episte-mological endeavor.

On the basis of a distinction, though not a dichotomy, between *explicit* knowing, which can be articulated and demonstrated, and *tacit* knowing, in which we always know more than we can say or prove, Polanyi sought to shift the focus of epistemological concern from foundationalism to a more viable center without falling into skepticism or relativism. The notion of a center, or axis, of knowing is crucial to a fresh and productive approach to epistemology because it allows for knowing to be grounded or integrated without the necessity of an immovable foundation. One can always ask what it is that holds up any given foundation, *ad infinitum*. However, an axis needs no support or justification other than itself.

In this way, then, we can see that while Polanyi was critical of mod-ernist thought, his criticism was aimed at what might be termed the "cultic" distortion of the insights that gave rise to modernism by those who have developed it over the past three hundred years. Thus, in Polanyi's view modernism does not so much need to be set aside or gone beyond as it needs to be reformed or reconstructed. In particular, he was opposed to the foundationalist thrust of modernist efforts to establish knowledge in an absolutist manner. For, in Polanyi's view knowledge can be and is reliable without being static and impersonal.

One way to focus this distinction is to contrast Polanyi's approach to knowledge with that of Karl Popper's well-known essay "Epistemology without a Knowing Subject" (an address given in 1967 at the Third International Congress for Logic, Methodology, and Philosophy of Science). In this essay, Popper seeks to eliminate entirely the personal element in knowledge claims and to make all such claims wholly explicit in nature. Surely, this approach represents the ultimate extreme in the effort to interpret the modern understanding of knowledge.

However, Polanyi has sought to interpret or reinterpret the modern approach to knowledge by placing the epistemic process squarely within the context of the personal and social dimensions of human experience. It is his conviction that his not only renders our understanding of it more responsible and accurate, but renders it honest as well. Knowledge is, after all, a decidedly human enterprise, and we only lie to ourselves when we distort the modernist concern to define it by pretending that it can exist independently of humans.

Perhaps this is as good a place as any to offer a few words by way of introducing Michael Polanyi to those who may not be familiar with his life and work. Polanyi was born and educated in Hungary, receiving his medical degree from Budapest University in 1913. After a distinguished career as a theoretical chemist, in both Hungary and England, his scholarly interests turned to social philosophy and economics. After World War II. Polanyi moved more and more into the field of philosophy where he focused primarily, but by no means exclusively, on epistemological issues.

Polanyi's major books include *Personal Knowledge; The Tacit Dimension; Science, Faith and Society; Knowing and Being; The Study of Man;* and *Meaning* (with Harry Prosch.) Polanyi held academic positions at Manchester and Oxford Universities and visiting professorships at, among others, the University of Chicago, Yale, Stanford, and Duke University. Those who had the privilege of knowing Michael Polanyi personally were consistently enriched by his quiet, gentle manner and his genuine concern for people.

For several decades now Polanyi's insights into the basis and structure of knowledge have generated interest across a wide and diverse range of scholarship throughout the world. Philosophers in general and philosophers of science in particular have been joined by thinkers in fields such as political theory, social science, history, educational theory, theology, and literary criticism in an effort to grasp and explore the ramifications of his journey toward a postcritical understanding of the basis and structure of knowledge. Polanyi's work constitutes an authentic pivot point in contemporary philosophy.

The following presentation of the central features of Polanyi's reconstructive approach to postmodern philosophy will not aim at a step-by-step, chapter-by-chapter format. Rather, I shall treat the main emphases of Polanyi's thought around two major foci: locating a fresh axis (part 1) and tracing the patterns thereof (part 2). I begin by considering the basis of traditional modern philosophy as found in the work of Descartes, Hume, and Kant (chapter 1). After exploring Polanyi's analysis of the structure of experience (chapter 2), I shall take up his examination of the dynamics of knowing (chapter 3). Part 1 concludes with a comparison of Polanyi's *re*constructive postmodernism with that of the major *de*constructivists (chapter 4).

In part 2 the patterns or ramifications of Polanyi's perspective to be traced are those of science and political theory (chapter 5), language and education (chapter 6), and art and religion (chapter 7). Chapter 8 will trace the similarities and differences between the foregoing interpretation of Polanyis work and that of several other thinkers. The concluding chapter will seek to show in what ways this Polanyian approach to the shortcomings of modern thought serves to reconstruct it rather than merely deconstruct it.

A wise and knowledgeable person once said that in his estimation Polanyi's *Personal Knowledge* is the most important book written in the last four hundred years. This, of course, would take us back to Descartes's day and would include all of the thinkers who actually shaped the modern era. Whether or not one agrees with this person's judgment, it is highly appropriate that Polanyi's work be considered in relation to that of these thinkers since it aims to take us beyond them. Let us now see how this is to be done.

Part One

LOCATING THE AXIS

1

THE BASIS OF MODERN THOUGHT

Although nothing in history, especially in the history of thought, ever really begins at a specific point in time, it is fairly commonly agreed that the modern era began after 1500 A.D. The discovery of the New World, the reformation, the rise of science, and the free thinking introduced by the philosophers of the sixteenth and seventeenth centuries all coincided to form what we know as the modern sensibility. The intellectual dimension of the way the West has come to understand itself roughly began with the innovative insights of Rene Descartes, who is often referred to as the "Father of Modern Philosophy." Thus, it is appropriate the begin our consideration of what Polanyi calls "critical philosophy" with a brief account of his critique of Descartes's system of thought. Afterward, we shall complete our analysis of modernism in philosophy with a distinctively Polanyian treatment of the epistemologies of David Hume and Immanuel Kant.

DESCARTES'S RATIONALISM

Descartes was a brilliant mathematician, and thus it is no surprise to find that he, like Plato before him, sought to build his approach to knowledge on the same grounds as does mathematics, especially geometry. Drawing on the work of Euclid and Newton, Descartes argued that the only sure foundation for totally reliable knowledge, knowledge that provides certainty, would be self-evident axioms, that can be taken as intuitively true. As is well known, he sought to find such axioms by systematically doubting every form of knowledge that conceivably can be doubted. If there is some claim that cannot be doubted at the cost of self-contradiction, then it can be taken as a self-evident starting point in the search for other reliable true claims.

Thus Descartes' epistemological approach was founded on *intuition* in the mathematical sense of the term. He likened his methodology to that of Archimedes, who argued that if he could be given but one stable, immovable point in space, he would be able to move the earth using this point as his fulcrum. Descartes argued that if he could find one thing that is indubitably certain, he would be able to base all the rest of knowledge of it. Whatever forces itself on the mind "clearly" and "distinctly" in the *logical* sense of these terms will serve as a reliable source of knowledge. In Descartes's mind, such an indubitable foundation was absolutely necessary for knowledge, since for him knowledge had to be equated with rational *certainty* in the same way that it is in geometry.

After doubting any and all knowledge claims based on sense perception, since the senses often deceive us, Descartes even went so far as to doubt the principles of logic on the possibility that an evil demon exists who takes delight in deceiving us about what follows from what, rationally speaking. What he found he could *not* doubt, however, is the claim that he himself exists since even if an evil demon is deceiving him about everything else, he himself must exist in order to be deceived. Since doubting is a form of thinking, thinking necessarily *entails* existence. *Cogito ergo sum.* In this claim, then, Descartes concluded that he had found the ultimate intuitive foundation of all knowledge.

Once an absolutely certain point of departure had been located, Descartes was ready to embark on the search for other possible true knowledge claims. Here, again, he was committed to the methodology of geometry, which advances from its initial axioms to further theorems and postulates by means of pure *deduction.* Thus, only those propositions that can be logically deduced from the claim I think, therefore I am, could be certified as legitimate knowledge. Whatever was to be accepted as reliable knowledge, in the strictly logical sense, must be characterized by the same qualities of clarity and distinctness as is the original axiom. Here again we see Descartes's commitment to a definition of knowledge that equates it with absolute certainty. His reasoning up to this point is presented in the first two chapters of his *Meditations on First Philosophy.*

Shifting over to Descartes's companion volume, *Discourse on Method,* we find him spelling out exactly how this deductive procedure is to be applied in the search for reliable knowledge by providing four rules for governing how sound reasoning must proceed. Of course, the first rule is to be absolutely *certain* of one's beginning point; set aside all previous and/or merely probably claims to knowledge. The second rule is that of *division;* carefully analyze every idea and proposition into its smallest components so as to be able to discern clearly and distinctly what is claimed and what follows from what. Third is the rule of *order;* move carefully from one proposition to the next in logical order. The fourth rule is to *number* and continually *review* each step of the argument.

It is precisely this sort of "critical" posture that both defines modern philosophy and gives rise to various efforts to overcome it, such as those of the deconstructionists and that of Michael Polanyi. There are a number of unstated presuppositions at work in this methodology that both invest it with power *and* lead to irresolvable dilemmas. One such presupposition pertains to the nature of mathematical knowledge. Although in Descartes's day Euclid's axioms were thought to be the *only* axioms possible and to apply to the spatial world as it actually is. Over the last one hundred years, however, as a result of the invention of numerous non-Euclidian geometries and the work of Einstein, it had become apparent that deductive systems are strictly speaking a function of their original definitions and that any number of such systems can be devised, each true in the sense of being consistent with its initial definitions.

The epistemological result of these discoveries is that mathematical knowledge is essentially empty of factual truth about the world. Thus, the price to be paid for the sort of certainty that such systems provide is that they cannot be used to establish the truth of falsity of any proposition, except in relation to its consistency with the system's given definitions. Empirical, scientific knowledge about the world must begin with experiential data, and only then can reasoning move ahead by means of deductive inferences as to what follows from this data. So Descartes's efforts to based knowledge of the world on self-evident axioms of intuition was doomed from the outset.

Another way to put this difficulty is in terms of the impossibility of ever being able to establish the consistency of any given definitional system from within that system itself, something that Descartes clearly sought to do. As a result of the work of Kurt Godel, in what is termed "Godel's theorem," it is now clear that it is possible in any self-contained system to generate questions which cannot be answered within that system. Clearly, questions about how well the system as a whole matches up with the world outside of it are of this type. A system would have to be expanded to encompass such a question, but even though this can be done, the question can now be asked anew about the modified system. Trapped, as it were, inside of his own system, Descartes was unable to establish its applicability to reality.

Yet another presupposition of Descartes's approach to the knowledge question that continuously arises to haunt him pertains to the very possibility of systematic doubt. Is it actually possible, whether psychologically of philosophically, for a person to divest him- or herself of all previous beliefs and assumptions in order to begin the search for reliable knowledge? Clearly, this is highly doubtful. The whole idea of an absolutely fresh beginning point for cognitive activity is naive at best. Moreover, this presupposition flies directly in the face of the very meaning of the notion of doubt itself for doubt is something that arises when there is a *reason* for it. Cognitive activity cannot *begin* with doubt since first there has to be something to doubt. The concept of doubt is parasitic on knowledge.

In any case, once he had established the logical base for his project, Descartes moved ahead to see if it was possible to know anything more than his own existence. He reasoned that as long as there remained the possibility of an evil demon, who might still be able to deceive him about everything other than his own existence, he would not be able to advance his knowledge. So the next task was to prove the existence of a good, all-powerful God. This he did to his own satisfaction by means of various causal arguments (Meditation Three) together with "ontological argument" (Meditation Five). In essence, this latter "proof" argues that the very *idea* of perfection, which is the heart of the notion of God, logically entails existence since anything that did not exist would clearly not be perfect.

Many philosophers have pointed out that not only does it seem clear that this argument begs the very question that it is trying to prove, but Descartes's entire effort at this stage of his project is circular since he is *using* the very reasoning process he is seeking to legitimize by proving the existence of God in the first place. Space will not permit further discussion of the viability of Descartes's method. Suffice it to say that the difficulties in which he seems to become ensnared here serve to illustrate the types of deadends and convolutions that, according to the critics of modern philosophy, necessarily arise when one sets out to force human reason to conform to preestablished definitions and narrow, deductive techniques. The cognitive edifice constructed by modern, rationalistic thought is too confining.

Once he had established the goodness and power of God to his own satisfaction, Descartes turned his attention to the question of what else could be known in addition to his own existence and that of God. He moved rather quickly to accept whatever pressed itself upon him "clearly and distinctly" since an all-powerful, good God would not allow him to be deceived about such basic things. So he concluded that material bodies, including his own, can be known to be real. Thus, the existence of pretty much everything that he at first had to doubt could now be cognitively ratified. In short, what it took the God of the first chapter of Genesis six days to accomplish, Descartes managed to perform in a five-day sequence of meditations, after having devoted the first of his six meditations to questioning whether the world could be known at all.

One of the most interesting and important aspects of Descartes's expression of modern philosophy is his treatment of the relation between mind and body. In Meditation Two, where he discovered his pivotal proof of his own existence, he had concluded that since this proof was based on the thinking process, all that he could initially know about himself was that he is a *thinking* thing, a mind. The proof of his own physical existence was not possible until much later, after he had established the existence of God, and so on. Thus, it was necessary to conclude that mind and body are essentially quite different types of reality. While minds and ideas do not take up space and cannot be subdivided, all physical objects do occupy space and can be further divided.

This move, which seems to be necessitated by his line of reasoning, leaves Descartes in an extremely awkward position. On the one hand, he deserves credit for insisting on the reality of both mind and body, even though material reality is given a sort of second-class citizenship. On the other hand, however, he is now in the difficult position of not being able to explain how mind and body are connected since they have been defined as essentially different types of reality. How do thoughts affect bodies if the former have no physical reality? In short, once one has separated mind and body as thoroughly as Descartes has there is no way to explain their interaction, even though it is perfectly clear from everyday experience that they do in fact affect each other.

To be fair to Descartes, it must be admitted that there is no way, simple or even complex, to account fully for the relation between mind and body. Brain physiologists can trace impulses to certain areas of the brain, they can stimulate different parts of it and get certain results, and they can study the diverse functions of the two hemispheres, but none of this explains the point of connection between two seemingly distinct kinds of reality, namely mind and body. To be perfectly honest, no one can fully explain how it is that we can wiggle our index finger when we decide to and can refrain from doing so even though we are thinking about wiggling it. Philosophers have done little better in their efforts to resolve this dilemma.

Other modern philosophers have, to be sure, devised ways of treating this issue that are quite distinct from that of Descartes. The materialist tradition, which began in ancient times, begins by defining mind as simply a function of matter, an epiphenomenon that has no reality in and of itself apart from the body, especially the brain. The idealist tradition, which also stems from ancient times, takes the opposite tack and defines matter as simply a reflection of ideas. Thus, body turns out to be a function of mind. Pantheists, such as Spinoza, maintain that mind and body, like the rest of the cosmos, are simply dual aspects of a single, all-encompassing reality. The difficulty is that none of these "solutions" to the mind-body problem have proven to be especially convincing to very many thinkers. This dilemma represents yet one more indication of the inept character of modern thought in general.

While this is not the place to attempt to provide a final answer to the dualism and reductionisms that plague modern philosophy with respect to the mind-body relationship, perhaps a hint or two as to where to begin may be in order. It might prove fruitful to *begin* by affirming the ontological priority of relationality over both matter and mind. Once we have divided reality up into different kinds of entities and given them preferential existence, it becomes difficult, if not impossible, to connect them. Rather than thinking of relationships among entities as accidental and/or optional, it is more helpful to think of relationality as essentially real and entities as a function thereof.

Two thinkers who have developed approaches that are in accord with the above suggestion, albeit from quite different initial postures, are Peter Strawson and Alfred North Whitehead. Strawson, in his book *Individuals,* argues that it high time we simply acknowledge human beings to be at bottom creatures that are characterized by two integrated, nonreducible qualities, namely the physical and the mental. We must begin by affirming the bipolar, symbiotic nature of reality, as mysterious as this may be, and stop insisting that every aspect of it must be reduced to one main aspect. Stawson argues that the concept of persons is "logically primitive" rather than being derivative from mind or body.

Whitehead, for his part, accused modern philosophers of committing the "fallacy of misplaced concreteness" when they seek to define reality in terms of either mind or body alone. Like Spinoza, Whitehead saw these two basic aspects as dynamic, symbiotic outworkings of the relational, interactive *process* within which they arise, rather than as qualities of a single unified being. Thus, for Whitehead all reality is bipolar in structure, and the mind-body "problem" ceases to be a problem. As we shall see, while Polanyi did not approach this difficulty in the same way as Strawson or Whitehead, he did seek to begin by acknowledging the bipolar character of human existence, knowing, and reality, Moreover, he also negated the tendency of modern philosophy to ignore the role of the body in cognition.

THE HUME'S EMPIRICISM

The other major dimension of modern philosophy is that of empiricism. The first clear-cut practitioner of this mode of thought was John Locke, but the most consistent and influential representative was David Hume. Empiricism, like rationalism, embodies a foundationalist approach to questions of epistemology in that it seeks to begin with a rock-bottom analysis of human cognitive experience upon which to construct the structure of knowledge. The basis of all human knowing, according to the empiricist, is *sensory experience,* the data of empirical input into the mind. The key idea here is that of the mind being empty, like a blank slate, of any and all informational content when it first arrives in the world.

The empiricist beginning point, then, is to provide an analysis of the process by means of which sensory experience conveys information about the world to the mind. In addition, the empiricist employs sensory experience as the test of whether or not a given idea or knowledge claim is reliable. If they cannot be traced back to some basis in sensory input, such ideas and claims are merely the creation of the imagination. It becomes extremely important, then, for the empiricist understanding of knowledge to be able to identify the initial building blocks of sensation and to follow their development throughout the intricacies of complex knowledge. A brief summary of empiricist psychology will be helpful here.

In section 2 of his *Enquiry concerning Human Knowledge,* Hume discusses the "Origin of Ideas." Borrowing the basic structure of his analysis, while altering the terminology, from Locke's earlier efforts, Hume divided the "perceptions" of the mind into two classes, ideas and impressions. The latter are said to come directly into the mind through the senses, while the former are formed in the mind by these impressions and remain as their representatives. The data of thought, then, are supplied by the senses in the form of "impressions," and the memory they leave in the mind are what Hume calls "ideas." He says that impressions are much more "vivid and lively" than their corresponding ideas and that either of these can be and generally are combined in complex and diverse patterns.

In addition, impressions, which form the basis of all knowledge, are of two distinct kinds or come from two quite different sources. There are those that come *directly* through the senses, called "sensations," and there are those that are *derived* from reflecting on the processes of the mind as it organizes these sensations, called "reflections." These organizational principles and activities of the mind Hume calls the "Association of Ideas," and he designates three: "Resemblance, Contiguity in time and space, and Cause and Effect. By means of these principles of association, the mind processes and organizes the sensory and reflective data provided by experience, depositing them in the memory. From this memory bank, the imagination can create fresh combinations, but the results are not to be confused with knowledge.

Up to this point, Hume can be said to have followed the empiricist philosophy in orthodox fashion. He accepted the grounding of all knowledge in sensory experience and the use of such experience as the test of every knowledge claim. He was adamantly opposed to the possibility of there being any sort of "innate ideas" already present in the mind at the outset of experience. The empiricists all rejected any rationalist claims, such as those of Descartes, Spinoza, and Leibniz, to certain a priori concepts and/or axioms contributing to the formation of experience and knowledge. The exact standing of the principles of association in relation to the possibility of such a priori factors has never been entirely clear in empiricist thought, but this is not the time or place to go into a detailed discussion of the issue.

After having established this seemingly solid basis for empiricist epistemology, Hume began to have second thoughts. In particular, he began to raise deep questions about the associative principle of cause and effect. It seemed clear to him that this principle serves as the lynch-pin of the entire knowing process since being able to anticipate future experience on the basis of prior experience, the very definition of knowledge, absolutely depends on being able to establish causal connections between events. Without such connections, we would simply bounce from one thing to another, unable to determine what might be coming up next. However, Hume was not so sure that the notion of causation can be found to have any rational foundation.

Early on, Hume had introduced a distinction between two kinds of kinds of knowledge claims, namely those that pertain to matters of fact and those that pertain to the relations between ideas or concepts. Roughly, this is the difference between empirical or scientific claims and those of logic. When it came to searching for the foundation of the notion of causation, then, it was only natural that he would seek to ground cause and effect in one or both of these types of knowing. The empirical or experiential knowledge claims are generally said to yield "a posteriori" knowledge and the ones involving conceptual definitions, or logical relations are said to yield "a priori" knowledge.

So, when he turned to the task of finding a rational basis for causal judgments, Hume asked if such judgments are grounded in or arise from perceptual experience, from empirical sensation. Try as he might, he could not establish such a basis for the simple reason that we do not, in fact, ever *actually* see, hear, or touch causes. What happens, according to Hume, is that when we are repeatedly confronted with the "constant conjunction" between event A and event B, we fill in the gap, as it were, between them by positing or inferring their connection. Clearly, causes have no color, no weight, no solidity in and of themselves, so they are not experienced per se by sensation. The fact of the matter is, according to Hume, we are *conditioned,* much like Pavlov's dog, by our repeated exposure to this conjunction of events to expect a B every time we are confronted with an A. However, expectation is not a matter of empirical experience.

Next, Hume asked if causality could possibly be a matter of *logical* necessity entailed by the very definitions of events A and B. Perhaps there is a "necessary connection" between the ideas involved in the two events such that the latter is required by the former. However, a closer look at this possibility makes it clear that this is not the case. There is no *necessary* connection between throwing a rock at a window and the window breaking, for example. It is not logically contradictory that the window might do something entirely different when struck by the rock. Although such an occurrence would be extraordinary, to say the least, there is nothing in the very *idea* of rocks hitting glass that requires them to break. As Hume said, this expectation is established through what we today would call "operant conditioning," but this connection is neither empirical nor logical in nature.

Finally, Hume noted that it is tempting to attempt to provide a rational ground for causality by means of the pragmatic appeal that making such judgments about the future on the basis of previous experience has always worked in the past, so it makes sense to trust this process in the future. However, he made it abundantly clear that this move will not work because it actually begs the question at issue. For it once again relies on past experience for predicting the future. There simply is, according to Hume's analysis, no perceptual or logical reason for *assuming* that the world will continue to behave as it has in the past. Assumptions about the "uniformity of nature" have no rational foundation.

A great many criticisms can and have been raised by other modern philosophers about Hume's analysis of the foundations of knowledge. To begin with, there is something suspicious about the effort of empiricist thinkers to break experience up into its so-called smallest basic elements. The fact of the matter is that neither perceptual nor reflective experience comes to us in simple, independent units which can be said to constitute the building blocks of thought. The atomistic character of Hume's assumptions about the nature of sensory perception and analytic thinking have been controverted by both the findings of Gestalt or "holistic" psychologists and the explorations of phenomenological philosophers. Human cognition cannot be understood by means of an approach that begins by dividing experience up into isolated items or data since such an analysis betrays the structure of experience itself.

That this is so becomes painfully clear when we consider Hume's efforts to locate the datum of causation in sense perception. He speaks of events, like A and B, as if they exist and show up on some sort of mental screen as isolated entities. In addition to separating the sensory qualities of any object of experience, such as color and shape, from one another in analytic fashion, as if they could actually be known in this manner, Hume expected to be able to identify and isolate a perceptual item which could be labeled "cause." Whatever it might turn out to be, it should be clear from the outset that the notion of causation does not derive from sensation.

A similar line of criticism can be followed with respect to Hume's attempt to see if causal judgments can be grounded in logical necessity. After having completely separated logic from factual experience, rendering it empty of any connection with the way the world is, it is hardly surprising that Hume was unable to find any necessary relation between the events comprising our experience of the world. If the order of things as we encounter and interact with them is assumed to be completely arbitrary and disconnected at the outset, and each and every relationship must be justified independently of the others as one goes along, it is clear that all is lost before we begin. One is reminded of Kierkegaard's insight that teaching someone to understand by first teaching them to doubt makes about as much sense as trying to teach someone to stand up straight by first getting him or her to lie down in a heap.

Another way to put all this is to point out that every attempt to explain one thing on the basis of another is doomed to failure from the beginning since either one becomes engaged in an infinite regress and can never really begin at all, or one is forced to bring the process to an end at some seemingly arbitrary point. Reductionism in any form is doomed from the outset. As Wittgenstein reminded us, explanations must come to an end, otherwise they would not be explanations. Following another of Wittgenstein's words to the wise, what is needed at this point is the willingness to begin at the beginning and stop trying to go further back. Polanyi's concept of tacit knowing will prove to be of great help in showing how this way of beginning can be achieved.

Similar difficulties arise when one examines Hume's criticism of the assumption that the future will be like the past. His way of setting the issue up forces him to take one of two options: either one despairs entirely of ever finding a rational basis for knowledge, which results in skepticism, or one falls back on simple pragmatic justification alone, which provides no rational foundation whatsoever. Either way, Hume's approach places itself in a no-win situation. The chief problem with this way of coming at the whole matter is that it *begins* by requiring that every belief, including presuppositions, must be justified in terms of another. Hume defined rational warrant in such a way that he systematically eliminates the possibility of fulfilling it. No wonder he ended up confused and disillusioned.

The lesson to be learned from these considerations is that whenever one's angle of approach leads to a choice between two dead-end alternatives, it is time to reconsider the original point of departure. In his own day, Thomas Reid, whom Hume ridiculed, tried to point out this line of thought to Hume, but to no avail. Reid, in essence, argued that the principle of inductive inference, which serves as the fulcrum for all knowing, neither can be nor needs to be justified. It simply is one of the principles by means of which human life is governed. Contemporary thinkers, such as Wittgenstein, wonder what one means by the term *grounds* when asking how the past can serve as grounds for beliefs about the future. If the past does not constitute 'grounds' in such cases, what would? Hume boxed himself in by defining rationality too narrowly.

Here again we see the commitment to foundationalism that characterizes what is called "modern philosophy." It is assumed at the outset that every aspect of and step in the rational process must and can be articulated in terms of another until one reaches a point of bedrock. If we cannot find such a point, then the whole chain of reasoning comes to naught. Both rationalists and empiricists were confident that they found this bedrock, in intuition and deduction and sensory perception, respectively. This confidence leads, in the view of postmodern thinkers, to unfounded arrogance. Hume, to be sure, undermined this confidence with his skeptical analysis, thereby setting the stage for both Kant and the postmodern movement.

Before moving on to a consideration of both Kant and various postmodern thinkers, including Polanyi, it will prove worthwhile to tabulate the sorts of dilemmas that Hume was led into by virtue of his empiricist and skeptical posture. In addition to being unable to find a rational basis for the idea of causation in either sensation or logic, he was unable to find any grounding for the ideas of the self, other persons, and God. The entities represented by these concepts can be neither sensed nor defined as existing. Thus, he concluded that they are bogus notions that have no bearing on cognitive experience. Such skepticism may well be the logical outcome of a rigorous application of the empiricist approach to epistemology. Hume was thus able to "save" religious belief from rational criticism by placing it outside of the cognitive realm altogether.

In some ways, these negative conclusions to which Hume came as a result of his investigations epitomize the serious limitations of modern thought as seen from a postmodernist point of view. In addition to the ironic, if not downright contradictory character of a full-scale demolition of the possibility of rational processes being offered in terms of an extremely articulate, rational argument in Hume's work, there is the highly embarrassing fact that this work was written so that other thinkers might be convinced by the arguments therein, even though one of the conclusions was that there is no rational basis for the idea of other persons in the first place. These paradoxes are not just "cute" sidelights to the history of philosophy. They belie its claims.

By far the most excruciating paradox of all is that produced by Hume's serious but futile effort to locate any logical or experiential grounding for the idea of the self, including his own. In essence, he says, "I look and I look, but I fail to find a self, only a continuous flow of data." What is actually pathetic here is his complete failure to notice his own *necessary* employment of the very notion that he claims has no basis in experience. One is reminded of Descartes's starting right out with the idea of his own selfhood, even *before* having proven its rationality, when he reasoned "I think, therefore I am." It is, of course, quite rational and necessary to function this way; the difficulty lies in being able to explain the nature of this cognitive necessity. We shall return to this issue in chapter 2.

KANT'S TRANSCENDENTALISM

It is generally understood that Immanuel Kant developed his approach to modern philosophy in an attempt to provide a *synthesis* of both rationalism, in which he had been trained, and the empiricist skepticism of Hume, who awoke him from his "dogmatic slumber." Kant began by acknowledging that Hume was absolutely correct in claiming that all knowledge *arises* from experience; but he went on to insist that this does not entail that all knowledge is *derived* from experience. On the contrary, Kant maintained that while the content of knowledge is supplied by sensation, the structure of knowledge is provided by the formal character of the bond.

In this way, rationalism can be seen as correct in stressing the role played by the mind as the source and test of knowledge but as incorrect in assuming that the mind contains ideas or principles that constitute the material make-up of knowing. Likewise, empiricism is on the right track in emphasizing the part played by sensation, but errs in claiming that it is sufficient to account for knowledge in and of itself. It is clear, according to Kant, that sensory perception and the structure of the mind must work together in forming human cognition. As he said, "Concepts without percepts are empty and percepts without concepts are blind." By thus shifting the focus of knowing from passive perceptual input alone to the activity of the mind, Kant claimed to have established a "Copernican revolution" in epistemological thought.

Kant argued, in his famous *Critique of Pure Reason,* that by separating out the content of experience, the data of sensation, we can, by the process of elimination, discover the formal structure or "categories" of the mind that shape cognitive activity. He called this process a "transcendental dialectic" since it provides us with an understanding of the workings of the mind without claiming to stand outside of the mind itself. In "backing into" the formal structure of the mind by first subtracting out the content thereof, we allow the categories that constitute the very conditions of knowledge to reveal themselves. This approach was thought by Kant to be far more humble than that of traditional rationalism and far more positive than skeptical empiricism.

In general, Kant claimed that the formal character of the mind is focused in concepts such as space, time, and, of course, causation. When we analyze our experience, he reasoned, it is clear that we never have sensory data of these concepts. We cannot see or touch them, as Hume noted, yet they are a crucial aspect of all our cognitive activity. Thus, it is only reasonable to conclude that such notions are grounded in the very structure of the mind itself. Even though we do not know what the content of experience will be in the future, we do know that it will be structured according to the categories of space, time, causation, and so on. In this way, we can deduce the nature and basis of human understanding from the inside, as it were, "transcendentally" rather than claiming to do so from the outside, "transcendently."

Kant's way of putting all this centered in the usual distinctions between *a priori* and *a posteriori* knowledge, on the one hand, and between *analytic* or logical propositions and *synthetic* or empirical propositions, on the other hand. Hume had claimed that while a priori knowledge provides certainty, it does so at the cost of being empty of information about the world because it must be expressed in analytic propositions; likewise, he maintained that a posteriori knowledge, which does offer factual information, always must be expressed in synthetic propositions. Thus, we can only be certain about the claims of logic, which are essentially a matter of definitions and consistency, while we can only obtain knowledge about the world through science, which only gives us various degrees of probability.

Moreover, Kant claimed that the knowledge derived from the categories of the understanding, while being a priori in character, since it is actually known before, or independently of experience, is also synthetic or factual because it does provide knowledge about the world. In this way, he claimed to have established the possibility and actuality of "a priori synthetic" knowledge that in effect guarantees predictability about future experience for claims that are based in the categories of the understanding. Kant offered the propositions of mathematics as examples of this type of knowledge. Arithmetic, being based on sequential understanding, is grounded in time, while geometry is clearly based on spatiality. Thus, these prepositions are both known to be true independently of experience and to tell us things about the world.

The possibility of knowledge in the realm of natural science was, of course, Kant's main concern because this is what Hume had denied. In Kant's view, the concept of 'causation' is grounded in the categorical structure of the mind, and thus it is not surprising that Hume was not able to uncover it by means of empirical analysis. This special grounding renders the concept capable of serving as the basis of scientific knowledge since it establishes its a priori character at the same time that it offers factual information about future experience. Although we never know the content of our future experience, as Hume so deftly pointed out, we do know that it will take place within the causal nexus provided by the structure of the mind. This is all that is necessary for science to function as a legitimate cognitive enterprise, and thus Hume's objections to the inductive process have, in Kant's view, been overcome.

Whereas Hume had maintained that attempting to ground causal judgment in the inability of the mind to function without it was not rationally justifiable, Kant argued that the inevitability of causality as a precondition of all knowing necessarily renders it rationally justifiable. What could it mean for an activity to be rational other than that it is what makes cognition possible? Hume insisted that all rationality must be based in sense perception and then was surprised not to find the notion of causation there. However, Kant posited causality as an inextricable quality and condition of the very act of reasoning itself.

While disagreeing with Hume about the rationality of science, Kant agreed with him on the application of the reasoning process to matters having to do with any supposed reality beyond the natural realm. In short, they both rejected the possibility of providing any sort of rational basis for metaphysical, aesthetic, and moral endeavors. It is built right into the very concept of a priori synthetic knowledge that it can only be said to apply to experienced reality in the natural realm, since it is a function of the categories of the understanding. These categories provide both the basis for scientific knowledge and its limitations. Thus, for Kant it would make no sense to attempt to apply these categories to the task of acquiring knowledge about something that by definition lies outside of their range and purpose. Kant labeled the realm that can be known by means of the structure of the mind the "phenomenal world" and that which cannot be so known the "noumenal world."

In his second major work, *Critique of Practical Reason,* Kant sought to uncover the basis of ethical judgments and reasoning. While such activities cannot be found to have any cognitive value in the way that science can, they do have a rationale of their own, according to Kant, in the realm of action. Moreover, moral behavior can be said to require certain assumptions or "postulates" in Kant's view since the concept of duty which governs it trades on the idea that we live in a moral universe. Such a universe requires us to postulate, but not prove, the existence of a moral ruler (God), an after-life (justice), and an ability to make moral choices (freewill).

It is highly likely that no other thinker has had as much influence on the formation of the modern mind as has Kant. Not only does he represent the high-water mark of the line of thought developed by Descartes, and others, he has also had inestimable impact on the shape of twentieth-century thinkers in nearly every field of endeavor. The stress on the active role of the mind in the formation of knowledge, often termed "Neo-Kantianism," has become commonplace in our time as a result of Kant's work. Nevertheless, there are a number of criticisms of his approach which are worth mentioning.

While Kant's effort to attain a transcendental understanding of the structure of human knowledge by means of his dialectical analysis is a highly creative proposal, and even a fruitful one epistemologically speaking, it is possible to question whether or not such a technique can in fact enable us to transcend our human pattern of thought. In other words, just what is the difference between Kant's claims to have uncovered the structural categories of the mind and metaphysical claims? Although he vehemently denied the charge, there are those who have accused Kant of being an idealist metaphysician. However, others have argued that he is really a positivist since he clearly wanted to reduce all cognition to empirical concerns and to eliminate metaphysics and ethics from the domain of philosophy. Kant saw his job as that of setting the limits of what can and cannot be and studied by both scientists and lay folk alike.

By far the most ingenious of Kant's insights was that of the possibility of an a priori/synthetic foundation for cognitive activity. His claim that there is a grounding for knowledge that provides a kind of certainty, while at the same time yielding information about the world, is at the least extremely interesting and at best downright brilliant. Unlike Descartes, Kant did not maintain that this bedrock is provided by abstract reason alone, and unlike Hume he did not expect to find it amidst the data of sensory experience. Rather, Kant placed the pivotal ground of knowing in the structure of the mind itself, in the way that it serves as the condition of the possibility of knowledge per se. There is something extremely right-headed about this move on Kant's part, as our presentation of Polanyi's views in the next two chapters will make quite clear.

Nevertheless, there are difficulties here as well. One pertains to the highly intellectualist character of Kant's treatment of the categories of the understanding. Although he acknowledges that the notions of space, time, and causation are absorbed by means of our *interaction* with the objects we encounter within these categories, Kant never returns to this important feature of cognitive activity. For all practical purposes, Kant's epistemology, like those of modernist thinkers before him, is completely devoid of any need for the *body* as a vital factor in the knowing process. The concepts and perceptions of which Kant speaks all exist in a disembodied mind as essentially passive constructs.

This complete lack of any appreciation for the cruciality of the body in acquiring and grounding knowledge is perhaps the major flaw in Kant's modernist philosophy. We shall return to this issue in some detail in the next two chapters. Another chief difficulty with Kant's case for the viability of a priori/synthetic knowledge derives from his use of mathematics as the chief example. The development of mathematical theory since Kant's time has rendered this view of the nature of arithmetic and geometry quite obsolete. The invention of non-Euclidean geometries in the late 1800s by Labochevsky and Reimann, as well as the proof that all mathematics is but a special case of logic by Russell and Whitehead in the early years of this century, make Kant's use of mathematics quaint at best and extremely misleading at worst.

Finally, the absolute dichotomy that Kant constructed between the experiential, phenomenal world and the transcendent, noumenal world may well be vastly overdrawn. Like the early Ludwig Wittgenstein, in his *Tractatus Logico-Philosophicus,* Kant sought to set the limits of meaningful thought and speech by insisting on separating pure from practical reason, the former yielding knowledge, and the latter failing to do so. Unfortunately, this dichotomy is entirely out of harmony with the way human experience actually comes in everyday life. Moreover, one can even argue that theoretic activity itself does not and cannot be made to conform to this total separation of cognitivity from values and emotions. Kant's dichotomy even undercuts itself because it exemplifies a value judgment in its formulation.

Before proceeding to a consideration of Polanyi's view of the difficulties and quandaries inherent within what is known as modernism, together with his resolution of these, it seems advisable to compile a summary of the main features of the modernist perspective that give rise to its limitations. While these limitations are also stressed by deconstructivist postmodernists, the negative character of their critique of modernism is not shared by Polanyi. Rather than seeking to "deconstruct" modernism, Polanyi sought to "reconstruct" it in such a way as to preserve its positive advancement over the authoritarianism of previous periods. This reconstruction was aimed at moving beyond modernism by uncovering the authentic axis of human cognition and value. But first, a summary of the shortcomings of modernism as instituted by the likes of Descartes, Hume, and Kant.

There is a distinctly *atomistic* flavor to the modernist approach to epistemology. The assumption seems to be that both reality and knowing not only can be divided up into ultimately simple units, but must be if they are to be understood. Not only does this assumption fly right into the face of actual human experience, but it leads inevitably to a commitment to reductionist analysis at each and every stage of thought, a commitment that in principle can never be fulfilled. Moreover, atomism and reductionism give rise to a desire, even a demand, to be able to control and manipulate both reality and the reasoning process, thus denigrating the role played by imagination and feeling in cognitive activity. Surely, this kind of narrow "positivism" sells knowledge short.

It is perhaps this *reductionistic* quality of modernism that leads to the undue confidence that twentieth-century thought has developed concerning the powers of scientific method and analytic processes. It has been tacitly assumed that the human ability to understand the world around us is essentially unlimited, that objective knowledge of reality is within our grasp. At the same time, however, there has been a strong tendency in the twentieth century to insist on the total relativity of all knowledge claims, a tendency that essentially undercuts the dream of the possibility of the "God's eye view" inherent within the goal of objectivity. Nevertheless, it is largely this sort of ethnocentric arrogance on the part of modern thinkers that gives rise to the postmodernist protest. As will become clear in the next two chapters, it was Polanyi's contention that it is not necessary to embrace relativistic subjectivism in order to avoid the difficulties of modern, critical thought.

Another disconcerting thing about modern philosophy is its tendency to lead to a *dualistic* treatment of reality. From Descartes' separation of the mind and the body to Kant's dichotomy between the knowable and the unknowable, we see the seeds of the dualism that has come to characterize nearly every aspect of our contemporary life and thought, from the separation of religion and politics to the reductionistic approach to medicine, and from the separation between social values and economic progress to the gulf between science and ethics. Any philosophy that divides the world into such distinct parts surely leaves a great deal to be desired.

In every version of modern philosophy there has been a commitment to establishing an unmovable foundation for all genuinely cognitive activity. This *foundationalism* has been shown time and time again to be essentially wrong-headed since about any given ultimate grounding of knowledge it is possible to raise questions as to the viability of its ultimacy. Intuitional self-evidence, sensory observations, and a priori/synthetic truths are all susceptible to serious criticism from a variety of angles and sources. The chief epistemological dilemma of modernism is that it forces us to choose between an indubitable grounding and open-ended relativism, between objectivity and subjectivity. Unfortunately, the former is impossible, and the latter yields no knowledge. What is needed is an epistemological approach that is able to locate a viable pivot point between these two extremes. Polanyi's philosophy of the tacit mode aims at doing just this, and in my judgment it accomplishes the task.

Finally, as was mentioned earlier, it has always been characteristic of modern thought to be excessively *intellectualist*. Both rationalists and empiricists, the latter's protest to the contrary notwithstanding, as well as Kantians carry on their analysis of cognition as if knowledge were an exclusively mental activity. What matters for all of them in regard to knowledge are the "ideas" that end up in the mind and the logical implications entailed thereby. The role of the body as it interacts with the surrounding environment is conceived of as incidental at best, and the mind is treated as not inextricably interwoven with somatic activity. There is surely something wrong with this picture of knowledge.

The reaction of those thinkers dubbed "postmodern" to the sorts of difficulties outlined above as endemic to the "modern perspective" is as important as it is forceful. However, the central thrust of this reaction has been primarily negative or "deconstructive" in nature. In their efforts to dismantle the presuppositions and arrogance of modernism, many postmodern thinkers have been guilty of throwing away the banana and eating the peel. Not only are there certain valuable insights inherent within modern philosophy, but the attempt to overthrow it by asserting that there are no viable criteria whatsoever by which to ascertain the meaning and/or truth of any statement is essentially self-negating and thus meaningless itself. The fact is, we do come to understand one another despite our biases and ethnocentric limitations; indeed, the very notions of misunderstanding and mistake are parasitic on their opposites for their meaningfulness.

It is at this juncture that the philosophy of Michael Polanyi becomes so relevant. In seeking to reconstruct modern, or what he calls "critical," philosophy, Polanyi sets about the task of locating an entirely different point of departure, or cognitive axis, for epistemological inquiry. He sets aside the "cult of objectivity" without setting aside the possibility of and need for criteria of meaning and evaluation in our search for knowledge. Polanyi introduces an understanding of knowing as grounded in the body, the society of knowing agents, and the affirmation of our cognitive powers of judgment. This posture enables us to act with both confidence and humility in the quest for knowledge.

2

THE DYNAMICS OF
COGNITIVE EXPERIENCE

In this chapter, the focus will be on presenting and exploring Polanyi's treatment of the structure of human experience with an eye to overcoming the errors of modernist philosophy. I shall begin with an account of his interpretation of what might be called the "awareness dimension" of experience and then move on to the corresponding "activity dimension." I shall conclude with a special emphasis on the cruciality of the body in all human experience, especially those aspects involving cognition. The stress throughout will be on the holistic, nonpassive, and nonintellectualistic character of the human encounter with the world, one that serves as its center of significance.

Finally these two dimensions, awareness and activity, will be integrated into yet a third dimension of human experience, that of cognitivity, thereby providing an overall schema within which to present and grasp Polanyi's theory of knowledge, which serves as the hub of his overall philosophy.

THE AWARENESS DIMENSION

In the preface to the second edition of his *Personal Knowledge,* Polanyi made the following statement:

> When we are relying on our awareness of something (A) for attending to something else (B), we are but subsidiarily aware of A. The thing B

to which we are thus focally attending, is then the meaning of A. The focal object B is always identifiable, while things like A, of which we are subsidiarily aware may be unidentifiable. The two kinds of awareness are mutually exclusive: when we switch our attention to something of which we have hitherto been subsidiarily aware, it loses its previous meaning. (p. xiii)

This statement introduces a major feature of the fresh axis of epistemological understanding being offered by Polanyi. Thus, it will serve as the pivot point for our discussion of the awareness dimension within Polanyi's understanding of human experience.

The term *dimension* is chosen with care here since it is absolutely crucial to distinguish Polanyi's view from more traditional and modern views at the very outset. Both the premodern and the modern interpretations of our encounter with reality have seen fit to divide the world up into quite distinct realms or levels, and this had led to the common practice of construing experience in terms of such divisions. While the more ancient world views sought to do this metaphysically, with higher and lower levels of reality, the modern Western view has done so epistemologically, with a basic dichotomy between the knower and the known, on the one hand, and experience comprised of distinct and independent units, on the other hand.

Contrary to these dualistic and atomistic understandings of experience, which lead directly to a compartmentalizing understanding of awareness, Polanyi begins by construing our experience as constituted of three simultaneous, interpenetrating dimensions, the first of which is awareness. In addition to avoiding the danger of thinking of experience and our awareness thereof as chopped up and isolatable, this way of modeling experienced reality also avoids the tendency of modern thought to separate the various aspects of knowing from one another. To speak of the dimensions of experience is to allow for far greater integration and interaction among its various aspects than is possible in the modernist model.

Polanyi's account of the awareness dimension of experience is quite straightforward and unproblematic. The vectorial character of human awareness is familiar to all of us. As the reader focuses on the meaning of these very words he or she is only subsidiarily aware of the fact that they are written in English and that they follow certain rules of grammar, and so on. Physiologically speaking, one is focally aware of the markings on the page but only at best subsidiarily aware of the movements of the muscles controlling the eyes. As Polanyi points out, these two poles of the awareness continuum are mutually exclusive, in the sense that one cannot focus on what is presently functioning subsidiarily, since by definition the vector of this dimension runs only in one direction.

At the same time, however, it is also true that what is focal in one context may well become subsidiary in the next and vice versa. Thus, the distinction between these two poles is also a relative one. A reader may begin to scrutinize the particulars of grammar and vocabulary in these present sentences, in which case their meaning may either switch to a subsidiary function or be lost altogether. Similarly, a physiologist may choose to focus attention on the muscular activity of the eye, in which case one can be said to be both focusing on and relying on this activity simultaneously. Actually, of course, there are many other factors comprising the awareness context in this case that fulfill the subsidiary function. In short, we rely on some things in order to focus on others; we attend *from* some things *to* others.

Furthermore, a dimensional construing of experience allows for what is best termed a "mediational" understanding of the structure of reality. The fact is that the world does not come to us in a flat, one-dimensional fashion; it is arranged in a hierarchy of levels of meaning, each richer and more comprehensive than the ones through which it is mediated. Thus, in the act of reading these words, the reader perceives the marks on the page as forming a pattern of significance, which we call "terms," "grammar," and "meaning" respectively, each being carried "piggy back," as it were, on the more simplified pattern beneath it. Some thinkers refer to this mediated quality of meaning as "supervenience," the richer and more comprehensive dimensions of meaning being discerned in and through the less rich and comprehensive.

It should be borne in mind that for the most part our discernment of meaning *begins* with these richer dimensions rather than with the simpler, more perceptual ones. Children first grasp the significance of statements, as commands, warnings, and encouragements, before they are aware of their grammatical patterns and vocabulary designations. The present reader generally discerns the overall significance of these utterances, often at the paragraph level, without even being aware of the specific terms and linguistic structures being employed. In short, they follow the *argument* of the text. Even though, from an analytical point of view, the richer dimensions of meaning are constituted by the less rich, they cannot be reduced to or exhausted by an account of them.

To give a more complex example, imagine several folks standing on a bridge watching a river flowing by below. Suddenly, one of the notices a child floating face-down in the current. It would be possible, and from a physicist's standpoint quite correct, for one of the observers to describe the scene in terms of so many pounds of protoplasm rotating at a certain rate and in a certain direction within a mixture of H_2O, and so on. But this is not what such folks, as members of the human community, would in fact say they perceive. One could even imagine someone giving an account of the aesthetic dimension of the scene in terms of colors, shapes, lines, and movement. But this, too, would be highly irregular. The scene normally would be discerned in terms of the *moral dimension* of experience, which is richer and more comprehensive than the others just mentioned. It is mediated through them without being reducible to an account of them.

Perhaps one more example, taken from the aesthetic level of experience mentioned above, will prove helpful here. In William Butler Yeats's famous question "How can we know the dancer from the dance?" the issue of the relationship between the parts and the whole is raised. The particulars of a specific dancer's characteristics, unique movements, and interpretive style are not identifiable with or equivalent to the reality of the dance, say of *Swan Lake,* itself. How is it that we can distinguish the one from the other, know the latter *in* the former without reducing it to or inferring it from the particulars comprising it? Clearly, we *discern* the richer, holistic reality as mediated in and through its individual parts.

The overall theme being developed here is that meaning in general, and specifically meaning in the more complex levels or aspects of experience, such as the aesthetic, is best understood as a function of the interaction among simultaneous and interpenetrating *dimensions* of reality. To return to Polanyi's favorite terminology, generally speaking, we come to know the richer and more comprehensive dimensions of our common experience by focusing on or attending to their meaning from or through the less complex particulars of which they are composed, Thus, the structure of the cognitive process is both *vectorial* and *mediational* in character. This dimensional model of experience and reality is best equipped to shed light on the nature of meaning at all levels.

While the more standard models offered by modern, critical thought are either reductionistic or dualistic, a dimensional model allows for a greater richness, on the one hand, and the essential wholeness of human experience, on the other hand. For to exist within simultaneously interpenetrating dimensions is to be aware of and participate in more than a single aspect of experience at once, while meaning itself can be viewed as inextricably bound up with perceptual and conceptual factors without being reducible to them. The dancer and the dance are inseparable, but neither is simply a function of the other, nor are they the same entity. Polanyi's schema for understanding the structure of experience goes a long way toward both clarifying and overcoming the errors of modern, critical philosophy.

Permit me to offer one further example, one that is even more abstract or existential in nature, of the dynamics of this vectorial and mediational model. Consider Ingmar Bergman's well-known film *Wild Strawberries*. Here is a simple story of a retired doctor-professor who drives from Stockholm to Lund to receive an honorary degree. The entire film is devoted to Isak Borg's one-day journey, interspersed with short side visits, dreams, and reminiscences. Yet one, if not *the,* clear meaning of the film pertains to Isak's journey toward self-understanding. In effect, the geographical journey serves to mediate, as a metaphor, the spiritual or existential journey. However, this mediated or metaphorical relationship is never stated as such in the film. Nor can it be said to "follow" logically from a consideration of the events and dialogues therein.

At the same time, however, it is of little help to maintain that this richer, more comprehensive dimension of meaning somehow exists on a higher level, independent of the more obvious features of the film comprising its lower level, and therefore can be grasped only by means of some sort of intuitive process. Such a dualism is as misleading as its more reductionistic counterpart. What *is* helpful, I submit, is to view the two journeys as interrelated dimensions of the same holistic experience, interacting with and illuminating each other. The richer dimension of Isak's journey is mediated to us *in and through* the particulars of his geographic journey; we attend to the former by means of and from the latter.

It is worth pointing out that this vectorial and mediational model of experienced reality entails an asymmetrical character. Mediated dimensions not only incorporate and rely on the specific features of those through which they are mediated, but in a sense they are controlled by them as well. For instance, even as the physical dimension gives rise to and is transcended by the aesthetic and moral dimensions, it also sets what Polanyi called their "boundary conditions," the parameters, as it were, within and according to which they function. The richer, more comprehensive realities can be said to emerge from the lesser dimensions, but they can never transcend them entirely; they are not reducible to these, but they cannot function without them, either. The hierarchy of dimensions that we normally encounter, range from the physical through the social, aesthetic, and moral, to the intellectual and spiritual; we see this asymmetrical, unidirectional pattern.

Polanyi delineated the relationship between the lower-level boundary conditions and the higher principles of meaning that govern their use in the following manner:

> [W]e recognize that in certain cases the boundary conditions of a principle are in fact subject to control by other principles. Thus the boundary conditions of the laws of mechanics may be controlled by the operational principles which define a machine, the boundary conditions of muscular action may be controlled by a pattern of purposive behavior, like that of going for a walk; the boundary conditions of a vocabulary are usually controlled by the rules of grammar, and the conditions left open by the rules of chess are controlled by the stratagems of the players. And so we find that machines, purposive actions, grammatical sentences, and games of chess are all entities subject to *dual control.*

Such is the stratified structure of comprehensive entities. They embody a combination of two principles, a higher and a lower. Smash up a machine, utter words at random, or make chess moves without a purpose, and the corresponding higher principle—that which constitutes the machine, that which makes words in sentences, and that which moves of chess into a game—will all vanish and the comprehensive entity which they controlled will cease to exist.

But the lower principles, the boundary principles of which the now effaced higher principles had controlled, remain in operation. The laws of mechanics, the vocabulary sanctioned by the dictionary, the rules of chess, they will all continue to apply as before. Hence no description of a comprehensive entity in the light of its lower principles can ever reveal the operation of its higher principles. *The higher principles which characterize a comprehensive entity cannot be defined in terns of the laws that apply to its parts in themselves.* (*Knowing and Being*, p. 217)

Thus, we see the mediated nature of experienced reality, along with its vectorial nature as delineated by Polanyi in the earlier quotation, explained in terms of the principles inherent within boundary conditions. The two structural aspects work in harmony with each other to govern the dimensional interaction that characterizes the world.

The contrast between this way of construing the structure of experienced reality and that presupposed by modern thought can best be demonstrated by comparing the key images or root metaphors involved in each. In contrast to the dualistic image of the cave as presented by Plato, which postulates the existence of two worlds or *levels* of reality, Kant offered a more modern, if reductionistic, image of an isolated island. Here is how he describes it:

This domain is an island, enclosed by nature itself within unalterable limits. It is the land of truth—enchanting name!—surrounded by a wide and stormy ocean, the native home of illusion, where many a fog bank and many a swiftly melting iceberg give the deceptive appearance of farther shores, deluding the adventurous seafarer ever anew with empty hopes, and engaging him in enterprises which he can never abandon and yet is unable to carry to completion. (*Critique of Pure Reason*, p. 257)

Over against these dualistic and reductionistic models, consider that embodied in the image offered by William James, an image that, in my opinion, captures the essence of Polanyi's overall proposal. James presents his image in this way:

Hold a tumbler of water a little above your eyes and look up through the water at its surface—or better still look similarly through the flat wall of an aquarium. You will then see an extraordinarily brilliant reflected image say of a candle-flame, or any other clear object situated on the opposite side of the vessel. No ray, under these circumstances gets beyond the water's surface: every ray is totally reflected back into the depths again. Now let the water represent the world of sensible facts, and let the air above it represent the world of abstract ideas. Both worlds are real, of course, and interact; but they interact only at their boundary, and the *locus* of everything that lives and happens to us, so far as full experience goes, is the water. We are like fishes swimming in the sea of sense, bounded above by the superior element, but unable to breath it pure or penetrate it. We get our oxygen from it, however, we touch it incessantly, now in this part, now in that, and every time we touch it we turn back into the water with our course re-determined and re-energized. The abstract ideas of which the air consists are indispens-able for life, but irrespirable by themselves, as it were, and only active in their redirective function . . . This shows how something, not sufficient for life itself, may nevertheless be an effective determinate of life else-where. (*Pragmatism*, pp. 127–28)

In place of Plato's two–world model and Kant's one-world model, which separate off or deny the existence of richer, more comprehensive realities, respectively, we now have the model suggested by James's image and devel-oped by Polanyi. It construes reality as structured according to a hierarchy of dimensions that interpenetrate and mediate one another in a vectorial pattern by means of boundary conditions and rules. The richer, more comprehensive dimensions are mediated in and through the lesser, without being explainable in terms of them.

THE ACTIVITY DIMENSION

The *awareness* dimension of experience is, according to Polanyi's analysis, intersected by the *activity* dimension. These two dimensions pretty much cover the range of human experience, functioning as "input" and "output" respectively. Whereas in the former case, the dynamic is between the focal and subsidiary poles, in the latter case, it is between the "bodily" and "con-ceptual" poles. This section will aim at unpacking the nature and interactive character of this activity dimension, which is fundamentally symbiotic in quality. The poles in both of these dimensions of experience function very much like those of an electromagnetic force field in that they serve both to define and to sustain each other; neither can exist or operate without the other.

All human activity takes place along a continuum between its bodily and conceptual poles. Although we do, at times, engage in activities that are nearly exclusively physical or mental, as in strenuous exercise or abstract thought, respectively, even in these extreme cases there remains an element of the opposite pole. We are still conscious while running the one hundred meter dash, and we still get hungry and tired while doing mathematical equations. Thus, the vast majority of the time human action is a blend of the bodily and the conceptual, with the interaction of body and mind being the norm rather than the exception. In this way, we can see that Polanyi, contrary to modern thought, begins by affirming the unity of the human person.

It is important to acknowledge that, as with the awareness dimension, the activity continuum of experience is characterized by a vectorial or unidirectional thrust that runs from the bodily pole toward the conceptual pole. After all, when we first arrive in this world, we are nearly all body with precious little in the way of mental activity. Thus, our growth into adult maturity involves moving along the activity continuum toward increased intellectual achievement. The reciprocity between bodily and conceptual action creates and allows for a highly complex integration of these two qualities within the human person. Our mind-body reality constitutes a unique mode of existence in the world as we know it.

Perhaps the clearest manifestation of this unique unity is our participation in language. On the one hand, speech is fundamentally a physical activity, whether by sound, signing, or writing. Without certain somatic equipment, it is impossible to become a member of the human community in the favored sense of that term. By participating in language at the imitative level in the beginning, a child slowly acquires the ability to express intentionality and conceptual understanding. Even though speech becomes a highly intellectual activity, it never ceases to be a physical one in the process. Writing and reading these words, for instance, which are exceedingly abstract and conceptual in nature, involves a mysterious mixture of mind and body, one that generally goes unappreciated by virtue of its familiarity.

To anticipate a bit, in Polanyi's scheme of things, the intersection between the awareness and activity dimensions, with their respective poles, gives rise to yet a third dimension or continuum, namely that of cognitivity. We shall explore this dimension more fully in the next chapter. I mention it here because having the full picture before one, at least in outline form, enhances the understanding of how the awareness and activity dimensions interact with each other. As can be seen from the following diagram, the focal and conceptual poles combine to produce what Polanyi terms "explicit knowing," while the bodily and subsidiary poles combine to form what he calls "tacit knowing." These two modes of knowing constitute the poles of the third dimension of the structure of human experience.

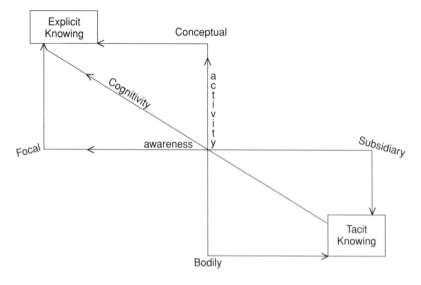

Figure 2.1

Returning now to the actual dynamics of the activity dimension, between its bodily an conceptual poles, it is helpful to consider how Polanyi
himself expresses the movement from the former to the latter. In one place,
he puts it like this:

> I have shown how our subsidiary awareness of our body is extended to
> include a stick, when we feel our way by means of the stick. To use
> language in speech, reading and writing, is to extend our bodily equip-
> ment and become intelligent human beings. We may say that when we
> learn to use language, or a probe, or a tool, and thus make ourselves
> aware of these things as we are our body, we *interiorize* these things
> and *make ourselves dwell in them.* Such extensions of ourselves de-
> velop new faculties in us; our whole education operates in this way; as
> each of us interiorizes our cultural heritage, he grows into a person
> seeing the world and experiencing life in terms of this outlook. (*Know-
> ing and Being,* p. 148)

Thus, we can see how everything from specific motor skills, including
those involved in speech, to enculturation comes about as a result of our
vectorial movement from physical activity toward conceptual activity. By
means of our embodiment, we come to live in or "indwell" the things and
ideas, people and institutions, that make up the natural and social worlds that
surround us. Of course, once we are participants in conceptual reality, we find

that our ideas, as well as those of others, may cycle back to have an effect on our bodily activity in the form of instruction and motivation.

It is extremely important to bear in mind that for Polanyi the awareness and activity dimensions of experience are neither passive nor blind, respectively. The dominant modernist model of awareness, excepting that of Kant, construes it in terms of simple sensory perception, as a kind of passive exposure to data that are imprinted on the senses. Thus, this view turns out to be essentially intellectualist in nature, an account of awareness that is entirely devoid of any somatic aspects whatsoever. However, as has been firmly established by Gestalt psychology and other perceptual studies, awareness is a highly active phenomenon, one in which the senses themselves play an important formative role. Not only do we generally perceive the sort of things we go looking for, as a result of the enculturation process, but the very structure of the sense organs themselves largely determines what we will see and hear.

Thus it is that in a significant sense Kant was correct when he suggested that the knower contributes a great deal to the character of the known. Unfortunately, however, he limited his insight to the nature of the mind, rather than extending it to encompass the whole mind-body person as the knower. Therefore, Kant's categories of the understanding were understood in a passive way, as a kind of static filter system, rather than as an active process of interaction between the mind-body and the surrounding environment. However, Polanyi's way of construing awareness insists on stressing the active, somatic nature of awareness as indicated by the vectorial character of the relation between its focal and subsidiary poles. This relationship precludes viewing awareness as passive exposure.

In a similar way, it is extremely important to interpret the activity dimension of experience as anything but blind. Human action is characteristically both purposive and cognitive. The reductionism that is inherent within the modern interpretation of human behavior seeks to explain and understand our activity strictly in terms of responses to various stimuli, or as B. F. Skinner preferred to call it, "operant conditioning." The ironic and contradictory character of this approach to understanding human action is clearly demonstrated in the title of Skinner's well-known book *Beyond Freedom and Dignity*. The entire argument of the book, as well as of modern reductionism in general, presupposes the very notions it seeks to eliminate or get "beyond" since it urges us to choose to move beyond traditional concepts such as 'freewill' and take control of our own destiny. The obvious implication is that in so doing we will also move beyond the traditional idea of the superior dignity of human beings, and thus we will partake of an even higher form of nobility. Clearly, concepts such as 'freedom' and 'dignity,' in the sense of moral character, are pivotal to any understanding of human behavior, and they necessarily entail viewing human activity as purposive rather than as blindly conditioned responses. Phenomenologists prefer to call this quality of human action "intentionality," and Polanyi would have no difficulty accepting this term.

Not only is human action not blind, but in Polanyi's view it also involves a distinctly cognitive aspect. Any reflection on the dynamics of simple bodily activity will reveal what may be called a "dimension of assessment." When we walk through a room or look in the direction of a sound, to say nothing of when we catch a ball, go dancing, or drive a car, we necessarily make judgments about the speed and/or position of various objects, including our own bodies. These judgments are clearly cognitive in nature because they can be either correct or erroneous, right or wrong, and so on. We make assessments or judgments, and these require the use of our cognitive powers just as engaging in abstract thought does. Thus, in Polanyi's interpretation of the activity dimension of experience, the body as well as the mind plays an important role. We shall explore this role more fully in the next section.

An especially clear example of the interplay between the awareness and activity dimensions can be seen in complex situations, such as athletic contests and computer games, as one takes in information and makes judgments about how best to respond to it. This sort of interaction can take place at extremely fast speeds and within quite confined contexts, thus demanding a very high level of coordination and integration of thought and skill. After such activities have been engaged in or indwelt for a significant length of time, they can become a matter of "second nature" or even of reflex. Carrying on a conversation also can exhibit this sort of integration of awareness and activity, requiring a great deal of perceptive discernment and cognitive judgment.

The sort of integration and coordination mentioned above involves what some have designated as "synaesthesia," the symbiotic interaction of all the senses, together with the participation of the mind, providing both the structure and the dynamic of experience. It is an obvious and significant fact about modern philosophy that it generally has carried on its analysis of sensory experience as if each of the senses operated independently of one another. The eye is said to process color, size, and shape; the ear treats pitch, volume, and rhythm; and touch deals with weight, texture, and solidity. The fact of the matter is, however, that our perceptions and judgments with respect to these different concepts are highly interrelational in nature. Our experience of any one of them is to a large degree dependent on how our other senses come into play.

Interesting research has been done in this field by various Gestalt psychologists. One study that is especially fascinating is that done in connection with the notion of key in music. Trained keyboard and string musicians can recognize in what key a particular performance was originally played after the music has been put through a computer that changes nothing but the key.

As they say things like "Well, I'm hearing it in E, but it was played in F," they invariably move and "listen" to their fingers as if they themselves were doing the playing. Also, whole groups of musicians have been fooled by being told that a "rigged" piano had changed the key of the piece they had watched a pianist play when in fact it had not. (Geoffrey Pazant, "Subsidiary Musical Awareness," unpublished manuscript).

Polanyi himself references the work of Gestalt investigators, although he points out that they have been slow to draw the important epistemological conclusion entailed by their work.

> They were probably unwilling to recognize that knowledge was shaped by the knower's personal action. But having realized that personal participation predominates both in the area of tacit and explicit, we are ready to transpose the findings of Gestalt psychology into a theory of knowledge. (*The Study of Man,* p. 28)

Among the many examples of the integration of awareness and bodily interaction offered by Polanyi are those pertaining to simple perceptual operations, especially vision. He frequently describes how the minute muscles of the eye work to control the focus and coherence necessary in distinguishing moving objects from one another and from their background.

> When I move my hand before my eyes, it would keep changing its color, its shape, and its size, but for the fact that I take into account a host of rapidly changing clues, some in the field of vision, some in my eye muscles, and some deeper still in my body, as in the labyrinth of the inner ear. My powers of perceiving coherence makes me see these thousand varied and changing clues jointly as one unchanging object, as an object moving about at different distances, seen from different angles, under variable illuminations. A successful integration of a thousand changing particulars into a single consistent sight makes me recognize a real object in front of me. (*Knowing and Being*, pp. 138–39)

The intricate character of the relation between the awareness dimension and the activity dimension of experience is discussed by Polanyi in terms of the role that authority and connoisseurship play in acquiring knowledge. He puts it like this:

> To learn by example is to submit to authority. You follow your master because you trust his manner of doing things even when you cannot analyse and account in detail for its effectiveness. By watching the master and emulating his efforts in the presence of his example, the

apprentice unconsciously picks up the rules of the art, including those which are not explicitly known to the master himself. These hidden rules can be assimilated only by a person who surrenders himself to that extent uncritically to the imitation of another. (*Personal Knowledge,* p. 53)

As John Dewey said, we learn by doing. In attempting to practice an art or skill, we indwell it to the extent that it eventually comes to indwell us, even though we generally cannot say how this happens. In learning a new dance step, a new language, or how to think philosophically, there simply is no substitute for practice. We imitate, are corrected, try again and again, get corrected again, and gradually get better at the task. Perhaps the ultimate example of this process is exhibited by those folks who are trained to be "chicken sexers." Even though there is no simple way to tell the sex of a tiny chick, people can be taught to sort the males from the females by apprenticing themselves to those who already know how to do so. Their awareness becomes a function of their activity.

The intellectualist thrust of the modernist approach to human experience, which requires it to separate awareness from activity, received its initial impetus from Plato's commitment to vision as the paradigm case of knowing. This commitment is highly evident in the image of the cave in Plato's *Republic.* Here various levels of reality and knowledge are focused in the story of how people must liberate themselves from the tyranny of the senses by relying on the mind to lead them out of the cave of ignorance to the light of pure ideas. The mind, as the eye of the soul, is portrayed as seeing reality correctly only in the light of reason, especially mathematics and logic. It goes without saying that such a view of knowing has no use for the somatic aspects of awareness and judgment. Modernist thinkers, from Descartes to Kant, followed directly in Plato's steps in this regard.

Once again it is in language that we encounter the most sophisticated form of this integration of awareness and activity. Children do not first put speech into their minds and then learn to express themselves through the activity of talk. Rather, they enter into speech, if ever so minimally, and *by* speaking they become speakers. Polanyi puts it well:

We must realize that to use language is a performance of the same kind as our integration of visual clues for perceiving an object . . . or our integration of muscular contractions in walking or driving . . . all of which are performed by relying on our subsidiary awareness of some things for the purpose of attending focally to a matter on which they bear. (*Knowing and Being,* p. 193)

Here is a concrete example from our common experience with language wherein we can see the integration of parts into wholes by means of the inter-action between awareness and action. Whenever we are learning a language other than our mother tongue, or when we are straining to understand a speaker with a heavy accent, we frequently find that the particulars of the utterances we encounter are experienced as just so many unintelligible sounds until one of them is recognized as a meaningful whole. At that point, when some significant foothold has been gained, we suddenly recognize the previous random sounds as meaningful parts of a larger, holistic pattern of meaning. Once the big picture makes sense, we are in a position to comprehend its parts. It is as if we must first find the frequency or wavelength of the communication and then work our way backward to the meaning of the sounds.

What is extremely important to grasp here is that we do *not* work our way from the parts to the whole, but rather from the whole to the parts. To be sure, the parts constitute the whole ontologically speaking, but our com-prehension of the parts *as parts* depends upon our first grasping some mean-ingful whole. The notion of "part," after all, only makes sense in relation to the whole of which it is a part. Parts do not just float around as independent entities; they take on their reality as parts and their significance as units of meaning in relation to their respective wholes. With respect to a foreign language, we begin with individual words, but these are already units of holistic meaning when they are given to us as vocabulary, and so on. Only as such can they enable us to work our way toward an understanding of the other particulars comprising the language.

> We may say that when we comprehend a particular set of items as parts of a whole, the focus of our attention is shifted from the hitherto uncomprehended particulars to the understanding of their joint mean-ing. This shift of attention does not make us lose sight of the particu-lars, since one can see a whole only be seeing its parts, *but it changes altogether the manner in which we are aware of the particulars. We become aware of them now in terms of the whole on which we have fixed our attention.* I shall also speak correspondingly of a *subsidiary* knowledge of such items as distinct from a *focal* knowledge of the same items. (Polanyi, *The Study of Man*, pp. 29–30)

The Cruciality of Embodiment

The dynamic character of the awareness and activity dimensions of experi-ence in Polanyi's interpretation combine to underscore the crucial role of the body in the shaping of our interaction with the world. Not only is awareness very largely a function of sensory perception and physical engagement, but all human behavior is expressed in and through the body. Polanyi focuses the significance of our embodiment in the following manner:

> The way the body participates in the act of perception can be generalized further to include the bodily roots of all knowledge and thought. Our body is the only assembly of things known almost exclusively by relying on our awareness of them for attending to something else. Parts of our body serve as tools for observing objects outside and for manipulating them. Every time we make sense of the world, we rely on our tacit knowledge of impacts made by the world on our body and the complex responses of our body to these impacts. Such is the exceptional position of our body in the universe. (*Knowing and Being*, p. 147).

In explicating his view of the cruciality of embodiment, Polanyi was influenced by the work of Maurice Merleau-Ponty in his phenomenological analysis of experience and knowledge. Merleau-Ponty, in seeking to overcome the extreme intellectualism of modern philosophy, posits the body as the axis of the human way of being in the world. In his view, it is our unique point of entry into, our mode of engagement with both the social and physical realities in which we find ourselves. In contrast to the prevailing Western dualistic view of mind inhabiting, as it were, the body, Merleau-Ponty insists that our personhood is inextricably bound up with mind as embodied. The body is the pivot point of human existence in the world.

One way to make this point extremely vivid is to reflect on the fact that a person's body is the only physical object in the entire universe from which he or she cannot walk away. Moreover, our relationship to our own body, a physical object in its own right, is entirely different from our relationship to other physical bodies. The difference, for instance, between the act of picking up a rock or drinking glass and picking up our own hand is qualitative in nature. When we scratch our own itch or probe for a sliver in our own finger, we act as both subject and object of the same activity. Thus, our bodies are both in the world as physical objects and the means by which we come to know the world through interaction with it. Of no other aspect of reality is this true. Merleau-Ponty, speaking in his own concrete, poetic fashion said: "Our own body is in the world as the heart is in the organism; it keeps the visible spectacle constantly alive, it breaths life into it and sustains it inwardly, and with it forms a system" (*Phenomenology of Perception*, p. 203). Like the heart, which is both part of the body and the fulcrum of its life, the body provides the bridge between ourselves and the world by participating in both. We do not, properly speaking, *have* bodies; we are, in truth, embodied creatures.

There are, to be sure, those who speak of what are called "out of body experiences," but at least at this stage of scientific knowledge it is unclear just what such experiences might involve. For one thing, like the claims made by those who say they have come back from the dead, these claims may very well be dreams in which the subject is projecting from embodied experience to some imagined disembodied state. Moreover, it is important to note that more often than not these "experiences" are said to involve someone floating above her body, who, nevertheless, is at the same time still in what is termed her "astral body." Even here, then, embodiment turns out to be crucial.

The crucial role played by embodiment in the formation and integration of the awareness and activity dimensions of experience is focused in Polanyi's notion of indwelling. As was mentioned earlier, it is the interaction between subsidiary awareness and bodily activity that gives rise to tacit knowing, one of the poles of the cognitivity dimension of experience. This interaction is accomplished by our bodily participation or dwelling-in the particulars of which we are but subsidiarily or subliminally aware. These particulars are not initially encountered as meaningful units but as a random flow of unrelated elements or sensory data. The key to indwelling is to allow ourselves to participate in these particulars as if we already knew what they mean. We do this by imitating the meaningful behavior of those around us even though we do not understand them fully, because we expect to be able to do so. Moreover, such imitation is accomplished through our embodiment, through putting ourselves in the place of others and behaving as we see and hear them doing.

The acquisition of one's own natural language is a powerful and clear example of how indwelling works. Tiny infants are surrounded with meaningless sounds and actions by the members of the speaking community to which they belong. Very early on, they begin to mimic these sounds, and later on they begin imitating the corresponding behavior as well. In short, infants indwell the subsidiary input in which they are bathed, and by means of this process of "osmosis" these random elements take on meaning and come to indwell the children. Thus, the body is the bridge or the axis that makes knowledge possible, even conceptual knowledge such as language.

As one immerses oneself in the various disassociated particulars of subsidiary awareness by indwelling them through repetitive imitation, at some point they come together in a holistic pattern of meaningfulness. For example, chess players come to understand the minds of great chess masters, as well as the deeper strategies of the game itself, by studying and *replaying* their crucial games. Young athletes come to embody the skills necessary to their sport by dwelling in the moves and styles of the stars thereof through repetitive imitation. These separate particulars come together as embodied skills, according to Polanyi, by means of what he calls an "integrative act."

An integrative act takes place when the particulars of subsidiary awareness coalesce into a meaningful whole, when that which the learner has sought to indwell comes to indwell the learner as a cognitive skill. Learning to ride a bike or to swim clearly demonstrates this phenomenon. One struggles to master a whole host of what at the outset are experienced as distinct tasks, and often they come together quite suddenly to form a single, unitary skill. This is accomplished by placing one's body in the midst of the diverse particulars and interacting with them as if one already had integrated them as a cognitive whole. When my eldest son was five, he insisted that he could not go swimming until he first learned how to swim. It took some persistence on my part to convince him that it is by swimming that one learns how to swim. This sort of knowledge is nonetheless cognitive for being bodily in character.

It is to be acknowledged, of course, that the individual particulars into which one immerses oneself by means of bodily indwelling are in themselves unitary wholes of previous integrative acts. However, they themselves came to be such as a result of the same dynamic of embodied participation in a previous cognitive context. Only infants could be said to start from "scratch," by virtue of not possessing any specific skills when they arrive on the scene, but current research in this field would seem to suggest that infants come into the world with certain predispositions to seek and to know meaningful wholes. Within a matter of days, they can distinguish voices and faces, grasp objects, and even exhibit a walking reflex. In any case, once such cognitive wholes are in place, they serve as the unrelated particulars of still other, more complex, and yet to be integrated units of meaning, which in turn become the particulars of further integrative acts, and so on.

By way of a further example, I well remember learning to drive a stick-shift car when I was about fourteen. The process of seeking to integrate all the separate subsidiary elements comprising this skill, even though each was a unit of focal awareness in its own right, was truly overwhelming. I had already mastered the individual skills of shifting, steering, using the accelerator and the clutch, and braking. However, attending *from* these skills *to* that of driving was quite a different matter. Fortunately, by means of repeated bodily indwelling, these individual skills came to form a new, more complex skill as an integrated act.

The essential difference between knowledge that arises from the interaction of subsidiary awareness and bodily activity, on the one hand, and that resulting from a combination of focal awareness and conceptual activity, on the other hand, lies in the distinction between *integration* and *inference*, respectively. The process of inference, whether that of deduction, as in logic, or of induction, as in science, is central to what Polanyi calls "explicit knowing." This is the sort of knowing that has been enshrined within the world view of Western modernism, knowledge that can be identified and articulated.

In fact, it is a cardinal rule of this view that if one cannot focus and articulate an idea or theory, one has no right to lay claim to knowledge at all. Also, in the inferential process it is possible, as Descartes stressed, to move either from the premises or data to the conclusion, or from the conclusion back to the premises or data. In other words, the inferential process is essentially reversible.

However, an integrative act is not reversible in this fashion. Once an integration has taken place, one cannot go back to the beginning and operate as if it had never been accomplished. Surely, one can pretend that one does not know how to swim, speak English, or drive a car, but one cannot actually unlearn the cognitive skill once the integration of previous particulars has occurred. Again, one can forget or become rusty in the use of the skill, but this is not the same thing as reversing the direction of thought as in the inferential process. Following the steps of an inference is quite different from integrating parts into a whole through bodily indwelling.

As can be seen, the nature of an integrative act is grounded in the vectorial structure of the intersecting dimensions of awareness and activity. This vectorial quality is neither static nor passive but requires the embodied participation of the knowing agent. As one attends from the subsidiary particulars in and through bodily action to their intended focal meaning, these particulars coalesce into a unitary, holistic grasping of this meaning. Sometimes, of course, this participation must be repeated many times in order for this integration to take place. Once it has taken place, however, as with being able to "see" the pattern in a puzzle picture or understanding a spoken sentence, it remains as a meaningful whole. Integrative acts, then, function as the matrix or loom out of which meaning emerges and abides. Polanyi summarizes this overall point in the following way:

> There is a fundamental difference between the way we attend to the pointing finger and its object. We attend to the finger by *following its direction* in order to look at the object. The object *is then at the focus of our attention* whereas the finger *is not seen* focally, *but as a pointer* to the object. This directive, or vectorial way of attending to the pointing finger, I shall call our *subsidiary awareness of the finger.* It is our subsidiary awareness of a thing that endows it with meaning: with a meaning that bears on an object of which we are focally aware. A meaningful relation of a subsidiary to a focal is formed by the action of a person who integrates one to the other, and the relation persists by the fact that the person keeps up this integration. (*Knowing and Being,* pp. 181–82)

It is now time to bring this analysis of Polanyi's main ideas concerning the structure of experience and the crucial role of the body to bear on the difficulties and dilemmas of modern philosophy in general and epistemology in particular. It will be recalled that one fundamental problem for modern thought is that it begins by separating the knowing subject from that which is to be known. This tendency to assume that what is to be known must somehow lie at a cognitive distance from the knowing agent can be traced all the way back to Plato's commitment to vision as the paradigm case of knowing. However, it was Descartes who transposed this commitment into the modern sensibility when he began his investigations by assuming that the knowing subject-to-be is locked up in his own individual mind must initiate his quest for knowledge from there.

Hume and other empiricists followed suit by assuming that the mind is devoid of any and all knowledge at the outset and must somehow find a way to bridge the distance between itself and the so-called outside or external world. Kant, in his own way, also construed the relationship between the knower and that which is to be known in terms of this "inside-outside" structure. Thus, once again, the knowing agent turns out to be a prisoner of the mind itself. Throughout the nineteenth and twentieth centuries, modern Western thinkers have continued to work within the confines of these assumptions, whether to extend them to their extreme limits, as in the case of contemporary analytic philosophy and social science, or to seek to overthrow them, albeit in self-contradictory fashion, as with existentialism and deconstructionism.

Over against this modernist view, which posits what turns out to be an unbridgeable gap between the knower and the known, stands Polanyi's approach to the basic issues of epistemology. By placing the embodied activity at the center of human cognitivity, he provides a way to connect the knowing agent and that which is to be known by simply denying the dichotomy before it gets off the ground. As a matter of fact, we are never shut up within our own minds as knowing agents, cut off as it were from the social and physical worlds that surround us. On the contrary, we arrive on the scene already connected to and interacting with the environment. The capacities for relationship and cognitive activity are already in place, and they form the framework within which we function as knowers, even when we do so erroneously. Moreover, it is the body that serves as the pivot point of this interactive connection, and this is precisely what has been left out of the modernist approach.

In his preface to *Phenomenology of Perception,* on which Polanyi draws quite heavily, Merleau-Ponty introduces the notion of "intentional threads" as that which connects us to the world from the very beginning. These threads form the fabric out of and with which we engage in cognitive activity, and they are constituted by means of our embodiment. Although we cannot let go of these threads in order to examine reality in and of itself, Merleau-Ponty suggest that we do "slacken" them in such a way as to be able to achieve an understanding not only of the world but also of the threads themselves. The infamous egocentric dilemma of modernism is thus dissolved.

Following up on Merleau-Ponty's image of intentional threads, I would like to propose yet another image that may serve as a fitting conclusion to this chapter. It is helpful to think of our relationship to the world as that of a *dance,* wherein we are inextricably connected to our dance partner, reality, by means of our bodies, including language, and we are dancing in the dark. Thus, although we cannot cognize our partner directly in and of itself, and thereby it remains somewhat mysterious and intractable, we can and do acquire knowledge of reality by means of our interactive dancing with it. Sometimes we can actually predict what it is doing to do and sometimes not; at other times we can actually alter its behavior and thereby contribute to the very character of reality. This way of viewing cognition eliminates the need for a way to bridge the subject-object gap bemoaned *and* created by modern philosophy since it does not posit or require a gap in the first place.

It only remains to be said that we are not participating in this dance of cognitivity as individual knowing agents. Rather, the dance must be seen as a common group effort on the part of the entire human community. Thus, we are dancing in a large circle, joined through our respective embodiments, to each other and to the surrounding world. Sometimes we agree on the proper moves to make, and sometimes we do not; sometimes we agree on the nature of reality, and sometimes we do not. But by means of our common dance, we can and do correct our views and come to a knowledge of the world, one another, and even of ourselves.

3

THE STRUCTURE OF KNOWLEDGE

Before turning from the foregoing summary of Polanyi's account of the dynamics of cognitive experience to his approach to the structure of the knowledge that results from this dynamic, a fuller discussion of the cognitivity dimension is in order. It will be recalled that Polanyi begins with an account of the awareness dimension of experience as projected along a vectorial continuum between its focal and subsidiary poles. This dimension is intersected, as illustrated in the previous diagram, by the activity dimension of experience, which has as its poles conceptual and bodily activity. The third dimension, that of cognitivity, arises out of this intersection, with the interaction between focal awareness and conceptual activity giving rise to *explicit knowing*, on the one hand, and the interaction between bodily activity and subsidiary awareness yielding *tacit knowing*, on the other hand.

Thus it is that according to Polanyi cognitivity is a function of the interplay between the explicit and tacit components of human experience. Since the main emphases and concerns of explicit knowing have received such thorough treatment throughout the history of Western thought, especially in the modern period, Polanyi devotes the majority of his efforts to expounding and exploring the nature of tacit knowing. Along the way, to be sure, he finds opportunity to criticize and revise the modern view of explicit knowing as well.

As we have seen, tacit knowing is accomplished through what Polanyi calls "indwelling," the process of immersing oneself in the particulars of subsidiary awareness by means of embodied activity until these particulars come together as a meaningful whole in an "integrative act." When this act takes place, the knowing agent interiorizes the holistic Gestalt, or locus of meaning, and thus can be said to be indwelt by it. Both physical and conceptual skills and understandings are claimed by Polanyi to be achieved in this manner since even somatic judgments entail cognitive claims, while intellectual understanding always involves the acquisition and employment of specific skills. In Polanyi's view, then, knowledge emerges as a function of the interaction of these two cognitive poles, but the tacit pole provides the matrix out of which all knowledge flows.

There are at least two radical ramifications of this postcritical epistemology that warrant special attention. The first is that Polanyi is challenging the traditional modernist view that all knowledge is and must be explicit in nature. Part and parcel of the modernist philosophy is a commitment to the necessity of full articulation and objectivity in any definition of knowledge. Since Plato, the Western tradition has insisted that only one knows when one can say what one knows. All of the modern thinkers, each in his or her own way, have stressed the ultimate importance of absolute clarity and value-free reasoning in approaching questions of knowledge and reality. Twentieth-century thought either has affirmed this commitment, in spades, or has rejected it out of hand.

The term *objectivity* has become the password for knowledge in the modern era. Indeed, the two terms are almost synonymous in our contemporary understanding of cognitivity, thereby reflecting the fundamental dichotomy between the subject and the object of knowledge that modernism has been unable to overcome. The knowing agent and all the aspects of what Polanyi calls "personal knowledge"—such as commitment to truth, individual judgment, and intersubjectivity—are completely separated from what is to be known from the very outset. This modern "cult of objectivity" is especially predominant in our understanding of science as it seeks to divide facts from values. Here is Polanyi's critique of this view of science:

> The prevailing conception of science, based on the disjunction of subjectivity and objectivity seeks . . . to eliminate from science such passionate, personal, human appraisals of theories, or at least to minimize their function to that of a negligible by-play. For modern man has set up as the ideal of knowledge the conception of natural science as a set of statements which is 'objective' in the sense that its substance is entirely determined by observation, even while its presentation may be shaped by convention. This conception, stemming from a craving rooted

in the very depths of our culture, would be shattered if the intuition of rationality in nature had to be acknowledged as a justifiable and indeed essential part of scientific theory. That is why scientific theory is represented as a mere economical description of facts; or as embodying a conventional policy for drawing empirical inferences; or as a working hypothesis, suited to man's practical convenience—interpretations that all deliberately overlook the rational core of science. (*Personal Knowledge*, pp. 15–16)

The whole of Polanyi's work is to be understood as an attempt to counteract this one-sided emphasis on objectivity in modern epistemological thought by establishing the personal dimension of cognitive activity. In brief, he argues that the entire scientific enterprise presupposes (1) a belief that knowledge of reality is possible, (2) a personal commitment to the search for truth, (3) an affirmation of the reliability of human cognitive capacities, (4) a reliance on the imagination for the creation of hypotheses, and (5) an acknowledgment that scientific truth is the result of social interaction and convention. Each of the above aspects of cognition represents an aspect of what Polanyi terms the "personal coefficient" necessary to all knowing, and each of them is systematically eliminated from the modern, critical account of science and epistemology.

This way of confronting the issues involved in defining knowledge makes those committed to the modernist point of view quite uncomfortable because it raises the ghost of wild subjectivity and seems to undercut objectivity. However, Polanyi contends that any account of cognition that leaves the above factors out not only produces an erroneous understanding of knowledge but is flatly self-contradictory. A more complete treatment of the way science actually operates will have to wait until a later chapter. At this junction, the following remarks of Polanyi must suffice:

> The arts of doing and knowing, the valuation and the understanding of meanings are thus seen to be only different aspects of the act of extending our person into the subsidiary awareness of particulars which compose a whole. The inherent structure of this fundamental act of personal knowing makes us both necessarily participate in its shaping and acknowledge its results with universal intent. This is the prototype of intellectual commitment.
>
> It is the act of commitment in its full structure that saves personal knowledge from being merely subjective. Intellectual commitment is a responsible decision, in submission to the compelling claims of what in good conscience I conceive to be true. It is an act of hope, striving to fulfill an obligation within a personal situation for which I am not

responsible and which therefore determines my calling. This hope and this obligation are expressed in the universal intent of personal knowledge. (*Personal Knowledge* p. 65)

The second radical ramification of Polanyi's approach to the structure of knowledge pertains to his claim that in the final analysis all knowing is or derives from tacit knowing. In other words, for Polanyi, tacit knowing is logically prior to explicit knowing and hence is the fulcrum or axis from which the latter acquires its possibility and significance. This logical priority of tacit knowing is depicted in the figure 2.1. The vectorial character of the awareness and activity dimensions of experience provides the basis for a similar vector in the resulting cognitivity dimension. Thus, cognition always moves from the tacit pole toward the explicit pole. This is a radical ramification because it scandalizes the modern insistence on full articulation of meaning and rationale as a requirement for knowledge.

The main point that Polanyi wishes to make is that because tacit knowing is the anchor or tether for explicit knowing, it necessarily follows that we always know more than we can tell. This is to say that because tacit knowing centers in embodied indwelling of factors of which we are but subsidiarily aware, and not in conceptual analysis, we never can articulate these factors fully while we are yet relying on them in order to focus on more explicit factors. Indeed, Polanyi argues that we never can fully articulate the various cognitive conditions and frameworks that make knowing possible since they are imbedded in our embodiment and common social life. Although these conditions and frameworks are clearly exhibited, and thereby validated, in our cognitive activity, they are not subject to *full* articulation at the explicit level because they are, in the final analysis, bodily and communal realities, not conceptual ones.

Once again, the specter of subjectivism raises its ugly head in the minds of those committed to the modernist or critical point of view because this placement of tacit knowing at the center of cognitive seems to undercut any possibility of verification and/or validation of knowledge claims, whether in science or in logic. But the fact of the matter is that the criteria for both scientific and logical knowledge claims cannot themselves be established by means of explicit conceptual articulation or rationalization. The criteria are already imbedded and embodied in our natural and common search for knowledge, in the cognitive powers and capacities with which we are endowed from the outset of life. As Polanyi says:

For we can derive rules of observation and verification only from examples of factual statements that we have accepted as true *before* we knew these rules; and *in the end* the application of our rules will necessarily fall back once more on factual observations, the acceptance of which is an act of personal judgment, unguided by any explicit rules. And besides, the application of such rules must rely *all the time* on the guidance of our own personal judgment. This argument formally confirms the participation of the speaker in any sincere statement of fact. (*Personal Knowledge*, p. 254)

Thus, although the ultimate ground of all knowing resides within embodied activity rather than articulatable cognition, this does not undercut the possibility of determining whether or not a given knowledge claim is to be accepted as true. The reason that this is the case is to be found in the fact that even the very possibility of raising such issues trades on or presupposes the employment of the very standards and criteria in question. In short, one could say that these latter are validated and confirmed by their very embodiment in the cognitive process of determining them. They show themselves even though they cannot be said.

This whole issue of the relation of tacit knowledge to the question of verification or confirmation is of course quite critical. Polanyi is not saying that every claim to tacit knowledge is to be accepted as veridical, any more than every claim to explicit knowledge is to be accepted as true. In each case, there are criteria and procedures for assessing whether or not a given knowledge claim is warranted. However, there are different criteria for tacit knowing from those appropriate to explicit knowing, due to the nature of their representative natures. While we are quite familiar with the criteria for explicit knowledge, we are much less so with those for tacit knowing, partly because they are so obviously a part of our everyday lives, and partly because the modernist definition of science systematically ignores them.

The criteria for adjudicating between assertions that fall within the range of explicit knowing can be articulated in advance because they can be identified and defined through focal awareness and conceptual activity. However, those that are appropriate to claims to tacit knowing cannot be so identified and defined because they are already in use in the very process of seeking such identification and definition. This is true of logic as well as of science since no "logical" proof of the principles of logic can be offered without presupposing the very principles being defined. These principles and criteria are demonstrated in their use and vindicated thereby as well since without them there can be no talk of truth at all, let alone a proof of it. This demonstration cannot be provided apart from bodily activities such as formulating syllogisms and testing them by means of Venn diagrams, for example.

A somewhat different way of approaching this same issue involves exploring the implications of the embodied character of tacit knowing for the question of verification or vindication of claims thereto. When one is asked to confirm a given claim to explicit knowledge, one expects to be shown certain recognizable data or premises from which one can infer the proposed conclusion. When one is asked to confirm a claim to tacit knowledge, however, what one expects to be given is an embodied demonstration thereof. One shows that one has acquired a certain set of skills, such as actually speaking Finnish or solving a mathematical problem. The same holds true of the skills involved in validating logical claims as well, since they too must and can only be demonstrated through practice. Likewise, the confirmation of a scientific hypothesis requires the use of skills and insights that themselves lie outside of empirical demonstration.

Tacit knowing is, then, clearly more fundamental than explicit knowing, since the latter can be carried out only on the basis of the former, while tacit knowing can and does take place without relying on explicit knowing. The kinds of discernments and judgments involved in tacit knowing form the axis for all other knowledge and as such cannot be explained or justified in terms of any form thereof. As Wittgenstein said, what is required is to be willing to begin at the beginning without trying to go further back. In placing tacit knowing at the center of all knowing, Polanyi has sought to follow this advice: "The premises underlying a major intellectual process are never formulated and transmitted in the form of definite precepts. When children learn to think naturalistically they do not acquire any explicit knowledge of the principles of causation" (*Science, Faith and Society*, p. 42).

In many ways, the goal of all modernist philosophy is summed up in the ideal offered by the mathematician LaPlace that if we could know everything there is to know about everything at any given moment, we would be able to know all there is to know about the whole universe, past, present, and future by direct inference. This ideal has been called the "God's eye view" and lies at the heart of the modernist definition of and quest for knowledge. It would set aside the fact that knowing is a capacity and act achievable only by human persons, on the basis of their embodiment of specific skills and values, in favor of a definition of knowledge without a knowing subject. Polanyi criticizes this line of thought in the following fashion:

> But this ideal is logically absurd. Imagine a set of mathematical formulas that would answer any question that we might ask about matters of experience. The object of such experience must be other than the mathematical formulas which are to explain it, and hence these formulas are meaningless unless they bear on non-mathematical experiences. In other words, we can use our formulas only after we have made sense of the word to the point of asking questions about it and having established the bearing of the formulas on the experience that they are to explain. (*Knowing and Being*, p. 175)

One of the fundamental difficulties of modern thought is its commitment to some form of foundationalism, as we saw in chapter 1. Even those who deride modernism in the name of subjectivity, relativity, or deconstructionism do not always fault it for seeking such a foundation for knowledge. Rather, they fault it for not being able to achieve its stated goal. So from Polanyi's point of view, both modernism and the forms of postmodernism we encounter today are wide of the mark because they fail to acknowledge that knowing can and must have a place to begin that neither guarantees certainty nor leads to subjectivism. In short, they both accept the dichotomy set in place by modernism between fact and value, between objectivity and subjectivity.

I have chosen to call the place where Polanyi anchors knowledge its "axis" rather than its foundation because the latter term conjures up an image that inherently requires us to ask what it is that this foundation itself rests upon. Foundationalism only leads to an infinite regress or an arbitrarily chosen basis, and the rejection of foundationalism leads only to arbitrary relativism. The genius of Polanyi's approach is that by placing tacit knowing at the center, at the axis of knowledge, he avoids this dilemma of choosing between these equally inadequate alternatives. For the image of an axis suggests an anchoring that is not fixed and in need of further support. Tacit knowing begins within the embodied interaction of human beings with the surrounding physical and social environments, and it needs no other justification than that it vindicates itself in the lives of these human beings, even when and as they discuss whether knowledge is possible at all. The image of an axis enables us to begin at the beginning and avoid arbitrariness at the same time. Tacit knowing as defined by Polanyi provides such an axis.

ACCREDITING OUR COGNITIVE POWERS

The final threat resulting from the assumptions of modern philosophy is that of skepticism. According to the accepted dogma of modern thought, if we cannot have objectivity and full articulation with respect to knowledge claims, then it is impossible to have knowledge at all. For if the gap between the knower and the known cannot be bridged by either sensory perception or logical necessity, as Hume clearly saw, then nothing can ever really be known but at best only believed. However, Polanyi has placed the body, together with its inherent cognitive capacities, at the center of human existence and has, thereby, eliminated the need for a bridge between the knowing agent and the world. Skepticism is predicated on the possibility, indeed, the necessity, of this gap, and so Polanyi's model of cognitivity does away with the threat of skepticism.

The famous skeptical dilemma was posted by Plato in the dialogue *Meno*. There it is argued that humans can ever acquire knowledge, since either they already have it, or they do not. If they have it already, they cannot acquire it anew, and if they did not already have it, they would be unable to recognize it when confronted with it. Thus, it is impossible to gain knowledge in any way whatsoever. Socrates' answer to this dilemma was simply to go ahead pursuing knowledge since it seems to work, and we will be better people for having done so. Polanyi's summary of the *Meno*'s contribution to epistemology runs like this:

> The *Meno* shows conclusively that if all knowledge is explicit, i.e., capable of being clearly stated, then we cannot know a problem or look for its solution. And the *Meno* also shows, therefore, that if problems nevertheless exist, and discoveries can be made by solving them, we can know things, and important things that we cannot tell. (*The Tacit Dimension*, p. 22)

Plato's answer to the dilemma, which was most likely different from that of Socrates, involved complicated views about the pre-existence of the soul, and so forth, an answer that only avoids the issue rather than resolving it. However, the notion of tacit knowing does resolve it by showing that the possibility of knowledge actually requires that we know things that we cannot articulate since otherwise we would not even be able to question its possibility in the first place. After all, one cannot meaningfully question the process of questioning, any more than one can meaningfully question meaningfulness. Moreover, skepticism itself trades on the very notion of the viability of knowledge since the concept of the absence or impossibility of knowledge actually entails its opposite, because it can only be defined in terms of it.

The only alternative, according to Polanyi, is to accept or accredit our inherent cognitive powers, as prone to error as they may be, since on the one hand to do otherwise would lead to a dead end, while on the other hand we do in fact come to know things. People survive together, raise families, build communities, make art, develop science, and even do critical and postcritical philosophy. The attempt to define knowledge according to modernist requirements seeks to eliminate the possibility of error by removing all personal and valuational aspects form the cognitive enterprise, but this also removes the very conditions that render knowledge a viable and valuable endeavor in the first place.

The fact that our cognitive efforts sometimes go awry or are less than perfect is not a weakness or inherent fault but is, rather, a necessary ingredient or counterpart to the very meaning of knowledge in the first place. Rather than view the participation of a personal, social, and valuational dimension in cognition as something to be overcome, or as a "contamination" as the social scientists would have it, what needs to be done is to affirm the potential for knowledge as we already have encountered it and to insist that certain criteria are employed in order to guard against unwarranted investigations and reasonings. We must begin where we are and strive to do better rather than despairing over the impossibility of ever exorcising the specter of skepticism.

Perhaps the most prevalent form of skepticism on the contemporary market is that of relativism, both cultural and epistemological. Polanyi counteracts this popular posture by pointing out that no matter how vehemently a person insists that all claims to truth are relative or subjective, it is the case that this very insistence aims to be understood and accepted as true by those to whom it is directed. He calls this aim "universal intent" and argues that it lies at the very heart of all meaningful cognitive activity. He says:

> While compulsion by force or by neurotic obsession excludes responsibility, compulsion by universal intent establishes responsibility, compulsion by universal intent establishes responsibility. The strain of this responsibility is the greater—other things being equal—the wider the range of alternatives left open to choice and the more conscientious the person responsible for the decision. While the choices in question are open to arbitrary egocentric decisions, a craving for the universal sustains a constructive effort and narrows down this discretion to the point where the agent making the decision finds that he cannot do otherwise. *The freedom of the subjective person to do as he pleases is overruled by the freedom of the responsible person to act as he must.* (*Personal Knowledge*, p. 309)

To put this major point in a slightly different manner, it is of fundamental importance to remember that a "mistake" is precisely that, a "mis-take," a failure to get it right. But a failure to get something right is only recognizable as such because one already *knows* what getting it right would mean and be. This does not entail some sort of mysterious act of institution: it simply acknowledges that we are already embarked on the quest for knowledge and that we can and do often know, even though we may not be able to explicate it, what it is we are looking for and how to go about finding it. The doubting associated with skepticism is a parasitic activity; it presupposes that which it claims to undermine. We do, after all, doubt for a reason, not in general.

It is frequently the case that Polanyi's emphasis on the personal dimension of cognitive activity gets misread as an affirmation and defense of subjectivity as the basis of knowledge. I must admit that this was my own initial bias against his point of view. I thought he must be something of an existentialist in philosopher's clothing. However, the crucial thing to bear in mind is that Polanyi does not claim that it is the personal element within all cognitive endeavor that establishes the truth thereof. Rather, he is claiming that without this personal aspect the whole epistemological enterprise makes no sense because it constitutes the *raison d'etre* for seeking knowledge in the first place. Moreover, unless we accredit our cognitive powers of perceptual and logical discernment, we will be unable to proceed with the search for knowledge.

Once these acknowledgments of and commitments to the fundamental conditions of knowing are in place, then the usual standards and processes of science and logic must, of course, be strictly applied. However, to attempt to define and carry out the search for knowledge as if these conditions were unnecessary, even detrimental to the whole enterprise, as modern philosophy clearly has sought to do, is misleading at best and downright suicidal at worst. Thus, for Polanyi, the quest for knowledge clearly entails the assumptions that there is a world to be known and that we can trust our ability to come to know it, at least partially and usefully. These assumptions constitute the core of personal knowledge.

Polanyi himself anticipated this sort of criticism of his approach to epistemology, and he sought to address it directly in the following manner:

> My own attempt to acknowledge tacit powers of personal judgment as the decisive organ of discovery and the ultimate criterion of scientific truth, have been opposed by describing these agencies as psychological, not logical, in character. But this distinction is not explained by my critics. Is an act of perception which sees an object in a way that assimilates it to past instances of the same kind, a psychological process or a logical inference? We have seen that it can be mistaken and its results be false; and it certainly has a considerable likelihood of being true. To me this suggests that it is a logical process of inference even though it is not explicit. In any case, to perceive things rightly is certainly part of the process of scientific inquiry and to hold perceptions to be right underlies the holding of scientific propositions to be true. And, if, in consequence we must accept the veridical powers of perception as the roots of empirical science, we cannot reasonably refuse to accept other tacit veridical processes having a similar structure. (*Knowing and Being*, p. 173)

Aside from the fact that I think Polanyi should have used the term *integrative act* instead of *inference* in this context, which would be more in keeping with his basic perspective, the point he is making surely holds true. Unless we trust our powers of perception, scientific knowledge is clearly out of the question; likewise with our powers to make reasonable judgments in general. Neither of these capacities can be fully explained or justified outside of themselves since any such efforts must employ, and thus presuppose, the very processes being questioned. Thus, all cognitive activity emerges from and is justified by acts of tacit embodiment in which we necessarily know more than we can tell. As Aristotle so clearly understood, all deductive knowledge begins with inductively arrived at premises, and these in turn arise form our inherent ability to perceive and make judgments correctly.

By way of further exploration of Polanyi's concern to establish the fundamental character of tacit knowing to all forms of cognitive activity, I would like briefly to relate his insights to recent work in brain physiology pertaining to what is known as the "split-brain" phenomenon. There is an increasing amount of data accumulating that suggests and supports the theory that the human brain is structurally divided between its left and right hemispheres. The left hemisphere is thought to control right-handed behavior and such cognitive activity as language and analytic reasoning, while the right hemisphere, about which much less is known, would seem to control imaginative and intuitive judgments. The left hemisphere seems to be more involved in sequential and inferential thought, while the right hemisphere deals more with "lateral" thinking and gestalt awareness. On the surface, it would seem that there exists an obvious correlation between this phenomenon and Polanyi's distinction between explicit and tactic knowing.

The inferential quality and processes associated with explicit knowledge would seem to correlate directly with the functionings of the left hemisphere, while the integrative processes that define the character of tacit knowledge would correlate well with the activity of the right hemisphere. One way of viewing these correlations is to think of the right hemisphere as the axis of subsidiary awareness and bodily activity. By means of the interaction between apperception and embodied prehension, a tacit knowledge is acquired that provides the framework or context within which and out of which explicit knowing takes shape. Sequential and analytic thought can, after all, only take place within a broader context of meaningfulness. Parts and stages can be recognized *as such* only in relation to a previously, if tacitly, acknowledged whole. It is in this sense that tacit knowing, and thus the functions of the right hemisphere of the brain, must be admitted to be logically or conceptually prior to explicit knowing and the functions of the left hemisphere.

In other words, initially, we attend from our genetic and embodied capacities, immersed in physical and social reality, toward meaningful configurations that only take shape tacitly. Then we attend from these tacitly grasped wholes to the particulars and stages comprising them, as well as those comprising yet other holistic units of meaning. This account would suggest a symbiotic, bipolar relationship in which cognitivity is understood as a field or dimension within which neither pole can be said to exist or function apart from the other.

A considerable interest has developed in these issues on the part of cultural anthropologists as a way to deal with what has been termed the "culture/cognition paradox." On the one hand, anthropologists are nearly unanimously agreed that the human brain is the same wherever it is found, that preliterate and literate brains, for instance, are essentially the same, and so on. On the other hand, most anthropologists also maintain that what is "rational" in one culture may not be so in another, and so on. These two emphases within the field of anthropology create a degree of tension at the theoretic level that the split-brain phenomenon may be able to resolve.

According to this model, the bipolar structure of the brain could allow for a given culture, or even subculture, to emphasize the development of the right or left hemisphere more heavily and to thereby produce widely different patterns of cognitivity without questioning the similarity of brain structure. The ability of South Pacific island people, for instance, to navigate across vast expanses of ocean without the aid of instruments or land sightings, or the tendency of many African peoples to model reality in terms of spiritual forces and relationships, rather than substances and attributes, can be offered as phenomena that substantiate this theoretical hypothesis. Thus, it can be said that the same cultures or subcultures stress either the explicit or the tacit mode of knowing more heavily. This could even be said of different families and/or individuals.

It should not be thought that any culture or subgroup can dispense with either set of functions associated with the two hemispheres for all humans have practical needs and situations that call for both modes of thought. This holds true as well for the diverse emphases within our own culture on scientific and artistic endeavors. Not only do both approaches need one another, but each is itself a blending of both hemispheric functions. As Polanyi has made clear, science and logic only make sense and can be carried on within the context provided by the affirmation of meaningful wholes and creative formulation. Artistic creativity must, in turn, rely on the principles of order and concrete embodiment for its fulfillment.

Here again, however, the logical priority of tacit knowing over explicit knowing needs to be reiterated. In all cognitive contexts, no matter how precisely defined and focally explicit, "we know more than we can tell." There are always assumptions, skills, and commitments that not only are articulated, but that we are in principle unable to articulate because they are rooted in our subsidiary awareness and embodied existence. Experientially, then, all cultures and individuals exist within and employ both of these cognitive poles simultaneously and dialectically, but the vector of logical dependence nevertheless runs from the tacit mode of the right hemisphere to the explicit mode of the left hemisphere. In order to understand the dynamics of knowledge, it is necessary to affirm this asymmetric pattern.

THE SOCIETY OF EXPLORERS

One final aspect of Polanyi's account of the structure of knowledge remains to be discussed, namely that pertaining to the social or political dimension of cognitive activity. It will be recalled that at the close of the previous chapter, I introduced the image of a dance as a model of the relationship between our search for understanding of reality and its semi-intractable, somewhat mysterious, ever-opening nature. As we engage in this dance, we frequently can follow the world's lead; sometimes we wander in the dark; and from time to time we even seem to introduce steps and moves of our own. As I indicated at that time, it is important to bear in mind that we do not participate in this dance as independent, self-sufficient individuals but as a cognitive community. There is a horizontal as well as a vertical dimension to our dance, and thus we can think of it as a triangular reality constituted by our mutual interaction with the world and one another.

Polanyi called this social dimension of cognitive activity the "society of explorers." On the one hand, he wished to call attention to the necessarily conservative character of the scientific enterprise in particular and of the search for cognitive understanding in general. Once a given theory or conclusion has been established as reliable, those who know and care about that to which it pertains will naturally be very hesitant to modify or abandon it. On the other hand, however, science and the general search for truth are and should be vigilantly committed to testing and, in the words of Albert Einstein, "questioning axioms." This commitment represents the inherently radical nature of all responsible cognitive activity. Polanyi's image of a society of explorers aptly captures both aspects of knowing.

The notion of 'exploration' is central to what might be termed the "vertical dimension" of the search for knowledge, the effort to discover and confirm those ideas and insights that enable human beings to carry on and enhance their life together. The notion of a society is crucial to what might be called the "horizontal dimension" of the cognitive search, the continual cross-checking and validating of each and every claim to have found the truth. These two dimensions are related symbiotically in that neither of them can function without the other. If the vertical dimension goes unchecked, it generally leads to epistemological authoritarianism, as in the European Middle Ages and the recent Soviet Union. If the horizontal dimension gains ascendancy, the result can be a narrow, skeptical "positivism" that will only accept claims to knowledge that conform to its own limited set of definitions. In a well-functioning society of explorers, each of these dimensions serves to stimulate and balance the other. Thus, in Polanyi's words, "the authority of scientific opinion remains essentially mutual; it is established *between* scientists, not above them. Scientists exercise their authority over each other" (*Knowing and Being*, p. 56).

Polanyi mentions three main categories of criteria that cognitive activity must embody in order to ensure that the concerns of both of the above dimensions are fulfilled. The first is "a sufficient degree of plausibility" or of what some thinkers call "antecedent probability." To be sure, it sometimes happens that we overlook important data or ideas because we judge too quickly that they are too unlikely to be true. However, it simply is not possible to consider seriously every theory or suggestion made in a given context. We must trust that eventually even unlikely truths will force themselves upon us.

The second category is what Polanyi calls "scientific value," consisting of three different aspects: accuracy, systematic importance, and intrinsic interest. Obviously, a specific hypothesis may be backed up with extremely accurate data but be of no particular interest or worth in this time or place. Moreover, it may not harmonize well with what already is accepted as knowledge in a given field. These three aspects play off of one another in dialectical fashion checking and balancing each other repeatedly and cyclically.

Polanyi's third criterion is that of "originality." It may prove to be the case that a given idea or discovery has little systematic value or intrinsic interest but is so highly unusual in character that it warrants serious cognitive attention. This criterion, as well, factors into the various phases and processes of the cognitive enterprise, at times taking a dominant role in relation to the others and at other times being subservient to them (*Knowing and Being*, pp. 53–54).

The usual dilemma that emerges at this point is that of choosing between the dogmatism of authoritarian "experts" whether in science, art, religion, politics, or everyday life, and the cognitive anarchy imposed by skepticism and/or relativism. Polanyi's difficulty in presenting his mediating position is intensified by the fact that he must fight on both fronts simultaneously. Against relativism, including that inherent within deconstructive postmodernism, Polanyi argues that the search for knowledge in general and any specific knowledge claims in particular, once again including those of deconstructionists, necessarily entails the acknowledgment of and commitment to the possibility of truth. As we have seen, he designates this necessity "universal intent" and indicates that it lies at the heart of all cognitive activity. In short, all cognitive claims are intended to be taken as true universally. Polanyi says it this way:

> I speak not of an *established* universality, but of a universal *intent*, for the scientist cannot know whether his claims will be accepted. They may prove false or, though true, may fail to carry conviction. He may even expect that his conclusions will prove unacceptable, and in any case their acceptance will not guarantee him their truth. To claim valid-

ity for a statement merely declares that it *ought* to be accepted by all. The affirmation of scientific truth has an obligatory character which it shares with other valuations, declared universal by our own respect for them. (*The Tacit Dimension*, p. 78)

On the other front, namely against all forms of authoritarian positivism or politicalism, Polanyi argues that there is no such thing as an absolutely established truth within the range of human possibility. This is not simply because we are limited in our abilities and technologies, but because our search for truth takes place within a human social context that allows for, indeed insists upon, continual dialogue among its participants. Just as our commitment to the truth is expressed in the quality of universal intent that accompanies each and every cognitive affirmation, and thereby guards against relativism, so our affirmation of the social dimension of the cognitive process acknowledges the intersubjective character of knowledge and thereby guards against epistemological arrogance. Polanyi expresses the social quality of the cognitive search thus:

Let it also be quite clear that what we have described as the functions of scientific authority go far beyond mere confirmation of facts asserted by science. For one thing, there are no mere facts in science. A scientific fact is one that has been accepted as such by scientific opinion, both on the grounds of the evidence in favor of it and because it appears sufficiently plausible in view of the current scientific conception of the nature of things. Besides, science is not a mere collection of facts, but a system of facts based on their scientific interpretation. It is this system that is endorsed by a scientific authority. (*Knowing and Being*, p. 65)

Thus, according to Polanyi, knowledge is neither exactly what we think it is nor merely what we make it. The social dimension of the cognitive search does acknowledge a degree of truth in what is frequently referred to as the "social construction" of knowledge and/or reality. However, this aspect of our cognitive dance never has the final or exclusive say-so in determining what is accepted as truth for it is always balanced by our common commitment to the thrust of "universal intent." Thus, our freedom to create and/or construct knowledge and our responsibility to the truth go hand in hand to provide for a realistic and useful understanding of cognitive activity.

Let us now consider two corresponding examples of what happens when either of these two off-setting criteria fails to function properly. First, with respect to the social dynamic within the cognitive process, take the case of Immanuel Velikovsky. Polanyi raises this case as a way of indicating that the scientific community can, and sometimes does, overstep its bounds in an effort to control and determine what gets accepted, or even considered, as knowledge. Velikovsky, in his highly controversial book *Worlds in Collision*, offered a theory of the evolution of the solar system that was based on detailed examination of ancient mythological texts rather than on astronomical observation. He hypothesized that the earth had passed repeatedly through the tail of a comet between the fifteenth and seventh centuries. This comet later collided with Mars, which in turn nearly collided with the earth, causing a reversal of the poles and a great number of other catastrophies. The vast majority of astronomers rejected Velikovsky's ideas out of hand, even to the point of threatening to boycott the Macmillan book company for publishing his book (*Knowing and Being*, pp. 74–79).

A group of social scientists took up Velikovsky's cause, not because they were in a position to agree or disagree with his theory, but because the treatment he received from the natural science community seemed clearly to represent a position that contradicted the normal and just processes for establishing truth. Their account of the matter was published in book form as *The Velikovsky Affair* (edited by A. de Grazia) and served to focus the issues involved very clearly. This would seem to be a clear case of the scientific community overstepping its bounds without even giving this new theory a fair hearing. After all, Velikovsky had made several predictions based on his theory which had turned out to be correct. Among other things, he predicted that Venus, since it is a young planet, would be hot, rather than cool as accepted scientific theory held. He also predicted the existence of an antiradiation belt that protects earth from ultraviolet rays from the sun, a belt that has since been confirmed. As it turned out, when scientists sent the *Mariner II* to explore Venus in 1963, it actually burnt up at 800°F. Nevertheless, many scientists rejected Velikovsky's ideas without even having read his book.

The issue here pertains to the proper amount of weight to be given by the scientific community to the criterion of initial plausibility. Clearly, Velikovsky's hypothesis was highly original and somewhat systematic scientifically since it did explain some things that previously had gone unaccounted for. After reviewing the case quite thoroughly, Polanyi concluded that although the scientists involved were short-sighted at best, they did exercise their proper authoritative role in rejecting Velikovsky's theory, primarily because it was not based on observation and experimentation. In the dynamics of the social dimension of the cognitive enterprise, there is no guarantee that truth will not be overlooked, or even surpressed, but at the same time, it is not possible to pursue every single suggestion with equal energy. The long-term, rigorous application of the flexible standards that define the scientific community must be trusted to reveal the truth eventually. Even if Velikovsky's theory is confirmed at a later date as the result of astronomical investigation, that would not legitimate its acceptance at this time since it did not arise by means of the processes and techniques of acceptable cognitive exploration.

In this way, Polanyi suggests that while cognitivity is indeed a social enterprise, this does not mean that whatever we say is truth is, willy-nilly, the truth. These conclusions need to be hammered out in the give and take of responsible dialogue among those who know and care about the field of inquiry involved and under the sanctions imposed by our mutual commitment to the implications of universal intent. Here is the way Polanyi expresses what some philosophers refer to as the principle of "antecedent probabilities," which integrates already established theories into the this particular reasoning process as initial premises:

> Such premises indicate to scientists the kind of questions which seem reasonable and interesting to explore, the kind of conceptions and re- lations that should be upheld as possible, even when some evidence seems to contradict them, or that on the contrary, should be rejected as unlikely, even though there was evidence which would favor them. (*Science, Faith and Society*, p. 11)

The foregoing discussion illustrates the dynamics and difficulties in- volved in the efforts of the scientific community, or society of explorers, to maintain some measure of control over what receives acceptance as scientific knowledge. These same dynamics and difficulties obtain in all cognitive ac- tivity, at whatever level and in whatever context. Knowing is a human enter- prise and therefore must be carried on and regulated by human communities. Although this regulation is not *sufficient* to guarantee the achievement of knowledge, it is *necessary* to its achievement.

At the other end of the cognitivity spectrum, the notion of universal intent undergirds the search for truth by ensuring that knowledge claims are taken seriously as just that, namely claims to truth that should be accepted universally. Whereas the acknowledgment of the social character of knowl- edge guards against overconfidence or arrogance in cognitive activity, the affirmation of universal intent guards against the tendency toward skepticism and relativism. The former provides humility, while the latter provides real- istic confidence in epistemological endeavor.

However, even as the society of explorers sometimes becomes too rigid in the application of its criteria, so too the philosophers "in charge" of defin- ing and ensuring the attainment of knowledge occasionally become too strin- gent in setting the parameters for determining when and where knowledge is attained. A consideration of the following example should make clear just how this kind of malfunction can take place.

In the modern English-speaking, analytic philosophical tradition it has become standard practice to define knowledge in terms of the fulfillment of three separate criteria. A person is said to have knowledge, or knowledge is said to obtain, when these three criteria are met: (1) a person *believes* that a particular proposition is true, (2) a person has adequate *evidence* that this proposition is true, and (3) the proposition is, in fact, *true*. A well-known and fair presentation of this interpretation of knowledge is that of Roderick Chisholm in his book *Theory of Knowledge*. My concern here pertains to the over-protective character of this definition of knowledge, especially of its third criterion.

Since cognitive activity is a human endeavor, the relevance of the first two criteria is not at all difficult to ascertain. As Polanyi himself insists, all knowledge claims entail the belief that what is being asserted is the case. Also, to qualify as a knowledge claim, there must be reason or evidence for believing that what is being affirmed is true. These two criteria are not sufficient conditions for truth, but they are necessary conditions. The addition of the third criterion, that the assertion also be the case, is problematic, to say the least. It represents an attempt on the part of those imposing it to safeguard against the possibility that one's adequate evidence may be coincidental, but it clearly goes too far in this direction. The reason that this is so is two-fold.

The first difficulty with this third criterion is that it is clearly redundant. After having specified that a given assertion must be believed to be true and that there must be support for this belief, what is added by further stipulating that it also must be true? Putting it this way makes it sound as if fulfilling this criterion involves an additional step in the cognitive process, but it should be obvious that this is not the case. If we set out to determine whether or not the assertion is in fact true, we are immediately thrown back to the second criterion, namely, whether or not there is good reason to believe that this assertion is true. In short, there is no way to fulfill this so-called third criterion apart from fulfilling the second. The former collapses into the latter.

Moreover, this additional criterion is highly inappropriate as a standard of knowledge because it seeks to eliminate the human or social dimension of cognitive activity. To require that an assertion actually be the case in order to be counted as knowledge entails that someone can be in a position to judge whether or not this is so. But, of course, this can never happen since human knowers cannot transcend their cognitive context to see reality from the "God's eye" perspective. In the end, we are left with the first two criteria, belief in and evidence for the truth of an assertion. Any attempt to guarantee knowledge by eliminating its human or social dimension is both redundant and arrogant. Such efforts have been the stock-in-trade of modern thinkers since the Enlightenment. Polanyi's understanding of knowledge in terms of the society of explorers in particular and the dynamics of tacit knowing in general replaces this critical posture with one that is wiser and more useful.

There are those who continue to insist on the viability of this third criterion by invoking a distinction between the ontological and epistemological levels of cognitivity. They claim that we must not confuse the question of whether or not a claim is true with whether or not we can say or know that it is true. The former question is said to be independent of the latter; a proposition is or is not true quite apart from anyone's knowledge of its status. This distinction is said to be necessary in order for us to be able to withdraw our truth claim after it has been established that our statement did not correspond to the facts.

My rejoinder to this line of reasoning is three-fold. To begin with, it should be clear that whether or not a given claim is true is decided on the basis of an examination of the evidence for it, not by checking to see if it is true by some independent means. It is not even clear what this could mean. Second, the idea that something could be true totally independent of our knowledge that this is so is essentially circular. After all, *true* is an epistemological term that pertains to knowledge, which in turn is related to humans as cognitive agents. Indeed, it is humans who assert propositions, so what could it mean for truth to be independent of our knowledge of it? Third, even the distinction between the ontological and the epistemological is one made within human linguistic and cognitive activity, so once again we must acknowledge that even this effort to salvage the third criterion ends up being an instance of what it seeks to deny. As William James put it, every distinction must make a difference, otherwise there is no point to making the distinction.

4

DECONSTRUCTING DECONSTRUCTIONISM

As the subtitle of the present study indicates, Polanyi's approach to philosophy is a postmodern one. His own designation for it, in the subtitle of *Personal Knowledge,* was "post-critical." In the Introduction to this examination of Polanyi's thought it was further indicated that his specific version of postmodernism differs rather radically from the sorts of approaches that have come into prominence since the publication of his major works. This difference is focused in the contrast between the terms *reconstruction* and *construction.* After having explored the main themes and distinctions crucial to Polanyi's epistemology, we are now in a position to consider this difference more thoroughly.

In brief, it can and must be said that while the more predominant versions of postmodernism, such as those of Jacques Derrida, Michel Foucault, and Jean Francois Lyotard, are generally classified as "deconstructivist" in character, Polanyi's version is more properly termed "reconstructivist" in nature. Both Polanyi and the deconstructivists are concerned to identify and overcome the cognitive limitations inherent within the modern way of thinking, limitations that result from the presuppositions inherited from the overall philosophical posture taken by early Western thinkers, such as Plato and Aristotle. These presuppositions and limitations are especially evident in and crucial to the works of modern thinkers such as Descartes, Hume, and Kant, and this is why a chapter has been devoted to delineating Polanyi's critique thereof.

The deconstructivist thinkers also offer trenchant criticisms of the Western, and especially modern, way of thinking about language, knowledge, and reality. But whereas Polanyi sought to develop a post-modern philosophy that overcomes the modernist presuppositions and ensuing limitations without obviating the positive values inherent within this approach, deconstructivist thinkers for the most part have concluded that there is nothing of value to salvage from the traditional Western way of philosophizing. They seek, in their own words, to "deconstruct" this tradition by calling into question its fundamental assumptions and then to move on to more honest and open-ended way of doing philosophy. On the following pages, the main concerns of this deconstruction project will be presented, together with an account of how they differ from the major emphases of Polanyi's reconstructive understanding.

The Critique of Fixed Meanings

Throughout the history of Western philosophy, it has been assumed that the relation among language, reality, and thought was essentially one of the first phenomenon serving as the symbolic representation of the latter two phenomena. From Plato's time on through the logical empiricists in the early decades of the twentieth century, language has more or less been thought of as composed nouns which name objects and qualities in the world external to the mind or ideas and operations that are within the mind. This view has been called alternatively the "luggage tag" or the "picture theory" of meaning since according to it the purpose of language is to mirror or represent the world around and within us.

This way of construing the nature and function of language carries with it the unspoken assumption that the meanings of the words out of which language is composed are and must remain fixed, at least within the immediate context in which they are used in a concrete setting. Within this framework, ambiguity and vagueness have been understood as difficulties that can and must be overcome if true communication is to take place. The epitome of this representational approach to linguistic meaning was the "logical atomism" propounded in the works of Bertrand Russell and the young Ludwig Wittgenstein, the latter being famous for having claimed, "Whatever can be said at all can be said clearly; and whereof we cannot speak thereof we must remain silent."

In contrast to this standard way of construing language, Derrida, for instance, strives to point out the incredible fluidity of language and meaning, even within a concrete context. Indeed, he has insisted that any given utterance can and in fact must have as many different meanings as those who speak and hear it wish it to have. For Derrida, *difference* in meaning rather than fixedness is both the reality and the goal. For him, language is not about anything at all but is rather "about itself" in the sense that its meanings are systematically open-ended; language is nothing but a system of differential slippage and dissemination. "There is nothing outside of language . . . there is only the indefinite referral of signifier to signifier" (*Writing and Difference,* p. 25).

Actually, Derrida introduces his crucial concept of 'difference' in connection with the broader notion of a 'nonconcept' in the following passage:

> The notion of 'difference', for example, is a non-concept in that it cannot be defined in terms of oppositional predicates; it is neither *this* nor *that;* but rather this and that (e.g. the act of differing and of deferring) without being reducible to a dialectic logic either . . . There is no conceptual realm beyond language which would allow the term to have a univocal semantic content over and above its inscription in language. Because it remains a trace of language it remains non-conceptual. And because it has no oppositional or predicative generality, which would identify it as *this* rather than *that,* the term 'difference' cannot be defined within a system of logic—Aristotelian or dialectical—that is, within the logocentric system of philosophy. ("Deconstruction and the Other," in *Dialogues with Contemporary Thinkers,* p. 110)

As this passage makes abundantly clear, not only does Derrida express his ideas in complex, convoluted form, but he also enjoys playing with the self-reflective and potential for punning elements of language. Be that as it may, it is fair to say that Derrida seeks to undercut what he calls the "logocentric" pretensions of Western philosophy, the narrowminded overconfidence of philosophy and science that speech can accurately represent and analyze the physical and conceptual worlds. To borrow a line from Hamlet, there is far more to reality than can be crowded into our philosophies.

Another influential deconstructivist thinker who takes up this attack on the traditional Western understanding of the fixedness of linguistic meaning is François Lyotard. He is particularly animated by a concern to overcome the entire effort to reduce language to a systematic set of symbols, to which linguists and semioticists are prone. Lyotard attributes this way of thinking about language to the model proposed by Augustine in which words are said to stand for things and/or thoughts and then goes on to maintain that linguistic communication is far more subtle and supple than such a model will allow. He insists that it is now time to break the hegemony that this view has held over the theory of language. Lyotard puts it this way:

> Let's take up this business of signs once more, you have not understood, you have remained rationalists, semioticians, Westerners, let's emphasize it again, it is the road toward *libidinal* currency that must be opened by force. What the semioticians maintain as a hypothesis beneath

their discourse is that the thing of which they speak may always be treated as a sign; and this sign in turn is indeed thought within the network of concepts belonging to the theory of communication. (*Libidinal Economy,* p. 43)

Lyotard prefers the more fluid and paradoxical view of language proposed by the pre-Socratic Sophists to that of the Augustinian Western tradition. In large measure, this is so because he thinks that this traditional view was devised within a historical-political context in which religious conversion and oppression were at the top of the agenda. We shall return to this theme shortly, but first it will prove helpful to take note of Lyotard's more positive suggestions for opening up our view of linguistic communication. One of his key notions is that of the "differends," the as yet unspoken and undefined dimensions of thought and speech that get passed over by the traditional representationalist view of meaning and communication. This concept runs parallel to Derrida's analysis of the notion of "difference" as mentioned above.

Lyotard maintains that it is both arrogant and foolish to presuppose that every aspect of reality can be subsumed under a finite range of headings designated by nouns, verbs, and adjectives. Thus, room must be left for a way to deal with these leftovers, these differences that do not fit within the usual categories of language as we know and shape it. Lyotard makes his point well in the following remarks:

The differend is the unstable state and instant of language wherein something which must be able to be put into phrases cannot yet be. This state includes silence, which is a negative phrase, but it also calls upon phrases which are in principle possible. This state is signalled by what one ordinarily calls a feeling: "One cannot find the words," etc. A lot of searching must be done to find new rules for forming and linking phrases that are able to express the differend disclosed by the feeling . . . What is at stake in a literature, in a philosophy, in a politics perhaps, is to bear witness to differends by finding idioms for them. (*Peregrinations: Law, Form, Event,* p. 22)

THE CRITIQUE OF OBJECTIVE KNOWLEDGE

The deconstructivist approach to the concepts of 'truth' and 'knowledge' is grounded in what has come to be called the "situated" nature of all human cognitive activity. This is to say that it must be acknowledged that all our efforts to achieve and obtain knowledge take place within specific historical and social parameters that largely determine the way we go about acquiring data and reasoning from it toward reliable conclusions. According to the traditional Western definition of knowledge, it must be completely free from and uncontaminated by any and all factors other than those that strictly pertain to the issue or experiment at hand. In short, the modern understanding of the cognitive enterprise, which sees knowledge as absolutely "objective," must now be seen as both unrealizable and counterproductive.

Michel Foucault focuses his critique of the ideal of objective knowledge in terms of the notion of 'ideology.' For according to the accepted definitions of knowledge and truth, these concepts are contrasted to the concept of ideology, a false representation of reality that must be exposed by the efforts of science and/or philosophy. Foucault argues that it is crucially important to see that science and philosophy are themselves social practices and as such can never be free of the political pressures and agendas of those engaging in them. "Behind the concept of ideology there is a kind of nostalgia for a quasi-transparent form of knowledge, free from all error and illusion" (*Power/Knowledge,* p. 117). He goes on to offer his own working definitions of truth:

> (1) Truth is to be understood as a system of ordered procedures for the production, regulation, distribution, circulation, and operation of statements. (2) Truth is linked in a circular relation with systems of power which produce and sustain it, and to effects of power which it induces and which extend it. (3) This regime is not merely ideological or superstructural; it was a condition of the formation and development of capitalism. (*Power/Knowledge,* p. 133)

What Foucault is especially keen to point out, then, is the political and economic character of all epistemological activity, whether at the concrete or the theoretical level. In his view, it is impossible and even harmful to pretend to ourselves that we pursue and obtain knowledge apart from the social processes that surround and underwrite our investigations. We must always ask, about any claim to knowledge: Who is making this claim, why, where, when, and to and/or for whom? In short, there is no free lunch when it comes to the questions of knowledge and truth. Throughout history, those who have discovered and codified "the truth" have done so under the direction and control of those in power, whether it be the emperor, the church, the landed gentry, the state, or the capitalist. Foucault stresses the power of domination as the progenitor of all Western values:

> The domination of certain men over others leads to the differentiation of values; class domination generates the idea of liberty; and the forceful appropriation of things necessary to survival and the imposition of

a duration not intrinsic to them account for the origin of logic. (*Language, Counter-Memory, Practice*, p. 150)

Foucault is especially fond of the sort of philosophy found in the writings of Nietzsche, particularly that which focuses on the notions of "effective history" and "genealogy." Just as Nietzsche traced the genealogy of morals in his book by that name, so Foucault seeks to trace the genealogy of epistemological notions, to engage in a kind of "conceptual archaeology" aimed at uncovering the real roots of knowledge. This approach to philosophical investigation stands opposed to the ideal of objectivity because the latter is unrealistic and dishonest. It fails to admit that the very stuff out of which knowledge is made is in fact the particulars of personal and social life. About Nietzsche's way of doing philosophy Foucault has this to say:

> The final trait of effective history is its affirmation of knowledge as perspective. Historians take unusual pains to erase the elements in their work which reveal their grounding in a particular time and place, their preferences in a controversy—the unavoidable obstacles of their passion. Nietzsche's version of historical sense is explicit in its perspective and acknowledges its system of injustice. Its perception is slanted, being a deliberate appraisal, affirmation, or negation. (*Language, Counter-Memory, Practice*, p. 155)

Derrida, too, joins in this emphasis on the necessity of understanding the socio-political framework within which all epistemic endeavor takes place. This concern actually forms one of the more important features of his notion of deconstruction as a way of doing philosophy, as well as a way of reading other types of literature. Derrida addresses this whole issue quite pointedly in the following passage:

> It does, of course, contribute to our epistemological appreciation of texts by exposing the philosophical and theoretical presuppositions that are at work in every critical methodology, be it Formalism, New Criticism, Socialist Realism or a historical critique. Deconstruction asks *why* we read a literary text in this particular manner rather than another. It shows, for example, that New Criticism is not *the* way of reading texts, however enshrined it may be in certain university institutions, but only one way among others. Thus deconstruction can also serve to question the presupposition of certain university and cultural institutions to act as the sole or privileged guardians and transmitters of meaning. In short, deconstruction not only teaches us to read literature more thoroughly by attending to it *as language,* as the production of

meaning through *difference* and dissemination, through a complex play of signifying traces; it also enables us to integrate the covert philosophical and political presuppositions of institutionalized critical methods which generally govern our reading of a text." ("Deconstruction and the Other," in *Dialogue, with Contemporary Continental Thinkers,* p. 123)

This passage has been quoted in full because it focuses nearly all the different aspects of the deconstructionist critique of the ideal of objective knowledge, a critique that seeks to establish the role of political and other social factors in the search for and formulation of knowledge. Since this illusory ideal has come to be synonymous with the modern understanding of cognitive activity, the thrust of the deconstructionist critique entitles it to the title "postmodern" because the latter claims not to be based on the same assumptions.

Lyotard as well defines 'postmodernism' in terms of the need for skeptical questioning of all the epistemological and conceptual conventions that have been developed throughout the history of Western philosophy and brought to a head in the thought of the so-called Enlightenment. His detailed examination of this movement in *The Postmodern Condition* sees it as standing against all grounds of authority, assumption, or convention which have been codified in the past two centuries. Thus, it must be understood as a political as much as a philosophical critique. In the minds of the deconstructivists, these two are really one and the same reality.

THE CRITIQUE OF MONOLITHIC SYSTEMS

The above concerns of Lyotard lead naturally into this additional theme of the deconstructivist posture, namely, the critique of all ideological and philosophical systems of thought that seek and claim to encompass the entire truth about any aspect of reality. All authority and convention are suspect because they stem from the politically oppressive values and practices of those who are already in authority. Just as history is written by the victors, so knowledge is defined by those who determine the criteria for truth. Thus, the systems of thought devised within the parameters of the modern Western way of doing science and/or philosophy are extremely suspect from the outset. All system makers will end up justifying their own systems by means of the criteria that they themselves have devised, even as Hegel contended, "The proof of my system is my system."

In his *Discourse on Language,* Foucault focuses the constraints and conditions that give rise to the "truth" in any science, as well as the criteria by means of which all claims to the truth are judged. He argues that these sorts of factors actually control what we end up calling "truth" and "knowledge" and that they are more sociopolitical than epistemological. Thus, the various systems of thought or explanatory theories and laws developed within any scientific discipline should be suspect from the outset. It is the deconstructionist task to uncover and interrogate the presuppositions that hold such frameworks in place. Here is how Foucault expresses the point:

> For a discipline to exist, there must be the possibility of formulating—and of doing so ad infinitum—fresh propositions . . . These propositions must conform to specific conditions of objects, subject, methods, etc. . . . Within its own limits, every discipline recognizes as true and false propositions, but it repulses a whole teratology of learning . . . In short, a proposition must fulfill some onerous and complex conditions before it can be admitted within a discipline. (*Discourse on Language*, p. 223)

The conditions and criteria governing which propositions actually even get admitted for consideration within a given field of study are crucial to the determination of truth and knowledge in that field. Thus, the hypotheses, theories, and laws that embody the content of any discipline, the monolithic systems of thought that dominate the interpretation of our experience in a given dimension of reality are themselves subject to suspicion and critique as expression of modernism.

As some critics of deconstructionism have pointed out, it is difficult to know how one can criticize every system of thought without developing or presupposing a system of one's own. Derrida addressed this issue by speaking of locating a "non-site" or nonplace outside of any system from which to interrogate and reflect upon philosophy in an original manner. He concluded that such a nonsite could not be found within philosophy but could be found in the world of literature, especially in creative writing and poetry. The language of literature provides the needed "distance" to enable one to focus on philosophy as a kind of writing rather than simply as a conglomerate of theories and systems.

> This distance provides the necessary free space from which to interrogate philosophy anew; it was my preoccupation with literary texts which enabled me to discern the problematic of *writing* as one of the key factors in the deconstruction of metaphysics. ("Deconstruction and the Other," p. 108)

When the question is raised concerning the possibility of actually being able to stand outside of systematic thought in order to analyze and critique it from some cognitive "nonplace," Derrida admits that this is an exceedingly complex problem. He seems to think that even though systematic reflection is in fact still reflection, it can be engaged in such a manner as to provide a foothold that is at least partially situated in a "nonsite" with respect to philosophical systems of thought. Apparently, he thinks that by striking a literary posture one can approach philosophy by way of an angle that provides a fresh understanding of thinking in general. In the following passage, Derrida wrestles with this issue:

> In a certain sense it is true to say that 'deconstruction' is still in metaphysics. But we must remember that if we are indeed *inside* metaphysics, we are not inside it as we might be *inside* a box or a milieu. We are still *in* metaphysics in the special sense that we are *in* determinate language. Consequently, the idea that we might be able to get outside of metaphysics has always struck me as naive. So that when I refer to the 'closure' . . . of metaphysics, I insist that it is not a question of considering metaphysics as a circle within a limit or simple boundary. The notion of the limit and boundary . . . of metaphysics is itself highly problematic. My reflections on this problematic have always attempted to show that the limit or end of metaphysics is not linear or circular in any indivisible sense. And as soon as we acknowledge that the limit-boundary of metaphysics is divisible, the logical rapport between inside and outside is no longer simple . . . It is simply that our belonging to, and inherence in, the language of metaphysics is something that can only be rigorously and adequately thought about from another *topos* or space where our problematic rapport with the boundary of metaphysics can be seen in a more radical light. ("Deconstruction and the Other," p. 110)

Derrida's attempt to resolve this dilemma may or may not sound convincing to those who continue to ponder this issue. Be that as it may, it should be clear that he and the other leading deconstructionists stand four-square against the traditional Western insistence on approaching philosophical questions from within the monolithic systems of thought that this tradition itself has created. They contend that it is necessary to interrogate these systems from outside of them. Moreover, the deconstructivist project is in no position to claim any sort of privileged perspective on reality and the truth for the fresh nonplace from which it seeks to raise questions about modernist presuppositions is just another place among others.

This latter point is an extremely important one since unless deconstructivist thinkers acknowledge the nonsuperior character of their own point of view they would be subject to the very same criticisms that they level at other pretentious monolithic systems of thought. At the same time, however, it must be noted that on a significant number of occasions deconstructivist thinkers write as if they are operating from a privileged vantage point that seems to grant them some sort of special objectivity when criticizing traditional Western philosophy. Nevertheless, as Derrida makes clear in the following remarks, there is a puzzling ambiguity about the deconstructivist posture on this issue:

> Nor must we forget that deconstruction is itself a form of literature, a literary text to be read like other texts, an interpretation open to other interpretations. Accordingly, one can say that deconstruction is at once extremely *modest* and extremely *ambitious*. It is ambitious in that it puts itself on a part with literary texts, and modest in that it admits that it is only one textual interpretation among others, written in a language which has no centralizing power of mastery or domination, no privileged meta-language over and above the language of literature. ("Deconstruction and the Other," p. 125)

DECONSTRUCTION AS POSITIVE RESPONSE

In spite of all protestations to the contrary, it must be admitted that deconstuctivist thinkers conceive of their project as a positive one. Deconstruction is not equivalent to nihilism. The various quotations from Foucault and Lyotard offered on the preceding pages should make it abundantly clear that even though they are highly critical of modernism and the entire Western intellectual tradition, the overall purpose of their work is to open up a fresh way to conceive of philosophy, language, and reality. It is, for them, one thing to seek the deconstruction of modernity and quite another to claim that this deconstruction of modernity represents the end of all meaningful thought and language. After all, one protests for a reason, namely in an attempt to change things for the better.

Derrida, for his part, speaks directly to this issue in the following passage:

> Deconstruction certainly entails a moment of affirmation. Indeed, I cannot conceive of a radical critique which would not be ultimately motivated by some sort of affirmation acknowledged or not. Deconstruction always presupposes affirmation, as I have frequently attempted to point out, sometimes employing Nietzschean terminology. I do not mean that the deconstructing *subject* or *self* affirms. I mean that deconstruction is, in itself, a positive response to an alterity which necessarily calls, sum-

mons or motivates it. Deconstruction is therefore vocation—a response to a call. ("Deconstruction and the Other," p. 116)

As is clear in the quotation from Lyotard in the first section of the present chapter concerning the notion of fixed meanings, he too conceives of the deconstructivist task as one that seeks to rethink and open up our understandings of meaning, reality, and truth altogether. There he says that "a lot of searching must be done to find new rules for forming and linking phrases that are able to express the differend disclosed by the feeling . . . to bear witness to differends by finding idioms for them." So postmodernism seeks to replace modernism by first critiquing its philosophical presuppositions and its political oppressiveness and then finding new points of departure and conceptual formulations for expressing the aspects of reality and experience that have been covered over by the limitations of modernism.

Although Foucault seems far less ready to acknowledge that the deconstructionist project constitutes a positive response to the negativities inherent within modernism, there is in his writings an implicit goal or purpose that serves as a positive rationale for engaging in deconstructionist activity. When commenting favorably on Nietzsche's efforts to trace out the genealogical roots of the modernist way of construing reality and knowledge, for instance, Foucault says that modernism presupposes the existence of some sort of exact "essence" behind all appearances and assumes that this original reality can be found and known. The modern, scientific quest for knowledge continues to buy into the classical philosophy of Platonic forms that endow the world of experience with reality and being. The West continues to search for this primordial utopia, a quest that is in fact illusory.

This search is directed to 'that which was already there' the image of a primordial truth fully adequate to its nature, and it necessitates the removal of every mask to ultimately disclose an original identity. However, if the genealogist refuses to extend his faith in metaphysics, if he listens to history, he finds that there is 'something altogether different' behind these things: not a timeless and essential secret, but the secret that they have no essence or that their essence was fabricated in a piecemeal fashion from alien forms. (*Language, Counter-Memory, Practice,* p. 141)

It would seem that for Foucault the minimal positive rationale for deconstructive activity is to disclose the shortcomings of modernist pretensions through rigorous and unending "conceptual archaeology." Nevertheless, this task in itself constitutes something that he believes is of the utmost importance, something that has intrinsic value for humankind in general and for postmodern philosophy in particular. Even Nietzsche implicitly assumed positive value to his efforts to "transvaluate values," to "philosophize with a hammer."

One is reminded here of the words of Albert Camus when analyzing the logic of resistance and rebellion in his most powerful book *The Rebel:*

> In every act of rebellion, the rebel simultaneously experiences a feeling of revulsion at the infringement of his rights and a complete and spontaneous loyalty to certain aspects of himself. Thus he implicitly brings into play a standard of values so far from being gratuitous that he is prepared to support it no matter what the risks. (p. 13–14)

So even though Foucault seems to offer no directly positive goal for his deconstructive enterprise, there would seem to be one inherent within his and any attempt to overthrow a dominant way of doing philosophy since such efforts presuppose a standard of value by virtue of which one judges that this accepted way of doing things is not right. This standard of value, in turn, also entails implicit proposals for an approach to philosophy that should replace the current approach. Thus, all recommended change implies, at least indirectly, a positive response to the current situation.

One final matter. The statements of Derrida that were quoted at the outset of the first section of this chapter—"There is nothing outside of language . . . there is only the indefinite referral of signifier to signifier"—has given rise to a good deal of controversy. Critics have maintained that for the deconstructivists there is no reality beyond language itself, no world outside of speech to which the latter refers or seeks to represent. Indeed, if this were in fact the case it would seem that the entire deconstructionist project would necessarily implode upon itself since there would be no point to any linguistic activity, including that of the deconstructivists, other than the playing of some freefloating phonetic game. While its referential function may not be the only purpose that language serves, it must be admitted that it is generally taken to be an extremely important, if not the most important, one. When this question was put to Derrida himself by an interviewer, he offered the following response:

> It is totally false to suggest that deconstruction is a suspension of reference. Deconstruction is always deeply concerned with the 'other' of language. I never cease to be surprised by critics who see my work as a declaration that there is nothing beyond language, that we are imprisoned in language; it is, in fact, saying the exact opposite. The critique of logocentrism is above all else the search for the 'other' and the 'other of language' . . . Certainly deconstruction tries to show that the ques-

tion of reference is much more complex and problematic than traditional theories supposed. It even asks whether our term 'reference' is entirely adequate for designating the 'other.' The other, which is beyond language and which summons language, is perhaps not a 'referent' in the normal sense which linguists have attached to this term. But to distance oneself thus from the habitual structure of reference, to challenge or complicate our common assumptions about it, does not amount to saying that there is *nothing* beyond language. ("Deconstruction and the Other," p. 124)

While there remain serious questions as to whether this sort of response adequately extricates Derrida from the grip of this particular criticism, it is perfectly clear that he himself does not think that language stands alone as the only reality. Indeed, the above quotation would seem to indicate once again that Derrida, as well as others who engage in the deconstructivist enterprise, presuppose an implicit positive agenda within their critique of the arrogance and errors of modernism. It is time now to turn to an exploration of the differences between this *de*constructivist philosophy and the *re*constructivist mode of thought offered by Michael Polanyi.

A POLANYIAN CRITIQUE

As was mentioned at the beginning of this chapter, both Polanyi and the deconstructivist thinkers seek to formulate a philosophy that carries us past the limitations and inconsistencies of modern Western epistemology. That is to say, both are "postmodern" in their outlook, striving to overcome the arrogance and oppression of modernity. However, they do differ in their analysis of just where the difficulties of modern philosophy lie, as well as in what they think ought to be done by way of correcting these shortcomings. I have sought to capture this basic difference by contrasting the prefixes attached to the terms by which their respective approaches are designated: *de*construction versus *re*construction. While the former approach finds little if anything of value in the modernist way of thinking and thus seeks to dismantle it in toto, Polanyi's approach seeks to redirect or redefine the basic insights of modern thought, which have been distorted and inverted through inappropriate use.

Beginning with the question of fixed versus open-ended meanings, a Polanyian understanding of linguistic significance would take a middle position between these two extremes. To begin with, since for Polanyi meaning is a function of the interaction between subsidiary and focal awareness, on the one hand, and conceptual and bodily activity, on the other hand, on both the individual and social level meanings cannot be seen as finalized or fixed. The dynamics of tacit knowing preclude the possibility that any symbol can be thought of as attached to any referent in a permanent manner. Just as reality continuously reveals itself, so do linguistic meanings.

At the same time, however, this same tacit dynamic makes it clear that meanings cannot be open-ended in the absolute sense that seems to be implied by deconstructivist analysis. For there exists a vectorial relation between subsidiary and focal awareness whereby meaning can only arise and be maintained in a context where there is something concrete to which to attend. Polanyi expresses this point in the following way:

> It is our subsidiary awareness of a thing that endows it with meaning: with a meaning that bears on an object of which we are focally aware. A meaningful relation of a subsidiary to a focal is formed by the action of a person who integrates one to the other, and the relation persists by the fact that the person keeps up this integration. (*Knowing and Being,* p. 182)

When we reflect on the nature of the language acquisition process it is easy to see the cogency of Polanyi's position. On the one side, we are all familiar with the difficulty that children have finding their way through the labyrinthine logic inherent in the necessary vagueness and ambiguity of any natural language. Clearly, meanings are not fixed in some Platonic sense, as the evolution of grammar and slang surely demonstrate. On the other side, however, it is equally clear that if meanings were completely, or even largely, open-ended children would never be able to acquire a natural language at all, and thus there would not be any languages either.

There are times when one gets the feeling that deconstructionist thinkers received their initial impetus from having read Wittgenstein's critique of the notion of fixed meanings but then failed to grasp his equally strong critique of the notion of private language. Since linguistic meaning is a function of socially interactive "language-games" it can be neither fixed nor entirely open-ended in nature. Polanyi's treatment of linguistic meaning, as parallel to his treatment of cognitive activity within the "society of explorers," is in essential harmony with that of Wittgenstein on this matter. In their zeal to liberate cognitive and linguistic activity from the confines of the modernist way of thinking, deconstructivists have overshot the mark and placed themselves in self-stultifying and embarrassing position.

For once one construes meaningfulness as completely open-ended, it is no longer possible to say anything. There are times when the deconstructivists sound as if they believe that words and statements can in fact mean anything and whatever the speaker and/or hearer wants them to mean. But such a view is self-defeating because it entails that there is no way to determine what the statements that supposedly express this idea itself actually mean. The position that meanings are intrinsically open-ended is viscously circular in that it undercuts its own intelligibility. The notion of logocentrality is, to be sure, unduly confining, but its opposite is equally dysfunctional.

With regard to the deconstructivist critique of "objectivity," it is easy to see that once again Polanyi shares a common concern. The major thrust of Polanyi's postcritical philosophy is aimed directly at what he more than once calls the "cult of objectivity." Indeed, the title of Polanyi's most thorough work, *Personal Knowledge,* is meant to counteract the standard modernist notion that cognitivity can and must be defined exclusively in terms of objective knowledge. Moreover, the whole notion of tacit knowing, wherein we always "know more than we can tell," undermines the modern hegemony of explicitness and replicability as the criteria of legitimate knowledge. In this regard, as well, Polanyi and deconstructivist thinkers are on the same page.

In addition, Polanyi would agree that social and political considerations factor into the discovery and formulation of knowledge. However, his approach would have to part company with that of the deconstructivists over the proper interpretation of the significance of such factors. Whereas deconstructivist thinkers, especially Foucault, conclude that the cognitive enterprise is nothing but a series of power plays and domination, Polanyi maintained that it is this very social character of knowledge acquisition, as focused in his notion of the society of explorers, that guarantees that the search for knowledge avoids both narrow-minded objectivity and the slippery slope of subjectivism. For the simple fact that cognitive activity is a social phenomenon does not entail that it is bogus or that its results are unreliable.

It is the concept of 'universal intent' that distinguishes Polanyi's approach from that of the deconstructivists. He argued that the tendency toward subjectivity inherent in the sociopolitical matrix of cognitive activity is offset by the equally powerful drive toward a universally accepted truth. Even as Socrates argued against Thrasymachus, in the early pages of Plato's *Republic,* that the possibility of error entails the necessity of truth, so Polanyi insists that choice and/or power alone do not determine knowledge and truth. Here is how Polanyi himself expresses the point:

> While compulsion by force or by neurotic obsession excludes responsibility, compulsion by universal intent establishes responsibility. The strain of this responsibility is the greater—the other things being equal—the wider the range of alternatives left open to choice and the more conscientious the person responsible for the decision. While the choices in question are open to arbitrary egocentric decisions, a craving for the universal sustains a constructive effort and narrows down this discretion to the point where the agent making the decision finds that he cannot do otherwise. *The freedom of the subjective person to do as he pleases*

is overruled by the freedom of the responsible person to act as he must.
(*Personal Knowledge,* p. 309)

The tragic irony implicit within the deconstructivist posture is that the contention that in the final analysis it is political power and domination that determine the nature of truth must then be applied with equal force and rigor to the "truth" of the deconstructivist claims themselves. For surely the critiques of Lyotard, Foucault, and Derrida are meant to be taken as true vis á vis modernism; yet if these claims are, in fact, true, they are merely the outcome of the particular agendas that motivate these thinkers. The point is, one cannot have it both ways. Either there is some sense and validity to the notion of universal truth at which our shared search for knowledge aims, at least partially independent of sociopolitical forces, or the claim that this is *not* so itself makes no sense and can have no validity. There is little or no indication in the writings of deconstructionists that they are aware of this irony.

The final two themes making up the deconstructivist understanding of postmodernism, as presented in the early sections of this chapter, tend to merge together in relation to Polanyi's philosophy. The first has to do with the need to critique the Western proclivity for monolithic systems of thought, while the second pertains to the claim that deconstruction still must be seen as a "positive" response rather than as a nihilistic one. The main thrust of the latter claim seems to conflict with that of the former since this positive response has in fact grown into something of a monolithic system in its own right. In a word, in order to be able to critique other points of view, one must have a place to stand, a point of view, from which to do so.

The situation here is similar to that which obtains in relation to the Marxist treatment of the notion of 'ideology' For most thinkers, the term refers to any perspective or point of view; it is synonymous with 'philosophy' or 'system of thought.' For Marx, however, an ideology is, by definition, a *false* point of view or philosophy. Thus, while others try to evaluate Marxism as an ideology or system of thought, the Marxist insists that Marxism is not just another philosophy, but is rather a matter of science. The result is that Marxism becomes immune to criticism because it lies outside of the process of evaluation as a point of view or perspective. However, to follow in this line of thinking lands Marxists in precisely the position that they criticized Hegel for taking up, namely, that of having to claim that "the proof of my system is my system." For it should be perfectly clear that the insights and claims of Marxism are not really scientific.

The point here is that one cannot have it both ways. One cannot claim to be critiquing all other systems of thought or philosophies while standing outside of any system of thought oneself, and at the same time claim to be offering a constructive response or alternative to these philosophies that should be accepted as the proper understanding of the way things are. Yet this is what deconstructionist thinkers do when they claim not be offering a system of their own yet also claim to be serving as an alternative to modernism. Indeed, as Polanyi would be quick to point out, it is not really possible to critique other systems of thought from within a vacuum; all claims entail presuppositions and implications, and all claims must be generated from within some perspective.

Here again we see the relevance of Polanyi's concept of a 'society of explorers' as a kind of democratic check-and-balance dynamic that guards against any effort to place oneself and/or one's point of view outside of or above the evaluative process necessary to search for understanding. In a "society," everyone's point of view is on equal footing and must submit to examination and criticism from other members of the community. Polanyi's other term for expressing this point is the *republic of science,* in which the claims of all are both honored and subjected to criticism. No point of view can exempt itself from full participation in this egalitarian give-and-take in the quest for truth. However, it is clear that deconstructionist thinkers are often guilty of speaking as if they are immune to such criticism, while at the same time freely offering criticisms of other modes of thought.

The other side of the coin in this discussion from Polanyi's point of view is the notion of universal intent. The tendency to err on the side of absolutism or authoritarianism is guarded against by the participatory interaction of the society of explorers. The tendency to err on the side of relativism and subjectivism is guarded against by the reality that all thinkers and speakers implicitly presuppose a criterion of truth by which they intend their thoughts and claims to be judged. In brief, every claim, including those of deconstructionists, aims at being judged by others as in fact true. However, deconstructionists frequently write as if such a criterion were merely the invention of modern Western philosophers, and that no such standard of truth can be seen as universal.

Of course, the rub is that even this claim appeals to the very criterion that it seeks to overcome in that it too claims to be true and intends to be accepted by others as insightful and useful in moving toward a better understanding of how things are and should be. To attempt to undercut the generally accepted criteria for evaluating claims to knowledge is a self-defeating undertaking since it necessarily involves an implicit appeal to these very same criteria. It is a classic example of a vicious circle, whereas to claim that one's view conforms to such criteria by being true, even though it may not be true, reinforces these criteria and constitutes a nonvicious circle. Thus, to a large degree, the claims of the deconstructionists, from a Polanyian point of view, are proclamations that though full of sound and fury actually end up signifying nothing.

These then are the shortcomings and pitfalls besetting the *de*constructivist approach to postmodernism. However, Polanyi's *re*constructivist approach avoids these difficulties by affirming and accrediting both the individual's powers for cognitive achievement and humanity's capacity and process for evaluating claims to such achievement. Rather than debunk the fundamental concerns and criteria of modern or critical philosophy themselves, Polanyi aimed at criticizing the misapplication of these concerns and criteria by the majority of the thinkers within the Western tradition. In other words, he sought to reconstruct or reinterpret the way such factors are to be understood and employed in such a way as to facilitate a more accurate and fruitful account of the epistemological enterprise.

The acknowledgment of the tacit character of both the matrix and the criteria of knowledge does not entail that any particular claims to truth and/ or knowledge are themselves reliable, but it does entail the affirmation of the standards and dynamics that are necessary to any cognitive achievement whatsoever. The insistence and efforts of modern thinkers to render these necessarily tactic factors explicit is what has led to the distortions and arrogance so maligned by deconstructionists. With this criticism of modernism, Polanyi would agree. But he would not agree with the self-destructive nature of the deconstructivist attack on these abuses. We might here remind ourselves of Keirkegaard's remarks about Descartes's method of systematic doubt: "It is not advisable to first get a person to lie down in a heap in order to teach him to stand up straight."

Part Two

TRACING THE PATTERNS

5

IN SCIENCE AND POLITICAL THEORY

In the foregoing presentation of Michael Polanyi's postmodern reconstructive epistemology, care was taken to employ the image of an axis rather than that of a foundation. Tacit knowledge, in serving as the anchor or tether for more explicit knowledge, functions at the center of cognitive activity rather than as a basis for it. This distinction may seem like a matter of "mere metaphors," but such a view itself reveals a failure to understand the radical thrust of Polanyi's reconstructive philosophy. To think of the justification of cognitive judgment in terms of foundations and/or bases is to open oneself up to an infinitely regressive search for a yet more basic grounding of knowledge. However, the notion of an 'axis,' allows cognitive activity to have a center that itself does not require further justification. That it functions as the center is its justification.

After having located the axis of cognitive activity in tacit knowing, it is time now to begin to explore the implications and ramifications of construing knowledge in this way. Thus, here in part 2, we shall be concerned with tracing the patterns of various aspects of our common search for knowledge as they orbit around this center. We shall take up the main patterns or dimensions of human thought as Polanyi himself sought to address them, while allowing for a certain degree of interpretive freedom along the way as well. This chapter will focus on science and political theory, while the next will be devoted to a consideration of the implications of Polanyi's thought for language and education. An additional chapter will take up his views on art and religion, while another will explore other interpretive angles on Polanyi's thought.

As was made clear in the preceding chapter, Polanyi's understanding of the nature of scientific activity and knowledge stands midway between the more popular points of view. At one extreme stands the traditional "objectivist" view in which science is seen as the development of theories and laws that correspond to reality, theories, and laws that are grounded in hard facts verifiable by sensory observation. At the other extreme stands the more contemporary "conventionalist" view, which sees science as simply a convenient and useful way to organize empirical data and predict human experience. Actually, in Polanyi's view, these two extremes give rise to and feed off of each other since it is the failure of each that suggests the need for the other. Once it was acknowledged that a completely objective account of reality, as with the traditional approach, is impossible, it then seemed necessary for modern thinkers to reduce scientific activity to "mere" pragmatic and conventional behavior.

Polanyi argues that the objectivity of scientific knowledge does not depend on the elimination of the human factors of personal commitment and social processes. Rather, it depends on the character of our interaction with reality and with one another, an interaction involving both universal intent and the accrediting of our common cognitive faculties. It should be clear that the admission that we can never claim to possess absolute knowledge does not lead directly to skepticism. Sometimes it turns out that our cognitive judgments are wrong, but this claim itself only makes sense in relation to incidences of having been correct. By 'correct' here I mean that they are judged to best fit with what those who know and care about such things have come to believe. These judgments constitute what is meant by 'knowledge' as decided by the scientific community, by what Polanyi calls the "society of explorers."

As I understand him, Polanyi sought to overcome the familiar dichotomy between the correspondence and coherence theories of truth by acknowledging the human, social character of knowing, on the one hand, and insisting on the necessity of the drive toward universal truth, on the other hand. While we can speak of Truth with a capital T as an ideal, or as what Kant called a "regulative idea," we also must admit that it is we, as participants in the "republic of science," who decide what is and what is not true, with a small t. The former way of speaking guards against the threats of both skepticism and relativism, while the latter guards against the possibility of any individual or group claiming to have arrived at absolute truth. Thus, we can be said to seek correspondence but to settle for coherence. To my way of thinking, it is better to set these familiar ways of speaking aside in favor of a two-fold acknowledgment that (1) our cognitive judgments are characterized by a commitment to the best possible reading of the particulars and contours of experience and that (2) the continuing self-disclosure of reality requires us to affirm the limited and evolving character of all human knowing. In Polanyi's terms, we must both accredit our own cognitive powers to know reality and confess the social and personal dimensions of these powers.

Here, once again, is Polanyi's way of putting the issue:

> Yet the prevailing conception of science, based on the disjunction of subjectivity and objectivity, seeks—and must seek at all costs—to eliminate from such passionate, personal, human appraisals of theories, or at least to minimize their function to that of a negligible by-play. For modern man has set up as the ideal of knowledge the conception of natural science as a set of statements which is 'objective' in the sense that its substance is entirely determined by observation, even while its presentation may be shaped by convention. This conception, stemming from a craving rooted in the very depths of our culture, would be shattered if the intuition of rationality in nature had to be acknowledged as a justifiable and indeed essential part of scientific theory. That is why scientific theory is represented as a mere economical description of facts; or as embodying a conventional policy for drawing empirical inferences; or as a working hypothesis, suited to man's practical convenience—interpretations that all deliberately overlook the rational core of science. (*Personal Knowledge,* pp. 15–16)

What Polanyi means by this "rational core" of science is simply the belief that reality is there to be known and that it is knowable through human cognitive activity. The relational interaction between reality and cognition neither requires nor allows for a concept of knowledge parsed off from the world as a separate domain; nor does it entail some sort of subjective conventionalism or absolute relativism. It simply enables us to go on learning about the world around us. This learning process presupposes the possibility of coming to know reality and, in addition, the reliability of our cognitive powers for doing so. However, the reductionistic assumptions of modern science negate these very powers even as they must presuppose them, thus denigrating both the knower and the known. Polanyi focuses his criticism of this one-dimensional view of cognition in terms of the theories that are generally assumed to explain every level of reality by reducing it to an account of a simpler, more basic level. This reductionism is generally called the "critical method" of modern science.

> Backed by a science which sternly professes that ultimately all things in the world—including all the achievements of man from the Homeric poems to the *Critique of Pure Reason*—will somehow be explained in terms of physics and chemistry, these theories assume that the path to

reality lies invariably in representing higher things in terms of their baser particulars. This is indeed almost universally regarded today as the supremely critical method, which resists the flattering illusions cherished by men about their nobler faculties. (Polanyi, *The Study of Man,* p. 64)

SCIENCE, INTENTIONALITY, AND EMBODIMENT

An interesting and profitable way to gain a yet deeper understanding of Polanyi's interpretation of scientific knowledge is by means of an examination of the supposed differences between the natural sciences and the human or social sciences. One thinker who has focused this difference rather nicely is Peter Winch in his book *The Idea of a Social Science.* From a Wittgensteinian perspective, Winch establishes an absolute dichotomy between the natural and social sciences, affirming the possibility of objectivity in the former while denying it in the latter.

The basis of Winch's dichotomy is not the traditional existentialist move that while we can know the physical world indirectly from the "outside," we know ourselves directly and most truly from the "inside." Rather, he argues that the concepts, laws, and rules of inference by means of which we explain physical reality are not part of that reality, and thus they can be applied to it objectively and can be said to yield scientific understanding. However, the conceptual schema by means of which we seek to explain social reality is, in fact, a vital part of that very reality and thus can be applied only by one who is irrevocably a participant in it. Thus, the notion of scientific objectivity is out of the question with respect to the social dimension of human experience. Since social reality is linguistically constituted, any understanding of it is itself a social phenomenon and thus cannot be understood objectively.

Polanyi would surely agree with Winch about the impossibility of objectivity narrowly defined in relation to the social sciences, since they clearly do involve the use of concepts and procedures which fold back on themselves, so to speak, and thus preclude objective "distance" at the outset. However, Polanyi would go further and insist that even the physical sciences necessarily incorporate concepts and procedures that are inextricably interwoven with personal and social commitments and values. Moreover, and more to the point here, just as the social sciences can be said to rely on the conceptual and/or linguistic dimension of what Wittgenstein termed the human "form of life," and thereby preclude the standard definition of objectivity, so the physical sciences must be seen as relying on the embodied character of our form of life and exclude this understanding of objectivity as well.

Just as social reality can be understood only on the basis of concepts and inferences that are themselves embedded in that dimension of experience, so physical reality can be understood only by means of our bodily participation in that dimension of experience. All human understanding is predicated on embodiment, on our interaction with the physical and social dimensions of our shared world through our bodies and through speech. Therefore, any understanding of these dimensions must both employ and take into account this dual interaction, and these processes negate the traditional notion of objectivity from the outset. As Polanyi has made abundantly clear, the patterns and difficulties that Winch details in the following quotation apply with equal force to both the physical and social sciences. In short, even natural science is a human enterprises, and as such it must partake of the same processes and commitments as does the study of human reality. Consider Winch's remarks:

> The phenomena being investigated present themselves to the scientist as an *object* of study; he observes them and notices certain facts about them. But to say of a man that he does this presupposes that he already has a mode of communication in the use of which rules are already being observed. For to notice something is to identify relevant characteristics, which means that the noticer must have some *concept* of such characteristics; this is possible only if he is able to use some symbol according to a rule which makes it refer to those characteristics. So we come back to his relation to his fellow scientists, in which context alone he can be spoken of as following such a rule. Hence the relation between N and his fellows, in virtue of which we say that N is following the same rule as they, cannot be simply a relation of observation: it cannot consist in the fact that N has noticed how his fellows behave and has decided to take that as a norm for his own behavior. For this would presuppose that we could give some account of the notion of 'noticing how his fellows behave' *apart from* the relation between N and his fellows which we are trying to specify; and that, as has been shown, is untrue. (*The Idea of a Social Science*, p. 85)

While Winch fails to consider the possibility that both physical and social science must subscribe to the limitations that he outlines in the above quotation, it is even more significant that he never even addresses the role played by the body in all forms of cognitive activity. As Polanyi has pointed out, our conceptual capacities exist and function in symbiotic relation with our somatic potential and cannot be understood apart from them. Winch's mentor, Wittgenstein, clearly grasped this symbiosis in his notions of 'language-games' as forms of social and physical activity. For him, cognitivity was seen as involving both thought *and* action, as the following quotation makes clear:

> So you are saying that human agreement decides what is true and what
> is false?—It is what human beings *say* that is true and false; and they
> agree in the *language* they use. This is not agreement in opinions but
> in form of life. If language is to be a means of communication there
> must be agreement not only in definitions but also (queer as this may
> sound) in judgments. This seems to abolish logic but does not do so.—
> It is one thing to describe methods of measurement, and another to
> obtain and state results of measurement. But what we call "measuring"
> is partly determined by a certain constancy in results of measurement.
> (*Philosophical Investigations,* nos. 241–42)

Thus, language and action, concepts and embodiment, are crucial to cognition
whether in the social or physical sciences. In this way, Polanyi can be seen
as agreeing with Winch but as going beyond him as well.

Within the dynamics of tacit knowing, as developed by Polanyi, the role
of bodily activity in relation to subsidiary awareness is absolutely crucial. It
is by means of our embodiment that we indwell and interact with those
factors of our environment to which we are exposed. In addition, it is through
embodiment that we perform the integrative acts that form the fulcrum points
for further, explicit knowing. Thus, our understanding of any aspect or dimension of experienced reality can arise only from and revolve around our
bodily participation in it. We know social reality only as we function as
members of a community and especially as we participate in its linguistic
activity. In like manner, we come to know physical reality only as we operate
in relation to it through our bodies, both in speech and in action.

It was the very ubiquitous character of language and its role in cognitive activity that for so many centuries caused philosophers to ignore it in
their deliberations. It was not until the twentieth century that analytic thinkers
brought linguistic issues to the fore and increased our awareness of their
importance in questions concerning cognitivity. It may well have been this
same ubiquitous character of our embodiment that has caused philosophers to
overlook its centrality in cognitive processes. Only among recent phenomenological thinkers, especially in the work of Maurice Merleau-Ponty, do we find
serious consideration being given that our way of "being-in-the-world" is
structured, as is our way of knowing, by the somatic nature of our existence.

One of the fundamental difficulties in the Western epistemological tradition is its almost exclusive reliance on visual perception as paradigmatic of
all cognitive experience. From Plato on down, this undue fascination with the
metaphor of vision has resulted in our overwhelming tendency to equate
understanding with seeing. Thus, the mind has been construed as the "eye of
the soul" and we say that we understand things in our "mind's eye." This one-

sided emphasis carries with it certain implications that have in turn led to many serious problems in epistemological theory.

First, it must be noted that vision is largely a passive mode of perception. Objects and qualities pass in and out of our field of vision with little or no effect on our part. It is this passive quality of visual sensation that contributes to our thinking of scientific investigation and the knowledge derived from it as based in mere observation. As a matter of fact, of course, science is based more fundamentally on interaction, both with nature and with fellow scientists, than it is on observation. Indeed, the very heart of the scientific method is the crucial experiment, which involves the manipulation and control of nature and itself must be designed and/or constructed. In addition, none of these activities could be carried out unless the scientist involved had acquired the necessary bodily skills inherent in them. These skills, in turn, are acquired through physical practice, not mere thought. Thus, as Polanyi would have it, there is no scientific knowledge apart from "somatic knowledge."

Second, it is highly likely that our traditional reliance on vision as the paradigm of cognitive experience has led us to think of ourselves as knowers as identical with our minds, as separated and distanced from the so-called external world (including other minds) in the same way that we are differentiated from the objects in our visual field. Epistemic distance has been construed as essential to distinguishing between truth and error, even though it is clearly this "gap" between the knower and the known that has proven to be the key stumbling block in the effort to lay skepticism to rest.

However, the fact of the matter is we do not experience the world passively or "at a distance"; rather, we are engaged by and engage the world around us through bodily interaction and speech from the very outset of our existence. Our body is our entry point into the world, the medium through and in which our reality is constituted. This symbiosis between our bodies and social and physical reality not only overcomes the traditional dichotomy between the knower and the known, but it simply does not allow it to arise. As Polanyi has shown, the answer to skepticism does not lie in constructing some foundationalist bridge over this gap, but is rather to be found in a full appreciation of the role played by the body as it interacts with the environment in creating the dynamics of tacit knowing. It is the body that constitutes the "intentional threads" that Merleau-Ponty posits as the integral connection between the world and our understanding of it.

Third, it is extremely important to bear in mind that our embodied experience is *synaesthetic* in character. That is to say, our encounter with reality is that of a holistic, integrated being that interacts with the world in and through all the dimensions of bodily existence simultaneously. Too frequently those who have sought to understand perception, and thus sensory knowledge as well, have made the mistake of isolating one mode of sensation from the others. However, we do not construct the world out of various and diverse sense data that just happen to come packaged together fairly consistently. Rather, the world is experienced by us as we interact holistically with its different features. We see, feel, hear, smell, and so on within contexts and events that arise as meaningful wholes through our intentional, responsive activity.

Thus it is that Polanyi's position with respect to the controversy between nominalism and realism, between those who maintain that language and thought create the world and those who insist that they discover and represent it, would seem to be a mediating one. That is to say, though he stands four-square against nominalism and conventionalism, Polanyi cannot be classified as a straightforward realist either. Although he insists that the world is there to be discovered, he also acknowledges that (1) it can only be known through interaction, (2) it is the human scientific community that decides what is real and true, and (3) since we are finite and reality is inexhaustible, we can never claim to possess the final truth. Thus, he might best be classified as a "critical realist" or perhaps as a "symbiotic realist."

By calling him a "symbiotic realist," I mean he is one who sees reality as constituted by the mutual and reciprocal interaction between whatever there is of the world that has not yet been discovered and human cognitive activity. These two poles of reality are symbiotic in that they define and sustain each other in such a way that neither can be said to exist or be known apart from the other. This way of putting the matter goes hand-in-hand with Polanyi's concurrent insistence on both the necessity of universal intent implicit within all knowledge claims, on the one hand, and on the finite quality of all the efforts of the society of explorers, on the other hand. It is extremely important not to seek to separate these two aspects of Polanyi's thought about reality.

Perhaps it is helpful to put it this way. There is no point to pretending to be able to speak about "reality" as if it can be conceived of as existing independently of our efforts to know it since even this way of speaking is in fact an instance of our effort to know reality. All that can be accomplished by this way of speaking, after acknowledging it not to be what it sounds as though one is doing, is to remind us that we are, after all, seeking to know the world in a way that goes beyond bias and error. At the same time, however, we can and must avoid speaking about our cognitive efforts as if they produce nothing more or other than subjective and/or hopelessly relative expressions of ego- or ethnocentrism. To acknowledge the "situated" character of our knowing is not the same thing as rendering it useless. It makes little sense to speak of either reality or knowledge as independent of the other.

Let us now place this whole discussion more focally within the purview offered by Polanyi. The trouble is that we have become accustomed to think-

ing of scientific endeavor as a wholly explicit process of observing, constructing hypotheses and crucial experiments, making inductive and deductive inferences, and the like. We identify a problem, isolate its factors, define our
terms, substantiate our reasoning, and spell out our conclusions. This conception of science yields an emphasis on facts, objectivity, replicability, and
probability. Indeed, it has become the very definition of the scientific enterprise. All ideas, affirmations, and commitments that cannot be fitted into this
definition, no matter how useful, are judged extrascientific at best and mere
subjective folk wisdom at worst. Thus, creative insights and value judgments
are carefully excluded from scientific investigations and accounts, or they are
tolerated as necessary evils or as unavoidable contamination.

Within the parameters provided by this approach to science, knowledge
is conceivable only as an activity of the mind, as that which can be focused,
explicated, and stated in propositions. However, this approach overlooks the
tacit character of the cognitive dynamic that underlies the explicit processes
stressed by the standard view and sketched out in the above paragraph. While
this tacit dynamic cannot be fully articulated in explicit propositions and rules
of procedure, it clearly makes itself evident at every step in scientific investigation and justification. After all, we are as knowers in general and scientists
in particular, physical beings. Thus, not only is the physical reality we experience and know deeply enmeshed in the linguistic and conceptual dimension of
our existence, but more important for our present purposes, our knowledge of
nature is equally embedded in our own participation in, our own sharing of, the
physicality of nature. Our embodiment provides the tacit matrix out of which
arises our ability to understand physical reality. When this matrix is acknowledged, and any sound epistemology must acknowledge it, the limitations of
the accepted view of science as strictly objective are exposed.

At this juncture, it is common to hear those who advocate the more
traditional definition of science fall back on the standard dichotomy between
"knowing *that*" and "knowing *how*," granting cognitivity to the one but not
to the other. It is claimed that all hunches, insights, skills, and intuitions are
not strictly speaking knowledge until they can be articulated explicitly and
verified objectively. The difficulty is that this move is simply a reification of
the very posture that is being called into question by Polanyi. It is all too easy
to limit knowledge to that which can be explicated and substantiated by
means of propositions, but it hardly fits the way knowledge is encountered in
life, whether at the ordinary or at the scientific level.

To begin with, the line between the two "kinds" of knowledge is not so
easily drawn, as Wittgenstein's remarks about the symbiotic character of the
concept of 'measurement' and the activity of measuring, quoted a few pages
back, makes abundantly clear. Moreover, the fact remains that all propositional
knowledge arises out of, must be understood in terms of, and can only be

justified by means of nonpropositional knowledge that has been thoroughly incorporated into the perceptual, kinesthetic, and conceptual skills of the knower. The subtleties of the human form of life, together with its cognitive processes, cannot be taught by explicit rules and instruction. They can only be caught by indwelling the practices and procedures comprising the warp and weft of the fabric thereof. Only against the backdrop of embodied experience does propositional knowledge become comprehensible and useful.

In the final analysis, the justification of the scientific enterprise itself, which clearly lies outside both science and mere practical advantage, can only be said to lie in the nature and contours of human cognitive activity. To borrow a page from Immanuel Kant, the "postulates" of scientific investigation, like those of moral responsibility, cannot be "proven," but they can and must be lived. The belief that reality exists and can be known cannot be and need not be justified deductively, inductively, or pragmatically. Nor is it simply a matter of blind faith. Rather, such "postulates or bedrock beliefs or whatever they are to be called are justified in and through our embodied activity. Searching for the truth as if it can be known is something that all humans do; in this sense, it is its own justification.

Finally, at the deepest level, it must be admitted that the scientist's concern for knowledge and the truth is itself a basic value commitment that cannot be vindicated by means of logic or science. Moreover, the scientist's interaction with the environment plays an important part in constituting the very concept of 'reality' itself, as well as of various theories about its nature. This acknowledgment neither undermines the possibility of authentic knowledge nor acquiesces to the traditional "objectivist" view. It simply points out that cognitive activity is as basic to human life as are breathing and eating. Polanyi's way of addressing this issue varies in from, but the following remarks are representative:

> Many writers have observed, since Dewey taught it at the close of the last century, that to some degree, we shape all knowledge in the way we know it. This appears to leave knowledge open to the whims of the observer. But the pursuit of science has shown us how even in the shaping of his own anticipations the knower is controlled by impersonal requirements. His acts are personal judgments exercised responsibly with a view to a reality with which he is seeking to establish contact. This holds for all seeking and finding of external truth . . . Any conclusion, be it given as a surmise or claimed as a certainty, represents a commitment of the person who arrives at it. No one can utter more than a responsible commitment of his own, and this completely fulfills the finding of the truth and the telling of it. (*The Tacit Dimension*, p. 77)

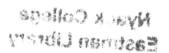

MARXISM, FREEDOM, AND MORAL INVERSION

We come now to the most difficult aspect of Polanyi's philosophy, that pertaining to political theory. It is the most difficult partly because his views
remain somewhat unclear and partly because in regard to political issues he
is furthest away from his own disciplines. Moreover, in my opinion, Polanyi's
political theorizing actually departs from the main thrust of his epistemological insights. Be that as it may, in these pages I shall simply try to present his
views, within a rather short compass, without attempting to analyze and
evaluate them in any great detail.

Actually, it was by way of political concerns that Polanyi was initially
drawn into the philosophical arena. After establishing himself in the fields of
medicine, physics, and chemistry, in both his native Hungary and England,
Polanyi devoted an increasing amount of time and energy combating various
aspects of the Communist philosophy emanating from the Soviet Union. He
was continuously at odds with the spread of this totalitarian ideology throughout
Eastern Europe, including his home country. The latter half of his career, at
the universities of Manchester and Oxford, was largely given over to the
philosophy of science in general and epistemology in particular. So in a sense
we have been exploring his ideas in reverse order from the way they were
chronologically developed. Of course, his later, more specifically philosophical insights not only stand on their own, but they do not in my view follow
logically from his earlier concerns at all.

The nub of Polanyi's critique of Marxism pertains to its basic claim
that the philosophy of Communism is actually grounded in a scientific law
concerning the nature and history of social reality. Both Marx and Engels
insisted that the relationship between economic production and the character of any given culture, as mediated in and through class struggle, can be
understood and expressed as one of strict causality. Thus, Communism was
said to be "objectively" true in the same way that Newton's laws of physics
have been established as true. There were two aspects of this claim that
troubled Polanyi. One concerns the contradictory manner in which this
alleged law was propagated.

As we have already seen, according to Polanyi, the modern concept of
'objectivity,' which Marxism clearly accepts, is itself badly in need of an
overhaul. For the main thrust of this concept is aimed at the elimination of
all personal and social factors from the scientific enterprise, and such a goal
not only is unattainable but is at odds with the way scientific investigation is
actually carried out. The modern "cult of objectivity" worships a false god
from the outset and thus fails to do justice to the real character of the cognitive processes involved in science. In like manner, then, Marxism must be

seen as grounding itself on a false conception of scientific understanding and as representing itself as "value free" truth when there can be no such thing. Thus, far from going beyond modernism, Marxism is simply a special case thereof.

The extremely ironic thing about the Marxist claim to objectivity, according to Polanyi, is the highly moralistic manner in which it is perpetrated. On the one hand, the form of objectivity inherent within Marxist "empirical science" systematically excludes any and all value judgments, be they personal or social. On the other hand, this so-called law of social reality was incorporated into Soviet culture and government in a highly totalitarian fashion and thrust upon the rest of Europe in an extremely authoritarian way. This "double-think" pattern, of denying on the one hand what is being claimed on the other, Polanyi termed "moral inversion." First, moral considerations and value judgments are excluded from consideration; then this exclusion itself is forcefully presented in a moralistic manner. In his view, the Marxist effort to exclude values and moral considerations actually only succeeds in inverting the traditional way of construing them without admitting it.

In commenting on the Marxist prediction that a proletarian revolution will necessarily bring a final end to the class struggle, Polanyi remarks:

> This affirmation satisfies the moral aspirations of Socialism, and is accepted therefore as a scientific truth by those filled with these aspirations. Moral passions are thereby cast in the form of a scientific affirmation . . . By covering them with a scientific disguise it protects moral sentiments against being deprecated as mere emotionalism and gives them at the same time a sense of scientific certainty; while on the other hand it impregnates material ends with the fervor of moral passions. (*Personal Knowledge,* p. 229)

It is important to see that Polanyi's critique of the moral inversion entailed by Marxism applies with equal force to all modern attempts to establish a political or social philosophy without reference to moral or value judgments. In a sense, it is characteristic of the modern age to attempt to do precisely this, and it is for this reason that Polanyi can rightly be classified as a postmodern thinker. The inconsistencies inherent within all such efforts, Eastern or Western, follow directly from the assumption that social reality can be understood without any reference to moral values whatsoever. However, this assumption undercuts the very possibility of such understanding since it undercuts the commitment to the value of knowledge made by the would-be knower. The search for truth presupposes the value of finding it, of telling the truth, and of understanding in general. Social science is impossible without these values.

The logical development of Polanyi's argument at this juncture is perhaps best understood when put the other way around, beginning with general human moral experience rather than with scientific judgments. Here is the way he puts it:

> The . . . argument is as follows: (1) All men, whatever their professions, make moral judgments. (2) When we claim that an action of ours is prompted by moral motives, or else when we make moral judgments of others . . . we invariably refer to moral standards *which we hold to be valid.* Our submission to a standard has universal intent . . . (3) Such a claim entails a distinction between *moral truth* and *moral illusion.* (4) This distinction in turn entails a distinction between two types of motivation. The awareness of moral truth is founded on the recognition of a valid claim, which can be reasonably argued for and supported by evidence; moral illusion, in contrast, is compulsive, like sensory illusion. (5) Thus once we admit, as we do when we acknowledge the existence anywhere of valid moral judgments, that true human values exist and that people can be motivated by their knowledge of them, *we have implicitly denied the claim that all human actions can be explained without any reference to the exercise of moral judgment* . . . (6) *This value judgment proves indispensable* to the political scientist's explanation of their behaviour. (*Knowing and Being,* pp. 33–34)

Moral inversion, then, according to Polanyi, involves attempting to understand and explain social reality without relying on the moral dimension of human experience, while all the while being logically dependent on it. The Marxist version of this fundamental error is particularly troublesome in Polanyi's view because of the authoritarian character of its albeit denied moral fervor. In short, he contends that Marxism cannot have it both ways; it cannot pretend to rise above all value judgments, which in itself is impossible, and at the same time urge its claims on others as being of utmost value. Such behavior is both logically and morally inadequate and inauthentic. One is reminded here of Nietzsche and B. F. Skinner, both of whom have urged us to get "beyond" such traditional moral concepts as 'good and evil' and 'freedom and dignity' but whose very urging trades on the traditional meaning of these terms. Clearly they, along with Marx, think it is *good* to exercise *freedom* in this way!

Perhaps Polanyi's most pointed definition of his idea of moral inversion is found in *The Logic of Liberty.* There he describes those persons who took up the totalitarian cause of Soviet Marxism as embodying this distortion of moral fervor in this manner:

In such men, the traditional form for holding moral ideals has been shattered and their moral passions diverted into the only channels which a strictly mechanistic conception of man and society left open to them. We may describe this as a process of *moral inversion*. The morally inverted person has not merely performed a philosophic substitution of moral aims by material purposes, but is acting with the whole force of his homeless moral passions within a purely materialistic framework of purposes. (p. 106)

The positive thrust of Polanyi's approach to political theory is focused in the concept of freedom. His basic model for the ideal society is what he calls the "Republic of Science," wherein the truth is aimed at through the free exchange of ideas. In like manner, Polanyi believed that the just society can, and only can, be attained through the democratic institutions forming the basis of Western civilization. According to this ideal, each person must be free to pursue his or her own truth and/or happiness and to urge it upon others as a universal goal. The tendency toward individualism inherent in this freedom is offset by the democratic process, which guarantees that the whole society must decide what is best for it.

Just as each individual scientist is free to express his or her own findings and rationale as the truth, but must also submit to the examination and judgment of his or her peers, so the individual citizen's freedom is limited by the judgment of other citizens comprising the body politic. In addition, just as the society of explorers is governed by a common commitment to certain rules of honesty, open-mindedness, and fair play, so the ideal community must be governed by clearly established laws guaranteeing equality and justice. Totalitarian governments systematically deny such fundamental rights and processes. Even though the democratic form of government, like the scholarly process, is often inefficient and sometimes unfair, Polanyi would insist, with Churchill, that "it is the worst form of government, except for all the rest."

Polanyi sees this democratic process, both in the pursuit of knowledge and in the pursuit of justice, as a system of "mutual authority" whereby both the freedoms of the individual and the overall good of the society are sought and preserved.

The freedom of a scientist or a judge is not one of simple self-assertion. It is a freedom to pursue certain obligations and to share in a system of mutual authority. Nevertheless, this freedom implies an absence of external restraint because it also entails a right to make personal judgments (often quite innovative). (*Meaning*, p. 202)

Mutual authority is seen as internal or lateral, as inherent within constitutional law and democratic processes, in contrast to the external authority of a totalitarian state.

In Polanyi's view, a free and just society can exist only within the context of a tradition and set of values that provides the framework necessary to the survival and growth of that society. Such a context, while guaranteeing the toleration of all ideas and lifestyles, cannot, of course, tolerate any ideas and actions that undermine or seek to undermine the values constituting this framework. Those committed to the absolute inviability of freedom and tolerance must restrain and resist any attempt to overthrow this commitment. Without a basic commitment to this set of values, the only alternatives are totalitarianism, wherein one point of view controls all others, or anarchy, wherein no society is really possible at all (*Meaning*, pp. 202–3).

This commitment to a tradition and set of basic values and laws, according to Polanyi, requires that all viable change must take place within the context provided thereby and never by means of a revolution that would seek to replace them. Only reformation, never revolution, can effect constructive change in the body politic without destroying it because some framework within which to accomplish this change is logically necessary. Thus, the American "Revolution" was actually a reformation taking place within the context of the European tradition, beginning with the Greeks, while the revolutions in Russia, China, and Cuba took place in societies that previously had been without any commitment to equality, freedom, and justice in the first place. Here is Polanyi's way of putting this point:

> Once we have fully grasped the import of the necessary limits on our ability to construct a perfect society and can dwell in that import, we will refrain from various sorts of radical actions aiming at the full establishment of justice and brotherhood. We will recognize that we can reduce unjust privileges, but only by graded stages and never completely. No single panacea for them exists. They can be dealt with only one at a time, never wholesale, since we have to use the power of the present system in order to make any changes in it. To try to reform all the power structures at once would leave us with *no* power structure to use in our project. In any case, we will be able to see that *absolute* moral renewal could be attempted only by an absolute power and that a tyrannous force such as this must destroy the whole moral life of man, not renew it. (*Meaning*, pp. 213–14)

Furthermore, according to Polanyi, an ideal society will govern itself within the dictates and dynamics of a free enterprise economic system since any attempt to control the economic activity of the market system for the greater good of society would in turn undermine the rights and freedoms of its individual citizens. Just as the search for knowledge must never be controlled by any centralized epistemological authority, so the exchange of goods in an industrialized society must not be governed by the state for the supposed good of the whole. "Even the economy . . . must be allowed its freedom to operate . . . by mutual adjustment of its participating parts through the mechanisms of markets and pricing and profits" (*Meaning,* p. 204). Polanyi does acknowledge the need for occasional regulation of the capitalist system for its overall preservation and the public welfare,

> but attempts to supplant it altogether by central planning would simply bring an industrial society to a halt, as well as place power to control all activities of groups and persons in the hands of public officials, since all working capital (resources) would be controlled and distributed according to their judgments. (*Meaning,* p. 204)

At this juncture, I will offer some reflections of my own on Polanyi's approach to political theory as outlined above. For there are a number of points at which I think he has not followed out the implications of his own philosophical posture in a consistent manner. I shall begin with some remarks about what I take to be his naive understanding of how the "republic of science" actually operates and then move on to an examination of his treatment of the relationship between democracy and capitalism. This too strikes me as naive.

Up through the first half of the present century, or until the end of World War II, the picture Polanyi paints of the dynamics and processes governing scientific inquiry is fairly accurate. Once scientists got out from under the thumb of the church, they operated with ever-increasing freedom throughout the Western world, regulated by their own interaction and mutual authority. By and large, scientific research was carried on in close connection with universities where the atmosphere was characterized by wide tolerance and a commitment to "knowledge for knowledge's sake." Here the concept of scientists constituting a society of explorers can be said to make a good deal of sense. In short, during this time, the search for knowledge was not directly connected to the domains of politics and economics.

During World War II, however, when war became a matter of big business and research, the connection among science, politics, and economics began to be much more direct. Since that time, the question of who funds what sort of scientific research has become a central concern in the quest for knowledge. What some have called "the Military-Industrial Complex" plays an increasingly dominant role in determining not only what sort of research gets done but what sorts of results are accepted as viable knowledge, as well. Weapons, drugs, space rockets, and petroleum production have all fared well, while environmentally sound processes and products, health sciences, and socio-economic conditions, together with their solutions, have done rather badly at best.

The truth of the matter surely seems to be that ever since the beginning of the industrial age, and increasingly throughout the electronic age, the encroachment of political and economic control into the scientific enterprise has and continues to be, at the very least, considerable. Polanyi's ideal of independent researchers pursuing their own investigations and submitting them to the examination and judgment of their peers for accreditation overlooks far too many parallel considerations to be realistic, even for science, let alone as a model for the ideal society. It is not that his ideas are wrong or irrelevant to either scientific endeavor or political theory; it is just that they seem to treat these considerations as if they existed in some sort of intellectual vacuum.

One way to put my reservations with regard to Polanyi's understanding of how scientific knowledge is acquired is to say that here he has failed to see that to a significant degree he has embraced a "modernist" interpretation of the way knowledge comes about. Perhaps the most valid aspect of the postmodernist critique pertains to the degree to which modern thinkers have neglected to admit the sociopolitico-economic dimensions of human cognitive activity. This critique applies with considerable force to Polanyi's account of the scientific community. It is not that these contextual factors necessarily undermined the possibility of knowledge, as Polanyi himself has clearly shown in establishing the tacit axis of all knowing. Rather, any epistemology that fails to take them into account will necessarily by misleading; moreover, Polanyi's epistemology is equipped to handle them.

What I mean by this last remark is simply that when he advocates the freedom of individual scientists governing themselves and one another through the mutual authority of their common commitment to seek the truth, Polanyi speaks as if this process did not involve any official bodies, such as journal editors, professional societies, and publishers. Surely, these centers of power, even when chosen democratically, operate as controlling agents in the "free enterprise" of the intellectual marketplace. They set policies, make rulings, and determine practice so as to mediate the efforts of the individuals within their jurisdiction. This is, in fact, precisely how the "republic of science" functions so as to balance individual freedom off against universal intent. The free-flow of ideas is not governed exclusively by the competition among individual thinkers but operates according to certain principles that in the long run serve the best interests of the truth.

When this model is transposed into the political domain, it carries inherent within it the necessity of control and regulation of individual enterprise by the democratically elected officials comprising the government. Of course, the complete control of all aspects of a society by such officials would constitute an excess, just as complete freedom on the part of individuals would. A planned economy, designed and run by democratically elected leaders who are subject to recall in no way resembles the totalitarian state feared by Polanyi. In fact, the social democracy of the Great Britain where Polanyi spent most of his adult life worked rather well.

The confusion involved in Polanyi's pejorative analysis of Soviet economics can be seen in his essay "Toward a Theory of Conspicuous Production" in which he criticizes Communist policies that sought to control production so as to meet the basic needs of all people. It cannot be denied that there is much to disagree with in the totalitarian economic system of the former Soviet Union, but Polanyi systematically refuses to consider the parallel dehumanization attendant to the capitalistic economy of the West. If the Soviet was guilty of promoting "conspicuous production," surely our system is guilty of promoting "conspicuous consumption." The narrowness of Polanyi's outlook is revealed in the following remarks:

> It may be objected that capitalism starves the collective interests of society and that the Soviet system restores this balance. Perhaps it does, through its authoritarian structure renders its assessment of collective satisfaction dubious; but even so, the major purpose of economic life remains the satisfaction of individual needs. (*Society, Economics, and Philosophy: Selected Papers,* pp. 180–81)

Not only does he regularly avoid dealing with how the capitalist system will meet the collective needs of society, but Polanyi also fails to provide any substantiation for his claim that the major purpose of economic life is the satisfaction of "individual needs." Surely such a claim begs the central question that is supposedly under debate in this discussion since it makes just as much sense to claim that the basic needs of the group should be the first priority.

This brings us to a consideration of Polanyi's account of the relationship between democracy and capitalism. In the discussion of the preceding paragraph, Polanyi would prefer to parallel capitalist business leaders to the editors and officers of professional societies as the proper governors of their respective domains (*Meaning,* pp. 204–12). But surely this is an inappropriate parallel since the only guide to behavior among the former are the competitive edge and increased profits. There are no common commitments to equality, justice, and truth inherent to the free enterprise system as there are underlying the search for knowledge as advocated by Polanyi in his philosophy of cognition. A just and fair society cannot be based on some vague notion of an "invisible hand" that will guide it to the truth. Elected officials, and those appointed by them, such as supreme court judges, must be entrusted with the power to monitor and alter the economic process so as to maximize the common good. This cannot be the responsibility of the marketplace even according to Polanyi's own model of the scientific community. This is not what is meant by "checks and balances."

What Polanyi seems to overlook is the fact that democracy and completely free enterprise are fundamentally incompatible for the simple reason that those who manage to acquire most of the wealth will be in a position to control the electoral process unless democratically elected officials have the political and legal power to regulate their activity. Either through so-called legitimate means, such as the lobby system and the media, or through illegitimate channels, those with money will completely control political processes. The nearly total disintegration of the American political process, to the point where only one-half of the people vote and tobacco, gun, and petroleum manufacturers dictate legislation, should be ample proof that more than mere freedom in the marketplace is required in order to guarantee a truly just and free society.

In my opinion, the heart of Polanyi's confusion here is a misunderstanding of the nature of the relationship between his notion of 'boundary conditions' and the richer, more comprehensive dimensions of human existence, such as the moral and religious. This misunderstanding is clearly at work in the reasoning expressed in the following passage in which Polanyi argues that the capitalist system is operating as well as can be expected of any politico-economic system.

> [W]e will perceive that it is operating well only if we manage to abandon our deeply ingrained moral perfectionism, one of the causes, we may recall, of moral inversion. We could do this, of course, if we were to dwell fully in the view developed here, namely that the moral level exists on the foundation of a lower, essentially nonmoral level and that the latter must inevitably place limits on the accomplishments of the higher level. It is not difficult to see the conceptual meaning and ontological validity of this principle, but it may be difficult for us to live with it. (*Meaning,* p. 213)

In my view, there are two fundamental errors in this line of reasoning, both of which are incongruous with Polanyi's overall point of view.

To begin with, there is nothing in Polanyi's concept of 'boundary conditions' that implies that they must dictate the quality and direction of the richer, more comprehensive dimensions of meaning that arise within and above them. As Polanyi has said, the boundary conditions of physics do not exhaustively explain, for instance, the nature and meaning of a clock, though these latter must function within the laws of physics. The sorts of limits that such boundary conditions place on what Polanyi terms "the higher levels" of meaning in no wise determine the values and significance of these higher levels, whether we are speaking of clocks or of societies. It is one thing to be a political realist, as both Polanyi and I are, and to thereby foreswear "moral perfectionism" in private as well as public life. It is quite a different thing altogether to insist that the economic order must in fact determine the character of the social order. To put it differently, Polanyi has confused his notion of boundary conditions with that of a foundation, which is the term he unfortunately employs in the above passage. Indeed, in this passage he sounds surprisingly like an inverted Marxist.

Second, it is in fact the character and purposes of the higher levels of political reality that determine just *what* aspects and qualities inherent within the lower levels will be made use of and just *how* they will be used to serve the higher levels. Although a clock does not transcend the principles of physics, its maker decides which principles will be incorporated in order to create a clock and not a truck. In the same way, those who guide and govern a society, if chosen democratically, should be in a position to decide which aspects and patterns of the economic order are best suited to the common good. To leave such matters to some "invisible hand" would be parallel to tossing a bunch of springs, boards, and gears up in the air and trusting that what falls to earth will be a clock. Polanyi's analysis of political reality is not only unduly conservative, but it does not follow from his own philosophical insights.

Before bringing this chapter to a close, it should be pointed out that Polanyi's political theory was not entirely devoid of any acknowledgment of the need for capitalism to be curbed and regulated by certain social values. Indeed, in the preface to *The Logic of Liberty,* he specifically rejected Karl Popper's notion of an entirely "open society," stating, "Private individualism is not an Open Society, but one fully dedicated to a distinctive set of beliefs." A brief consideration of what is meant by the latter phrase will be most helpful in rounding out this account of Polanyi's political views.

He did admit that certain moral difficulties inevitably arise within a capitalist system, due to the grossly unequal distribution of goods and capital, and that these inequities must be guarded against and rectified by governmental programs. Such adjustments should, in Polanyi's view, be limited to things such as education, health care, and other social amenities, as well as the protection of the general environment and the justice system (*The Logic of Liberty,* p. 149). Thus, our social values must control the economic process.

One of the driving forces behind Polanyi's more or less conservative political views is the realization that moral perfection on the social level of human existence is simply impossible. Polanyi was convinced that while the free enterprise system of economics acknowledges this fact and seeks to allow the system to correct itself, the collectivist system seeks to perfect human social and economic life by controlling it. Thus, there will always be a need for compromises and trade-offs between broader social welfare and the freedom of the individual. While self-interest must function as the basic force at the lower, economic level of our life together, the higher, moral level can neither be explained nor controlled by this lower level. We must remain committed to higher, more encompassing moral values, such as freedom and tolerance, without trying to force them upon our economic system.

As I mentioned a few paragraphs ago, I do not think this line of thinking correctly reflects Polanyi's deeper insights concerning the relationship between the boundary conditions imposed by the lower, economic order and the comprehensive reality of the higher moral and social order. While I agree that certain moral commitments, such as freedom, must be honored in order for there to be any real society at all, it does not follow from this that a nearly totally free market place must be insisted on. Surely, a commitment to meeting the basic needs of every citizen prior to allowing individuals to accumulate fortunes would seem fundamental. There must exist a middle ground between the "invisible hand" and totalitarian control since communal values are every bit as valid as are those of the individual.

6

In Language and Education

Two of the most interesting and influential applications of Polanyi's epistemological insights are those made to the question of the nature of language and to the philosophy of education. Although these two areas of concern may at first blush seem rather disparate, a brief moment of reflection should make it clear that they are, indeed, very closely related. After all, language is learned and thereby qualifies as a form of knowledge, while the vast majority of education is accomplished by means of language. In this chapter, I shall treat these two areas of concern from a Polanyian perspective, endeavoring to show how they can profitably be studied in terms of his insights. Most of the time, I shall rely on Polanyi's own writings in these discussions, but I shall also seek to connect his work up with that of other important thinkers in the field.

The Nature and Acquisition of Language

The most direct presentation of Polanyi's understanding of the nature of language is found in his essay "Sense-Giving and Sense-Reading." He begins with a brief account of the distinction between focal and subsidiary awareness, paying special attention to the vectorial character of the relation between them. Thus, our focal awareness can be said to be mediated in and through our subsidiary awareness. It may prove helpful at this juncture to take another look at figure 2.1. Polanyi applies this basic distinction to the question of meaning in the following way:

It is our subsidiary awareness of a thing that endows it with meaning: with a meaning that bears on an object of which we are focally aware. A meaningful relation of a subsidiary to a focal is formed by the action of a person who integrates one to the other, and the relation persists by the fact that the person keeps up this integration. (*Knowing and Being*, p. 82)

Polanyi divides up his account of the way language works into two parts, what he calls "sense-reading" and "sense-giving." The former has to do with the process of discerning the meaning of someone else's utterance, while the latter pertains to how it is that a speaker forms a meaningful utterance. In both cases, what is especially significant for coming to an understanding of how language works is the realization that grasping and imparting meaning through language is *not* fundamentally an intellectual process but is rather the result of the tacit integration of the particulars of our subsidiary awareness by means of our bodily interaction with or indwelling of them. Language does not simply float by and through our consciousness as a self-contained entity. On the contrary, it is encountered at the vortex of our involvement with other persons amidst our common tasks in the world around us. Thus, as we and others speak, we are ourselves on the move and are moving objects in the environment; in short, we get things done with language. Moreover, hearing and speaking are themselves bodily activities, which are learned and practiced through modeling and imitation.

Polanyi stresses this active character of sense-giving and sense-reading in the following remarks:

We must realize that to use language is a performance of the same kind as our integration of visual clues for perceiving an object, or as the viewing of a stereo picture, or our integration of muscular contractions in walking or driving a car, or as the conducting of a game of chess— all of which are performed by relying on our subsidiary awareness of some things for the purpose of attending focally to a matter on which they bear. "(*Knowing and Being*, p. 193)

As we grow beyond the most simple forms of communication of early childhood, we become increasingly aware of ever richer dimensions and circles of meaning, each of which infuses any speech with deeper and broader significance. This awareness is initially, of course, strictly a function of subsidiary factors and interactions, of exposure to and participation in the multileveled discourse and activity comprising the social and physical worlds that surround us. Amidst such exposure and participation, which are always largely somatic in character, we come to indwell the intended meanings of those members of the speaking community in which we find ourselves. We grasp these meanings by integrating them, at the tacit level, into significant wholes. Thus, we can be said to "read their sense" and in turn to "give them sense" as we ourselves engage in the give-and-take of everyday speech.

The deepest background against and within which we come to understand and participate in language consists of those wider contexts of meaning that pertain to the more complex dimensions of human existence, such as politics, art, and religion. These can be thought of in Polanyi's terms as providing the ultimate ground of subsidiary awareness from which we attend when we speak about and attend focally to less comprehensive meanings. The paradox is, to be sure, that in the beginning we attend from mere perceptual meanings to conceptual ones, which seems the reverse of the final dynamic. The key here is to understand that as the contexts of meaning widen and become more comprehensive, what was initially a matter of focal awareness becomes transformed through an integrative act into a subsidiary factor. Thus, linguistic understanding is characterized by a series of concentric circles of meaning, each vectorially related to the next, with the vector circling back on itself as it spirals toward each richer level of significance. Take, for example, the dynamics of understanding that transpire when a parent approaches an infant's crib and repeatedly asks, "Up?" "Would you like to go up?" and so on. At first the infant can only attend to the tone of these sounds, coupled with the parent's smiling face, past mornings, and so on, from its own bodily capacities of sensory perception, which function here only subsidiarily. Slowly, through repeated experience, the infant learns to separate out, in an integrative act, the sensations of being lifted into the parent's arms from the other aspects comprising the situation, such as opening the shades or singing a rhyme. Once this comprehensive whole of meaning is grasped, the infant incorporates it into its subsidiary awareness and uses it to attend from to yet further aspects of meaning inherent in the situation. These, in turn, also become part of the subsidiary fulcrum from which the child comes to work its way into the speaking community's world.

What one comes to know tacitly, by integrating subsidiary factors into meaningful wholes, thus forms the axis around and from which a native speaker operates in his or her own language. The concentric circles of significance begin as that to which we attend and then become that from which we attend. If and when such a speaker takes opportunity to study the language in a formal way, this tacit knowledge also can become explicit. In any case, Polanyi's analysis of language in terms of focal and subsidiary awareness, which give rise to explicit and tacit knowledge, is in fact quite useful. It enables us to understand the way in which individual utterances, whether simple or complex, function in relation to that of which they speak and in relation to the contexts of meaning within which they are uttered. This dynamic is but a specific application of the general analysis that Polanyi provides in the following remarks:

> When we are relying on our awareness of something (A) for attending to something else (B), we are but subsidiarily aware of A. The thing B to which we are thus focally attending, is then the meaning of A. The focal object B is always identifiable, while things like A, of which we are subsidiarily aware, may be unidentifiable. The two kinds of awareness are mutually exclusive. (*Personal Knowledge*, p. x)

This same vectorial dynamic is operative, according to Polanyi, in the symbolic use of language, especially that involving metaphor. In order to grasp the significance of a symbolic expression, we must attend to its meaning in and through the more literal meanings attendent to the words involved; these latter function at the subsidiary pole of awareness, while the former serves as the focal pole. In more straightforward discourse we attend from the particulars of perception and definition to the meaning of the utterance. However, in symbolic discourse, what is usually taken as the focus of meaning become the subsidiary factors from which we attend to the meaning of the fresh, nonliteral expression. Polanyi makes his point in the following way:

> The two constituent parts of a metaphor are made to bear on a joint novel meaning of them. We are aware of them subsidiarily in their joint focal appearance. This seems to hold also the formal features of a poem. In reading a poem we are aware subsidiarily of its rhythm, its rhymes, its sounds, its grammatical construction, and the peculiar connotations of the words used. Each of these components can be examined separately, in itself, but this inevitably dims and may even efface the meaning of the poem. Its meaning may be brought back to us with a deeper understanding when we shift our focal attention back upon the poem instead of upon its parts; . . . in any case, our awareness of the components, which we have focally examined, must once more become subsidiary if we are to see the poem's meaning. (*Meaning*, p. 80)

Polanyi's insistence on and development of the crucial role of the body in a sound understanding of the nature of linguistic activity and knowledge is similar to that of Maurice Merleau-Ponty. Moreover, his emphasis on the social character and pragmatic character of linguistic communication is quite parallel to that of the later Ludwig Wittgenstein. It will prove profitable to indicate briefly how these likenesses reveal themselves in the writings of these thinkers by offering a few direct comparisons.

Merleau-Ponty, like Polanyi, rejects what has been called the "picture theory of language" wherein statements are said to represent or mirror either the objects and qualities in the external world or the thoughts and processes in the speaker's mind. As he says:

> The reason why a language finally intends to say and does say something is not that each sign is the vehicle for a signification which allegedly belongs to it, but that all the signs together allude to a significance which is always in abeyance when they are considered singly, and which I go beyond them toward without their ever containing it. (*Signs*, p. 83)

Here we see clearly a vectorial pattern from the subsidiary and tacit toward the focal and explicit.

Furthermore, Merleau-Ponty maintains that the pivotal center of human linguistic activity is the bodily gesture.

> One can see what there is in common between the gesture and its meaning, for example, in the case of emotional expression and the emotions themselves: the smile, the relaxed face, gaiety of gesture really have in them the rhythm of action, the mode of being in the world which are joy itself. (*Phenomenolgy of Perception*, p. 186)

Polanyi's insistence that speech, like all cognition, consists of a "performance," of a bodily action based on an integration of subsidiary factors is echoed in Merleau-Ponty

> The phonetic 'gesture' brings about, both for the speaking subject, and for his hearers, a certain structural co-ordination of experience, a certain modulation of existence, exactly as a pattern of my bodily behavior endows the objects around me with a certain significance both for me and for others. (*Phenomenology of Perception*, p. 193)

Here they both remind one of J. L. Austin's claim that we do things with words only in reverse—we actually often say things without words by means of our bodies. It is clear that speech begins in gesture and never really outgrows its reliance on this original center.

Anyone who has read any of the works of Merleau-Ponty is well aware that he both thinks and writes in what might best be called the "metaphoric mode." His entire approach to philosophy requires a commitment to the notion that the world is best understood indirectly or "mediationally." Thus, it is not surprising to find that his understanding of language, like that of Polanyi, designates an important role for metaphor:

Language outruns us, not merely because the use of speech always presupposes a great number of thoughts which are covered by each word, but also. . . these thoughts themselves. . . were not at any time 'pure' thoughts either, for already in them there was a surplus of the signified over the signifying. (*Phenomenology of Perception*, p. 390)

This way of speaking clearly parallels Polanyi's understanding of the vectorial nature of linguistic meaning since it entails that in metaphorical discourse we "know more than we can tell."

Turning our attention to the insights of Wittgenstein, it is easy to find significant parallels to Polanyi's work here as well. Like Merleau-Ponty, Wittgenstein rejected the "picture theory" of meaning, even though he had been one of its primary advocates in his early work. He came to see that language is an extremely multifarious phenomenon, one which serves a wide variety of functions, depending on the purposes of its speakers and the context within which they speak. Thus there is, according to Wittgenstein, a decidedly pragmatic quality pervading language that far exceeds its representational use. For him, the meaning of an utterance is found in its *use,* in what tasks it actually accomplishes. In fact, Wittgenstein's major metaphor for speech was that of a tool box in which there is a variety of tools for every purpose. He offers the following list as indicative of the appropriateness of this metaphor:

Review the multiplicity of language-games in the following examples, and in others: Giving orders and obeying them—Describing the appearance of an object or giving its measurements—Constructing an object from a description (a drawing)—Reporting an event—Speculating about an event—Forming and testing a hypothesis—Presenting the results of an experiment in tables and diagrams—Making up a story; and reading it—Play-acting—Singing catches—Guessing riddles—Making a joke; telling it—Solving a problem in practical arithmetic—Translating from one language into another—Asking, thanking, cursing, greeting, praying. " (*Philosophical Investigations,* Macmillan, 1953, no. 23)

One cannot help but be reminded here of the many places where Polanyi employs the analysis of how tools are used as extensions of our bodies when we are engaged in cognitive activity. Frequently, in fact, he uses this analogy in connection with his discussion of how language works, comparing our deployment of speech to driving a car or moving pieces in a chess game as intentional extensions of our embodiment. The difference, to be sure, lies in the fact that speech, like our bodies, is much closer to the center of our existence than any tool, since we cannot really separate our selves from it.

Even deliberate silence is only meaningful in contrast to speech. The important point here, however, is that for both Wittgenstein and Polanyi language is an activity by means of which we accomplish things in the world, not some passive means of representing the world.

Wittgenstein's use of the notion of "language-games" in the above quotation serves to draw our attention to this active character of language. This term was not used by him to suggest that language is in any way trivial or arbitrary. On the contrary, his point was that language is something we do, a way of behaving that does in fact operate according to rules and patterns, even though speakers are not generally conscious of these rules and patterns. Wittgenstein's foregoing list enumerates and illustrates some of these language games that form the "middle-sized" context of speech. The immediate context, of course, consists of the people, objects, and individual purposes of a given time and place. The broadest context perhaps would be the values and commitments making up the character of the human "form of life."

The notion of language games also highlights another of Wittgenstein's main themes, namely that of the social nature of linguistic activity. Although it should be obvious enough, it is surprising how frequently those thinkers dealing with the nature and significance of language fail to take this all-important feature into account. Not only do all people learn speech initially from other people, but they carry on in it throughout their lives, even in times of great difficulty and during isolation. Indeed, it is possible to maintain that it is only by means of participation in language that we actually become human beings in the full sense of the term. Clearly, it is the rules and patterns of our symbiotic life together that are reflected in those of the language we use. Social reality is, in fact, largely constructed by and out of what Wittgenstein's followers have called "speech-acts."

Once again we can see the similarities between this way of thinking of language and that exemplified in Polanyi's approach. Not only does his concept of the social character of our quest for knowledge entail a parallel view of the nature of speech, but his analysis of language itself focuses on what J. L. Austin called the "performative" aspect of speech. The primary significance of this analysis pertains to getting things done with language within the social world in which we live, actually ordering and altering our social reality by means of our mutual interaction with each other and the physical environment. To borrow an idea from Martin Heidegger, people speak not only in order to be understood, in a specific instance, but because they already are understood at the general, more primordial level.

As with the nature of language, so with its acquisition, according to Polanyi's philosophy of tacit knowledge. Siding with Noam Chomsky against the empiricist or behaviorist attempt to reduce the learning of language to explicit factors of exposure and inference, Polanyi once again insists that any and all forms of explicit knowing must be derived from a tacit base. Chomsky maintains that children are born with the capacity for language, what he terms the Language Acquisition Device (LAD), already in place within the brain. Some thinkers, such as Steven Pinker *(The Language Instinct)* have sought to explain this inborn capacity as an instinct resulting from eons of evolutionary development. Chomsky himself has made no attempt to explain its presence. Polanyi is more interested in explaining how this capacity actually functions in bringing a nonspeaker into the speaking community, in the logic of language acquisition.

Unsurprisingly, he invokes the interaction between our subsidiary awareness and our bodily activity, which constitutes the process of indwelling, in order to account for how we move from square zero to square one with respect to speech.

> My view is that the use of language is a tacit performance; the meaning of language arises, as many other kinds of meaning do, in tacitly integrating hitherto meaningless acts into a bearing on a focus that thereby becomes their meaning. I would try to trace back the roots of this faculty to primordial achievements of living things. All animals are capable of tacitly integrating their bodily actions; indeed, meaningful integration can be found in the very process of coherent growth. *(Knowing and Being,* p. 196)

In addition to the involvement of somatic participation and imitation within the matrix of the emergence of speech, Polanyi also speaks of the role of the imagination. When we are beginning to indwell our bodies, we initially must operate strictly on the basis of our latent physical capacities, which provide the subsidiary pole of our awareness. The focal pole is provided by the imagination as we seek to imitate the behavior of those around us. Once these capacities and our imagination work together to produce an initial integrative whole, we then posses a rudimentary tacit knowledge from which to move on to other integrative acts. These in turn eventually give rise to various forms of explicit knowledge. Thus, language is acquired through the merging of bodily activity, subsidiary awareness, and imaginative projection toward a goal. Polanyi likens this process to that of an infant learning to keep its balance in walking or to a child learning to ride a bicycle. He summarizes his conclusion thus:

> To the question how a child can learn to perform a vast set of complex rules, intelligible only to a handful of experts, we can reply that the striving imagination has the power to implement its aim by the subsidiary practice of ingenious rules of which the subject remains focally

ignorant. This kind of rule can be acquired tacitly and *only* tacitly, and it can also be practiced *only* tacitly. The elaborate systems of grammar discovered by linguists in the speech of "the idealized native speaker" belong to this class of rules. (*Knowing and Being,* p. 200).

Space will not permit anything like a thorough analysis of the many issues involved in the question of language acquisition. However, it should not go unnoticed that Polanyi's treatment of this area of concern contributes a great deal toward an increased understanding of this extremely important and fascinating subject. Sad to say, the vast majority of those working in this field have approached it in a manner that almost completely ignores both the bodily and the social dimensions inherent within the process of acquiring language. The following quotations from a recent and very important book entitled *Language Acquisition* and edited by Paul Bloom both typify and demonstrate this highly unfortunate oversight by speaking of language acquisition as if it were strictly a mental process, isolated from the body and other speakers.

First Bloom himself:

> A constraint theorist might argue that regardless of how some mothers might aid children in the process of word learning, children are still faced with a logical infinity of candidate hypotheses—and psychologists have to develop a theory of the sorts of mental mechanisms that allow children to infer the correct hypothesis from the linguistic and nonlinguistic context that they are exposed to. (p. 17)

Next, consider Ellen Markman's remark: "The answer is that humans are constrained to consider only some kinds of hypotheses or at least to give them priority over others. This may be especially true for children first trying to learn the concepts that their language encodes" (p. 155). Finally, Melissa Bowerman: "As children begin to want to communicate, they search for linguistic forms that will allow them to encode their ideas" (p. 329).

Clearly, any analysis of language acquisition that speaks predominantly, if not exclusively, of "mental mechanisms," "hypotheses," "inferences," "concepts," and "encoding ideas" is entirely out of harmony with Polanyi's approach. Moreover, such an analysis is systematically ignoring the symbiotic, interactive, and embodied character of speech. In addition, a careful examination of the research methods generally employed by psycho-linguists working from this intellectualist model reveals an almost exclusive dependence on clinical situations in which children *sit* in front of TV screens and give responses to what they *see* and *hear.* Bodily activity and social interaction are *in principle* ruled out of these experimental situations, and thus so are the notions of indwelling, integrative acts, and tacit knowing. Polanyi's treatment of language acquisition in terms of these notions goes far beyond narrow experimentalism of psycho-linguistics.

In his highly profound book *What Computers Can't Do* (248–55) Hubert Dreyfus pinpoints the reason why the effort to understand human reasoning and language through comparisons with "thinking machines" cannot work. He argues that computers cannot really be said to think, not because they do not have minds, but because they do not have active bodies whereby they can enter into the vast and vastly complex modes of behavior that constitute the human cultural world. Polanyi's theory of language acquisition takes such factors into account by stressing the somatic and social matrix out of which all cognition, including language, arises and develops. In his view, these tacit factors play a crucial role in speech as well as thought.

The topic of language acquisition has been of special interest to me for a good many years and became the theme of my recent book *If a Chimpanzee Could Talk*. Throughout the discussion of a wide variety of cases, such as those of Helen Keller, feral children, chimps, and autism, Polanyi's insights into the tacit character of language acquisition were always at the forefront. These insights help to locate what I call the "threshold" of language.

The normal child acquires speech primarily through the "side door," or by "cognitive osmosis," rather than by explicit instruction. It is not possible to give a child a vocabulary list and the rules of grammar as a prerequisite to learning language. Even simple, ostensive definitions presuppose a tacit grounding in a myriad of previously shared activities from within which to grasp the significance of pointing and relative pronouns such as *this, that, here,* and *there.* The grasping of explicit designations and instructions draws heavily and parasitically on a whole host on nonexplicit interactions of both a linguistic and nonlinguistic nature. Songs, whispers, pattycake games, overheard conversations, and imperative utterances all form the subsidiary background that provides the tacit foothold for subsequent explicit verbal instruction and learning. When children "talk" on a play telephone, for instance, they make use of intonations and patterns of speech that express orders, jokes, questions, and declarations long before they have acquired any specific vocabulary. They are indwelling linguistic activity so that later it can come to indwell them.

Finally, I would like to finish up this section of the present chapter by connecting up Polanyi's approach to this topic with that of Steven Pinker as found in his recent and highly influential book *The Language Instinct*. Pinker distinguishes his own approach from that of both psycholinguistics and Noam Chomsky by insisting on the biological and evolutionary basis of language acquisition. As he puts it:

> Language is not a cultural artifact that we learn the way we learn to tell time or how the federal government works. Instead, it is a distinct piece

of the biological makeup of our brains. Language is a complex, special-ized skill, which develops in the child spontaneously, without conscious effort or formal instruction . . . [s]ome cognitive scientists have described language as a psychological faculty, a mental organ, a neural system, and a computation module. But I prefer the admittedly quaint term 'instinct.' It conveys the idea that people know how to talk in more or less the same sense that spiders know how to spin webs. (p. 18)

The chief difficulty with explaining that language acquisition is a func-tion of instinct revolves around the simple fact that instinctive behavior ex-hibits itself in the absence of external input from or interaction with the "social" environment. The spider will spin webs whether or not it has ever seen another spider to do so. But the very opposite is true of children with respect to speech; without some form of linguistic community and activity, children will not speak at all. As Pinker himself notes, albeit inadvertently, language is a "skill," and skills are learned.

Having explained the initial advent of the language "instinct" in terms of genetic mutation, Pinker faces the problem of explaining to whom the first being so programmed would have spoken. His answer to this crucial question turns out to be little more than a vague conjecture about other humans being able to at least partially understand "what the mutant was saying even if they lacked the new-fangled circuitry, just using overall intelligence" (p. 365). Thus, Pinker has people speaking before there are other speakers. Their prelinguisitic oral play must be engaged, stimulated, and expected if they are to become members of the speaking community. If this is true of children today, it certainly would have been true of any genetic mutant eons ago.

Once again, we see that the social and interactive context out of which language must arise provides the matrix for what Polanyi has described as the tacit dimension or component of human cognitive experience. The mystery of the tacit character of the ground of speech, as well as of all learning, runs counter to the fundamental atomism and reductionism of the modern Western heritage. In assuming that all phenomena will yield to an analytic breakdown of their basic elements, we also presuppose that knowledge is composed of a quantitative ac-cumulation of these essentially independent and isolatable conceptual units. However, the plain fact of both experience and logic is that no one has or can isolate any such atomic building blocks of meaning. The fundamental "given" of experience is far more holistic and organic than such a view will allow.

EDUCATION AS LEARNING TO LEARN

Polanyi himself nowhere directly addresses questions involving the philoso-phy of education. Nevertheless, his understanding of cognitivity as arising out of tacit knowing carries with it far-reaching implications for an approach to such questions, at both the theoretic and practical levels. In the remainder of this chapter, I shall trace out some of these implications, seeking to remain true to Polanyi's own development of tacit knowing as the axis of cognitive activity. The particulars of my remarks concerning the application of Polanyi's philosophy of cognition to education will of necessity be grounded in my own experience as a teacher of college and university students. A more thorough treatment of these issues can be found in my book *Learning to Learn*.

Discussions of the philosophy of education frequently revolve around three main questions, namely those of what is to be taught, to whom it is to be taught, and how it is to be taught. These questions, in turn, direct our attention to three areas of concern: the known, the knower, and the knowing process, respectively. In most cases, educational thinkers initiate their discussion of these areas by focusing either on what is to be taught or on the nature of those persons who are to be taught. The assumption behind this procedure seems to be that once we have an understanding of the subjects and the subject matter, we shall be in a better position to come to an understanding of the learning process, which brings the other two factors together.

On the basis of my own understanding of the interactive character of the cognitive process, however, it seems more sound to begin with a consideration of the dynamics of knowing and then move to an exploration of the implications thereof for an understanding of the knower and the known. In an earlier chapter, we considered the question of whether or not Polanyi was a realist, that is, whether he believed that reality exists independently of our cognitive interaction with it. Although there is some reason to conclude that he was, in fact, a realist, in my own view it is also possible to interpret him as a "critical" or "creative" realist. This would involve placing a good deal of weight on his analysis of the interactive character of cognition in relation to the object of knowledge. Since, in Polanyi's view, reality is in principle inexhaustible and our knowledge is perpetually open to fresh discovery, there is a sense in which reality itself is not truly static. Indeed, an extrapolation from Werner Heisenberg's "principle of indeterminacy" would suggest that our knowledge of any given aspect of reality actually contributes to its nature. Thus, the knower and the known can be construed as symbiotic in relation to one another.

The principle of indeterminacy stipulates that since the only way we can *know* the nature of subatomic reality is by *engaging* it, we necessarily alter or contribute to it whenever we seek to know it. Since the fundamental nature of this dimension of reality is organized energy in motion, and not tiny, indestructible particles, whenever we seek to observe it we introduce additional energy into it. Rather than thinking of this as a distortion of an infinitely inaccessible reality, since this would render knowledge thereof impossible, it is more fruitful to think of experienced reality as constituted by the interaction between that which is known and the knowing agent. It is this relationality that comprises the world as we know it, and the world as we know it is the only world about which we can speak. To speak of reality as existing independently of cognitive relationality is, to use a phrase from Whitehead, to commit the "fallacy of misplaced concreteness."

As I have indicated, it is unclear whether or not Polanyi himself would agree with this way of putting this issue, but it seems to me to follow from his equal stress on both the notion of universal intent and the social nature of the scientific enterprise. On the one hand, reality is said to be inexhaustible, which surely implies that we can never claim to know it in and of itself. This entails that the only meaningful notion of reality is one that is defined in terms of our interaction with it. On the other hand, even though we can know the world only through our interaction with it and with each other, the knowledge we gain thereby is sufficient for the purposes to which we put it, according to Polanyi.

Given this reading of Polanyi on the relation between the knower and the known, I suggest that it is best to begin a philosophy of education with a consideration of the knowing process in general and its tacit character in particular. If the matrix of understanding is taken to be the interaction between subsidiary awareness and bodily activity, which in turn gives rise to tacit knowing, this should dictate a good deal concerning the qualities of a sound educational process. Let me enumerate a few of the more significant implications of this point of departure.

To begin with, it should be clear that since tacit knowing consists in integrative acts yielding meaningful wholes, it is crucial for the person facilitating the educative process to enable the learners to grasp the overall significance or the "big picture" of that which is being learned. Individual aspects of reality must be encountered within the context of a sufficiently broad overview if they are to be incorporated into the learner's understanding. Far too often teachers immerse students in the details of an issue or a project without providing any background as to what the bigger picture is and why it is important, and so on. Knowing is a *relational* reality, and this pertains to the connection between parts and wholes as much as to anything else. The former can be grasped only *as* parts when they can be integrated into a significant whole.

Another aspect of this relational character of the knowing process is the importance of creating an engaging and exploratory approach to what is being studied. An atmosphere of discovery and imaginative creativity is extremely helpful in this regard, as is focusing on questions and possible answers rather than on information for its own sake. Even the sciences, history, and mathematics can be taught so as to engage students' imaginations and participation. Unfortunately, teachers who give any thought to such matters are exceedingly rare. The knower and the known can and must be approched as symbiotic realities for true understanding to take place.

In addition, since knowing is an active process grounded in integrative acts, the deepest form of understanding will not be expressed in explicit definitions and inferences, but will rather be embodied in the posture and behavior of the person acquiring it. Moreover, this active character of the knowing process requires that learners interact in some way with the materials and issues under consideration. There is no such thing as passive learning, although interaction can easily take a variety of forms. Field trips, projects, journals, and group discussions, as well as labs, studios, and practice opportunities, need to be explored as ways of engaging students in such a way as to engender involvement Thinking of learning as a participatory activity, perhaps as a dance, will greatly enhance the way one engages in it.

In my own field of philosophy, I long ago abandoned the lecture as the sole means of organizing the learning experience. Since philosophy is by nature a dialogical process, it seems natural to conduct classes on a discussion basis, but free-wheeling discussions soon degenerate into question-and answer sessions or mere bullsessions dominated by those who talk the most. So, instead, I divide the class into rotating discussion groups, one of which sits up front with me each class period, and use these groups to focus and spark discussion. Each member of the group that is up on any given day writes a two-page paper that identifies and develops a significant aspect of the reading for that day. Serving as both moderator and secretary of this discussion, I keep track of its progress on the chalkboard with diagrams, summaries, and so on. This method makes the discussion concrete and begins with the interests of the students, requiring their interaction.

The connection here between this type of pedagogical methodology and Polanyi's analysis of cognitive activity is two-fold. First off, it is clear that in any sound educational endeavor adequate attention must be paid to the role of the body in the learning process. Thus, thought must be given not only to the seating arrangement and use of the chalkboard but also to the possibilities for actual movement on the part of students. Even asking the students to sit in a circle contributes to this process. Ultimately, of course, what is learned must and will exhibit itself in the lives of the learners beyond the classroom. The point is simply that some degree of *somatic participation* is essential to genuine learning since tacit integration through physical interaction with the elements of subsidiary awareness is the matrix of all knowing.

Secondly, since the *social dimension* of human existence is every bit as fundamental as the physical, participation in this dimension is also absolutely basic to all learning. The main mode through which such participation takes place is that of language. For by means of our symbolic interaction with one another, in conjunction with our behavioral interaction, we are incorporated into the human speaking community and actually accomplish the various tasks comprising the human form of life. Thus, it is crucially important to maximize the social aspects of the classroom experience through various forms of active interchange, such as discussion and the creation of a friendly, nonthreatening atmosphere. Even the knowledge and use of students' names enhances what Polanyi calls the "conviviality characteristic of a society of explorers."

The conceptual pole of cognitive activity is, of course, essential to learning as well, especially in fields such as philosophy. The integrative acts that lie at the center of tacit understanding, and thereby give rise to holistic units of meaning, which form the leverage points for further learning, are, according to Polanyi, anchored in the interaction between subsidiary input and the imagination. Thus, the role of *imagination* is, in the conceptual spectrum of cognitivity, tantamount to that of somatic activity with respect to subsidiary awareness. Like bodily skills, conceptual skills also need to be developed through imitation and practice, in order for integrative acts to take place. In a discussion-based classroom, these imaginative skills have a chance to emerge in and through the give and take necessary to the exchange of ideas and reasonings. Conceptual "muscles" can and need to be built by means of imitation and imagination, as Polanyi says.

It must be borne in mind that the focus of such classroom discussions always should be the ideas and reasonings of the different philosophers being studied. Conceptual activity must be about something; there must be some type of cognitive "resistance," some problem or issue waiting to be resolved, in order for integrative acts to form and conceptual skills to develop. By means of this triadic interaction, among a text or a problem, student-learners, and the teacher-facilitator, a society of explorers can be created, cognitive skills can be developed and exercised, and issues and problems can be clarified, if not actually resolved. Education can be greatly enhanced by the appropriation of Polanyi's model of cognition.

Perhaps the most direct approach made by Polanyi to the crucial issues involved in the educative enterprise can be found in his discussion of the famous "Socratic paradox" offered in Plato's *Meno*. On the face of it, it would seem that to search for the solution to a problem is useless, since (1) either you already know what you are looking for, in which case there is no problem after all, or (2) you do not know what you are looking for and thus would not be able to recognize it when confronted with it. While dismissing Plato's solution to this paradox, Polanyi contends that the *Meno*

shows conclusively that if all knowledge is explicit, i.e., capable of being clearly stated, then we cannot know a problem or look for its solution. And the *Meno* also shows, therefore, that if problems nevertheless exist and discoveries can be made by solving them, we can know things, and important things, that we cannot tell. (*The Tacit Dimension,* p. 22)

Even as is evident in the process employed by Socrates in eliciting the Pythagorian theorem from Meno's slave boy, understanding emerges from our imaginative interaction with the particulars of our subsidiary awareness, on the backburner, as it were, particulars that provide clues to the solution of the problem with which we are concerned. This interaction yields integrative acts that, in turn, give rise to tacit knowledge, which may eventually emanate into an explicit solution to the initial problem. Polanyi agrees with Socrates when he says we will be better people if we believe that one must search for the things one does not know. We do after all come to know things by searching for them, and the logic of tacit knowing shows why and how this takes place. Thus, the educative enterprise should center therein.

A helpful way to gain an appreciation for the implications of Polanyi's understanding of cognitive activity is to compare and contrast them to the insights of several leading philosophers of education. Therefore, in rounding out this chapter, I shall offer a brief comparative analysis of the main motifs of Polanyi's thought with those of Alfred North Whitehead, John Dewey, B. F. Skinner, and Carl Rogers. While he clearly would have something with which to agree in each of these thinkers' angles of approach, it is equally clear that Polanyi would have to differ with each of them as well.

In many ways, the thoughts of Whitehead about education may be said to have a rather traditionalist ring to them. In his well-known book *The Aims of Education,* Whitehead outlines what he takes to be the main dynamics involved in the learning experience, together with his suggestions for curricular structure from grade school through university. Surprisingly enough, however, Whitehead's treatment of these themes and issues is relatively unorthodox, especially in relation to the educational practice in the early years of the twentieth century. In fact, it is not difficult to recognize intimations of his later, more radical philosophy, known as "process thought," tucked away within these pages.

To begin with, Whitehead construes human experience, even that of scientific investigation, as highly disorderly and diverse. Moreover, he contends that reality is constituted of ideas or energy rather than of simple material objects and that real knowledge consists in comprehending the connections among these ideas. Whitehead expresses his concern in this way: "My contention is that this world is a world of ideas, and that its internal relations are relations between abstract concepts, and that the elucidation of the precise connection between this world and the feelings of actual experience is the fundamental question of scientific philosophy" (p. 106).

Another rather surprising feature of Whitehead's approach to education is his affirmation of the fundamental importance of the notions of the 'present' and 'relevance' in relation to the learning process. He says:

> Pedants sneer at an education which is useful. But if education is not useful, what is it? . . . It was useful to Augustine and it was useful to Napoleon. It was useful because understanding is useful . . . I would only remark that the understanding which we want is an understanding of an insistent present. The only use of a knowledge of the past is to equip us for the present. The present contains all that there is. It is holy ground." (pp. 2–3)

Although there is no blatant contradiction between these ideas of Whitehead and those of Polanyi, neither is it clear that they would be in full agreement about these issues. It does seem possible that the notions of experienced reality as necessarily encountered and understood within the world of ideas is compatible with Polanyi's concept of reality as inexhaustible and emerging. Likewise, the notion that knowledge ultimately must be grounded in and relevant to contemporary experience would seem to fit within Polanyi's cognitive scheme. Tacit integrations of subsidiary awareness must, after all, occur in contexts formed by current experience.

The most obvious point of confluence between the educational philosophy of Whitehead and Polanyi's understanding of cognitive activity is found within the former's idea of the "rhythm" of the educative process. With respect to any particular learning experience or the cycle of an entire life time, Whitehead stresses the relevance of three basically distinct stages: romance, precision, and generalization. He insists that all learning must begin with kindled curiosity, move on to detailed analysis, and conclude by emphasizing the ramifications for and connections with other areas of life. "Education should consist in a continual repetition of such cycles. Each lesson in its minor way should form an eddy cycle issuing in its own subordinate process. Longer periods should issue in definite attainments, which then form the starting-grounds for fresh cycles" (p. 19).

This three-fold analysis of learning fits nicely with Polanyi's pattern of cognition in terms of the stimulation of the imagination by subsidiary factors that generate an awareness of a problem; an explicit, focal examination of the details and elements involved; and the return to the initial problem in order to trigger a tacit integration of a solution. Moreover, for Polanyi as well, any given solution then may become a point of departure for yet another cognitive cycle. In addition, both Whitehead and Polanyi place the emphasis in learning on cognitive activity and the skills acquired thereby, rather than on the specific information. Whitehead speaks of principles that have "soaked into you" as mental habits, of "the satisfactory way in which the mind will function when it is poked up into activity" (pp. 26–27).

It seems quite safe to say that the educational thinker with whom Polanyi's approach to cognition has the least affinity is B. F. Skinner. Skinner's understanding of learning revolves around the notion of 'behavior' and the "operant conditioning" thereof. According to his analysis, cognition is not a function of some inner mental process, but of an alteration in behavior toward a more favorable existenceby means of *reinforcement techniques*. As he puts it in his book *The Technology of Teaching:* "So far as we are concerned here, teaching is simply the arrangement of contingencies of reinforcement . . . Teaching is the expediting of learning" (p. 5).

While Polanyi, as well as others, talks of "awareness" and "integrative acts" as mental processes that exhibit themselves in overt activity, Skinner is content to focus on the overt activity itself. He sees no need to get all bogged down in nonobservable phenomena; behavior alone is what we can study and direct through education. Moreover, Skinner contends that most of what is learned in school can be taught much more efficiently and effectively by using teaching machines.

> Some promising advances have recently been made in the field of learn-ing. Special techniques have been designed to arrange what are called contingencies of reinforcement—the relations which prevail between behavior on the one hand and the consequences of that behavior on the other—with the result that a much more effective control of behavior has been achieved. (p. 9)

Therefore, insight and understanding for Skinner "are not behavior, but changes in behavior. There is no action mental or otherwise" (p. 120). Then, cognition is, simply the adopting of a new behavior pattern.

It is important to bear in mind that Polanyi's approach to cognition also emphasizes the basic cruciality of action or behavior. Indeed, the whole point of his stress on the role of the body in relation to subsidiary awareness is to overcome the traditional, as well as modern, tendency to construe understand-ing strictly in terms of the intellect. *Embodiment* is, after all, the axis or fulcrum of all tacit knowing, which in turn is the matrix of all explicit know-ing. Thus, for Polanyi as well as Skinner, bodily behavior must be the key to the educational process. However, Skinner's reduction of cognitive activity to mere behavior does not harmonize with Polanyi's philosophy.

Polanyi would contend that Skinner's account overlooks the importance of the vectorial character of cognition, with respect to both the role of the *imagination* and the concern for *universal intent*. For Skinner speaks of behavior as if it were nothing but responses to previous reinforcement, without any particular direction or imagined goal, while Polanyi is adamant in his insistence that imaginative projection of our subsidiary awareness by means of bodily interaction is what enables us to achieve behavioral change through integration. Furthermore, Polanyi's stress on the necessity of universal intent, whereby we implicitly seek the truth in all our knowledge claims, finds no place in Skinner's treatment of cognitivity. Ironically enough, Skinner's own analysis, which he clearly claims to be true, implicitly presupposes this notion of 'universal intent' even though it leaves no room for it. In short, he expects us to accept his claims, not just parrot them. These oversights in Skinner's approach to education make it far less helpful than Polanyi's model of cognition.

Another way to get at the difference between Polanyi's theory of cognition and that of Skinner is to focus on the *interactive* character of understanding. In order for someone or something to be understood, a whole host of subsidiary factors must be read or grasped as a comprehensive entity and distinguished from similar looking or sounding entities on the basis of context, intent, and historical background. The statement *The door is open* can mean a wide variety of things, depending on where it is said, to whom, why, and with what intonation and gestures. Skinner's account overlooks this interactive dimension. Here is how Polanyi makes the point:

> Words can convey information, a series of algebraic symbols can constitute a mathematical deduction, a map can set out the topography of a region; but neither words, not symbols, nor maps can be said to communicate an understanding of themselves. Though such statements will be made in a form which best induces an understanding of their message, the sender of the message will always have to rely for the comprehension of his message on the informal intelligence of the person addressed. (*The Study of Man,* pp. 21–22)

Another educational thinker with whom Polanyi would differ markedly, though for quite different reasons, is Carl Rogers. Whereas Skinner placed too little emphasis on the role of imagination and intentionality, in Polanyi's view, Rogers tends to stress these factors to the near total neglect of the more standard cognitive features of learning. In his book *Freedom to Learn* Rogers develops a case for individualized education that focuses on the affective aspects of human personality. Thus, for him the feelings and aspirations of the learner are of paramount importance, with motivation, self-esteem, and creativity being of crucial significance. Here is how he expresses his perspective:

> It seems reasonably clear that for the learning of the sort we are discussing, students must be confronted by issues that have meaning and

relevance for them. In our culture we try to insulate our students from any and all of the real problems of life . . . if we desire to have students learn to be free and responsible individuals then we must be willing for them to confront, to face problems. (p. 263)

And further on:

The locus of evaluation is again established firmly within the person. It is her own experience that provides the value information or feedback. This does not mean that she is not open to all the information she can obtain from other sources But it means that this is taken for what it is outside evidence and is not as significant as her own reactions. (p. 278)

The difficulty with Rogers's perspective, from Polanyi's point of view, is precisely the opposite from that of Skinner. In brief, where Skinner had paid too much attention to the explicit dimension of cognition, including behavior, Rogers devotes nearly all of his attention to the tacit, or affective dimension. Thus, he is more concerned with the psychological dynamics of human learning than with the actual process of acquiring knowledge itself. Polanyi, to be sure, would agree with Rogers that the "personal coefficient" is extremely significant in all learning, and he repeatedly emphasizes the importance of individual motivation and social conviviality. Nevertheless, Polanyi would see Rogers's educational posture imploding on itself because it fails to focus significant attention on the world that surrounds the learner. For him, the knower and what is to be known must be kept in symbiotic relation to each other for real learning to take place.

While he would be keenly interested in paying attention to environmental and emotional factors that make up the context of a given learning situation, Polanyi would at the same time insist that these factors are subservient to the actual task of acquiring knowledge, of finding a solution to the problem at hand, of devising a fresh hypothesis, and so on. Perhaps it can be said that cognition, like happiness, cannot be achieved when the subject focuses directly on the means to that end; it only takes place when the subject focuses on that which lies beyond him- or herself. An educative process that aims more at the psychological dimension of knowing than at the cognitive dimension will be less effective than one that reverses these priorities. Universal intent must be the goal of education, with motivational concerns as a means.

The educational philosopher with whom Polanyi has the most in common is most likely John Dewey. Their mutual emphases on learning through bodily activity and on the significance of social interaction place these two thinkers in approximation to each other. As is well known, Dewey pioneered an approach to education that stressed learning by doing instead of the traditional passing of information from the teacher's head to that of the learner. Moreover, Dewey taught that education is not primarily preparation for life in the future; rather, it *is* life itself, experienced in the on-going now of the present. Thus it is that the learner comes to understand him or herself in relation to the surrounding world, especially that of social reality.

Dewey was particularly enamored of the scientific method as the key to cognitive activity. He stressed defining the problem, formulating a hypothesis, gathering data by which to confirm or disconfirm the hypothesis, and applying the results, pro or con, to the initial problem. More specifically, Dewey focused on the experimental method as the best technique for gathering crucial data. In his own words:

> The experimental method of scientific inquiry is the only means at our command for getting at the significance of our everyday experiences of the world in which we live . . . it provides a working pattern of the way in which and the conditions under which experiences are used to lead ever onward and outward. (*Experience and Education,* p. 17)

This emphasis on cognition as problem solving, which characterized Dewey's approach to education, bears a strong likeness to Polanyi's concern with curiosity and imagination as the catalysts for integrative acts within the interactive dynamics between subsidiary awareness and human embodiment. In addition, his enthusiasm for activity as the key medium of real education, even with respect to so-called intellectual learning, places Dewey in a category amenable to Polanyi as well. For both of these thinkers, knowledge results from our *bodily participation* in the world, both physical and social, because it is the body that unites our minds and reality. For both Dewey and Polanyi, we are not minds encased within our bodies, a la Plato and Descartes, but holistic persons in whom minds and explicit knowing emerge out of the confluence of bodily perception and meaning-seeking activity.

At the same time, however, Polanyi would part company with Dewey over his failure to acknowledge the *tacit* quality of the fundamental pivot point of all knowing. On the one hand, Dewey speaks as if the scientific method of problem solving were a straightforward, fully conscious process of articulating the problem fully and then gathering data through experimentation and observation. On the other hand, Polanyi was convinced that at the most significant level the formulation of problems and hypotheses is essentially a tacit process. In like manner, even the confirmation or disconfirmation of an idea or theory may be more indirect than Dewey seems to have thought.

There is one other contrast between Dewey's account of cognitive activity and that of Polanyi. For Dewey, the process of learning is its own end or goal; it does not aim at anything beyond itself. At each succeeding stage of this process, as one achieves a sense of temporary closure, there is an awareness that growth has taken place, and this growth is the sole purpose of learning in general and education in particular. While he might well agree that the strengthening of one's cognitive capacities is a vital aspect of cognitive activity, Polanyi would go on to insist that we must affirm the value of goals and criteria by means of which to judge our own growth; otherwise, we have no way to distinguish between growth and mere change. Values such as truth and honesty are implicit within the search for knowledge, even as presented by Dewey. Once again, universal intent serves to balance the pragmatic and social processes involved in all knowing, whether in the classroom or in everyday life.

The following remarks from Dewey's *Experience and Education* clearly indicate the important differences between his view and that of Polanyi:

> Everything depends upon the quality of the experience which is had . . . There is an immediate aspect of agreeableness or disagreeableness, and there is its influence upon later experiences. The first is obvious and easy to judge. The *effect* of an experience is not borne on its face . . . Hence the central problem of an education based upon experience is to select the kind of present experiences that live fruitfully and creatively in subsequent experiences. (p. 27)

The obvious question that begs to be asked here is from whence do we derive the criteria by means of which to judge the "quality" of experiences, especially in terms of their "effects" on subsequent experiences? Polanyi would press for the answer to this question in terms of his notion of universal intent, stressing the drive toward truth, as a regulative idea, as that which helps us discern the fruitful experiences from those that will fail to produce growth. While growth itself is clearly to be valued, it is a meaningless concept apart from some notion of goal or purpose. Growth toward what? one might ask. For Dewey, growth itself is the only intrinsic value, while for Polanyi intrinsic value is to be found within the very structure of the knowing and valuing processes themselves. This structure provides the key to the criteria for judging the quality of experience.

In recent years, two additional concerns have taken center stage in the discussion about educational theory, namely the debate over imbalance of subject matter in traditional Western curricula and the trend toward increasing vocationalism at every level of the educational enterprise. While Polanyi did not address these concerns directly, his philosophy does contain some indication of how they might be taken up from a Polanyian perspective.

It would seem that while the current drive to broaden our educational curriculum to include the history and contributions of cultures other than that of traditional Western society (which is almost exclusively that of elite, white males) is in itself of real value, Polanyi would insist on stressing the continued importance of the values upon which Western culture has depended over the centuries. To the degree that other cultures and societies also have stressed these values, they will be seen to dovetail with and reinforce our own, and if they do not, they will perhaps detract from the latter. This issue is especially crucial to Polanyi's view of the nature and purpose of scientific inquiry on the one hand and interplay between exploration and universal intent on the other.

At the same time, however, it might be just as possible to interpret Polanyi's thought as open to a more universal perspective with respect to cultural values as actually maintaining that all cultures must have already incorporated the basic moral and epistemic values of cognition and community, otherwise they would not have been able to survive. This interpretive posture would then open the way for a more inclusive approach to the question of multiculturalism in the educational curriculum. A comparative study of the values and commitments of diverse cultures not only would be of value in and of itself, but it might well lead to a deeper and more comprehensive understanding of the nature of reality and knowledge.

The issue of increasing vocationalism in the educational curriculum most likely would be addressed by Polanyi in much the same way. To the degree that a vocational program of study reaffirms the basic structure and dynamics of tacit knowing and a stratified universe, it would clearly be viable. However, Polanyi would be quick to stress the dangers of reducing education to any form of training in which explicit formulas and rules of application might be substituted for cognitive skills and tacit integrations. In such programs, both teachers and students not only would cease to be learners in the truest sense of the word, but they may well lose sight of the more comprehensive, holistic nature of that which they are studying. Vocational emphases frequently reduce subject matter to separate and unrelated particulars.

Two examples in contemporary education suggest themselves in this connection. The first pertains to the way teaching itself has increasingly become a vocation in which there is so much emphasis on methodology that both the subject matter and the students are rendered secondary. The second has to do with the way medical education has more and more become a matter of isolated information about specific diseases and procedures, while at the same time becoming less and less a matter of fostering health among human patients.

7

In Art and Religion

Few would disagree with the claim that when we turn our attention to the patterns of the tacit mode as they play themselves out in the aesthetic and religious dimensions of human experience things get much more complicated. The richer, more comprehensive dimensions of life and reality are, by their very nature, a great deal more difficult to generalize about than those we have already discussed. Nevertheless, it is both valuable and interesting to attempt to trace these tacit patterns in relation to art and religion, especially since Polanyi himself actually addressed them in his later work. However, it must be acknowledged at the outset, that a good deal more interpretive effort will be required in this chapter, since Polanyi's writings contain far fewer references to these dimensions of experience than to those taken up in the preceding chapters.

Aesthetic Structure and Meaning

It is not surprising that when addressing aesthetic experience, Polanyi employed the same schema of cognitive activity that he developed in connection with his general account of knowledge as a function of the relation between tacit and explicit factors. The experience of both the artist and the prehender are to be understood in terms of the interaction between subsidiary awareness and bodily indwelling. Unlike scientific endeavor, however, aesthetic involvement never emerges into the explicit range of the cognitive spectrum; if it does so emerge, it fails aesthetically.

In Polanyi's view, the artist initially operates out of a broad base of subsidiary awareness that includes all of his or her own personal experiences, as well as the general background of cultural traditions and developments on the one hand and specific artistic trends and techniques on the other hand. More concretely, he or she interacts with such factors on a daily basis while indwelling particular aspects of the medium within which the work is being created. These latter aspects are primarily employed and experimented with in an indirect or unfocused manner, through bodily interaction, until integrative acts begin to coalesce around significant units of meaning. These meaningful wholes are then worked into a larger, more comprehensive entity that becomes a work of art or a part thereof.

This analysis applies quite directly to nearly all the arts. Composers and musicians work with tone, pitch, key, and rhythm, while visual artists work with space, line, perspective, and color, and creative writers employ denotation, connotation, rhythm, rhyme. Even sculpture, ceramics, architecture, photography, and film can be understood as instances of the interaction between subsidiary awareness and bodily activity from which arise acts of integration that produce significant units of meaning at the tacit level. As with other forms of cognitive activity, artistic indwelling is often embodied in and through the imagination rather than actual physical behavior. Even in such cases, however, the artist relies upon what is seen, heard, and touched in order to project what is yet to be created through the imagination.

In like manner, when a prehender encounters a work of art aesthetically, he or she interacts with it at the tacit level, indwelling its subsidiary particulars through embodied imagination and seeking to engage its foci of meaning. One does not focus on these particulars, but attends *from* them *to* their aesthetic significance. To be sure, these specific elements comprising a work of art may be focused on for detailed analysis and interpretation, but only as a means to the end of holistic comprehension. The parts are meaningless apart from the whole. Polanyi offers the example of poetic meaning in order to make this point, contrasting it to discursive discourse:

> But the damage done to metaphors and poems by specification includes a loss that is much more noticeable than the loss that is incurred when we break off the bearing of a word on its object by focusing our attention upon the word itself. The subsidiaries composing metaphors and poems are joined together by an imaginative performance much richer than any imaginative action required for linking a word to its meaning. To reduce a metaphor or a poem to its disconnected subsidiaries is to extinguish the vision which linked them to their integrated meaning in a metaphor or a poem. What is left is but a caricature of their true meaning. (*Meaning*, p. 82)

The fact that aesthetic significance, by definition, must remain at the tacit level, never being given a single focus of meaning, endows it with an open-ended character that is not present in more direct dimensions of experience, as for example in science. While creative imagination is clearly required in both artistic and scientific endeavor, once the latter has achieved explicit articulation, those seeking its comprehension need not enter into it through imaginative interaction and integration; they simply need to follow the empirical and logical factors so specified. As Polanyi says:

> *This is not the case in the arts.* The capacity of a creative artist's imaginative vision may be enormous, but it is only the vision that he imparts to his public that enables his art to live for others. Thus the meanings he can create for his public are limited by the requirement that they provide a basis for their re-creation by the imaginations of their viewers or readers. The *use* of a work of art by others is not, therefore, like the use of an invention . . . we do have to achieve an imaginative vision in order to "use" a work of art that is, to understand and enjoy it aesthetically. (*Meaning,* p. 85)

In the arts, then, both extremes must be avoided. The work must not specify its meanings too specifically or directly since this leaves no opportunity for the prehender to interact with it imaginatively. Similarly, if a work of art fails to present some degree of integrative significance, it will be impossible for the prehender to draw its parts together by any stretch of the imagination. This way of viewing the matter may be construed as an elaboration on the insight of Emily Dickinson when she said: "Tell all the truth, but tell it *slant.*" Polanyi's tacit-explicit schema enables us to understand how a successful work of art creates an arena for our imaginative and integrative interaction without articulating specific meanings.

Polanyi himself borrowed I. A. Richard's notion of the 'frame' into which aesthetic meanings are cast, so as to abstract them out from their psychological, historical, and political antecedents, by way of explaining the dynamics involved in producing and appreciating a work of art. Such a "framing" enables the aesthetic prehender to interact with a given work in a fresh manner without the interference of factors such as representation, connotation, and context. When treating the prehension of a poem Polanyi remarks:

> Something more than the integration of its frame and its story occurs in our grasp of the reality of a poem. The poem takes us out of the diffuse existence of our ordinary life into something clearly beyond this and draws from the great store of our inchoate emotional experiences a circumscribed entity of passionate feelings. (*Meaning,* p. 88)

Thus, it is clear that in Polanyi's view a work of art not only frames or brackets out the extraneous factors in the creator's life, but by means of this framing it elicits and focuses the prehender's mind and emotions in such a way as to project him or her by means of an imaginative integration into as yet unexperienced dimensions and modes of reality. Polanyi employs this same framing notion in his discussion of the interaction between religious ritual and myth.

> Each serves as a "frame" for the other's "story." And each frame is, in turn, incompatible with the contents of each story. An action in mundane time and space is framed by one that is outside mundane time and space, and vice versa. Yet they are joined together in a meaningful whole by our imagination. (*Meaning,* p. 154)

Let me offer a simple example of how this interpretation of the dynamic of aesthetic experience works itself out. Consider the song "Georgia on My Mind." The specific images composing the lyrics of this song have been chosen deliberately so as to create an ambiguous semantic reference. This ambiguity allows for, indeed it demands, a parallel or alternating interpretive pattern on the part of the prehender. The name *Georgia* functions either as the name of a woman or as the name of the southern state. Thus, the song is either about a person or a place or both, simultaneously. If the subject is taken to be a place, then the images of "arms" and "lips" are heard as metaphors for the human character of one's homeland. If the subject is taken to be a person, then the images of "moonlight through the pines" and "the road leads back to you" are heard as symbols of a romantic relationship.

The point here is that as we indwell the particulars of the song, and these include its rhythms and mood, we attend *from* some of them *to* others, depending on what we focus on as the "meaning" of the song. If we try to analyze these particulars in order to derive their meaning inferentially, we will be unable to do so. In fact, we may well destroy the significance of the song. By imaginatively indwelling these subsidiaries, however, we may be able to interact with them in such a manner as to integrate them into a meaningful whole. At the very least we should be able to appreciate the crucial ambiguity that lies at the heart of this familiar ballad.

Let me offer yet another example, this time from the visual arts, by way of illustrating the dynamics of aesthetic awareness from the perspective supplied by Polanyi's model of cognitive activity. One of Picasso's more well known paintings is commonly referred to as the "Blue Nude." It is safe to say that the painting conveys a mood of sadness. One might say that this is the focal "meaning" of the painting. We attend to this meaning, or are carried along *to* it, by and through, or *from,* the various particulars of which it is composed. Of course, one of these is the overall blue coloring of the painting. By itself, it might seem, blueness does not entail sadness, but we have in our culture come to associate this color with feeling sad, with having "the blues," and when this element of the painting is combined with its other elements, the overall effect is one of sadness.

Some of the other particulars through which this mood is conveyed are the heavy, oval shape of the figure's posture, the positioning of the head, and the absence of any other objects in the painting. Not only do we generally associate this posture with sadness or depression, but the "aloneness" of the figure, almost suspended in space, contributes to the feeling of isolation as well. It is interesting to note that the anatomical relationships of the figure's posture are quite out of proportion to one another. Not only is the left foot actually nonexistent, but the right leg cannot possibly be joined to the right hip properly. Moreover, the left shoulder and arm are much too small. In spite of these anomalies, or rather, by *means* of them, Picasso was able to create a figure whose shape conveys heaviness and isolation, thereby contributing to the overall mood of sadness. An anatomically correct figure would be far less weighty and less focused or intense than Picasso painted.

It is easy to see how the main features of Polanyi's analysis of the interaction between subsidiary awareness and imaginative indwelling are operative in our experience of this painting. When we first encounter the painting, we see the sadness as a comprehensive entity, as a meaningful whole in and of itself, without being focally aware of why this is so; we grasp the particulars of this whole, the overall mood of sadness, subsidiarily. These particulars are brought together by means of an integrative act and are thus known tacitly without having been articulated. When we do turn our attention to the specific elements comprising the whole, we can come to a more explicit understanding of the compositional dynamics of the painting. While engaged in this type of analysis, we lose our grasp on the overall meaning or focus of the painting, but we can once again turn our focal attention to this meaning, often with enhanced appreciation.

Another way to put all this is in terms of the notion of 'mediated meaning.' It is fair to say that in Polanyi's understanding of tacit knowing, which emerges from the interaction between subsidiary awareness and somatic and/or imaginative indwelling, the particular features of this painting combine to *mediate* its broader, more comprehensive meaning. The latter is carried in and through the former and thus can be said to be "supervenient" upon them. Although no account of these particulars can be said to exhaust or explain the meaning of the comprehensive whole, it is also true that the latter cannot be said to exist or be known apart from them either. Once again we encounter Polanyi's notion of 'emergence' within boundary conditions.

This introduction of the notion of 'mediation' opens the way to a discussion of still another application of Polanyi's approach to aesthetic awareness and meaning. For a number of years, I have taught a course entitled "Philosophy and Film," in which I have sought to make use of the dynamics of tacit knowing. The course is built around a three-fold model of film appreciation and understanding, which includes the perceptual dimension, the dramatic dimension, and themetaphoric dimension. The idea of this three-fold model is that the metaphoric dimension of a film, as distinguished from a "movie," is mediated in and through the dramatic and perceptual dimensions, while the dramatic dimension can be said to be mediated in and through the perceptual dimension. Although this schema greatly oversimplifies the rich and complex nature of film as an art form, it does provide a point of departure for an initial interpretive effort thereof. Also, it clearly embodies the main aspects of Polanyi's epistemology, as will be seen from the following discussion.

In spite of the fact that the present generation of students was literally raised in front of movie and television screens, it remains true that they, as well as those of us in an older generation, are essentially illiterate with respect to the dynamics of filmic comprehension and reality. For this reason, the main emphasis in this course is on the perceptual dimension of films by way of calling attention to those elements that largely go unnoticed because we are focusing on the storyline (dramatic dimension) or on the symbolism (metaphoric dimension) of a given film.

The perceptual dimension of a film is composed of elements such as lighting, framing, perspective, color, motion, sound, and editing. In addition, one can include emotional factors that are "perceived" internally, as it were, such as tension, sadness, joy, and confusion. All such particulars are generally only prehended subsidiarily and are interacted with and entered into at a basic perceptual and visceral level. Yet these elements constitute the parts out of which the larger units of significance, such as objects, characters and events, are constructed; they mediate the dramatic and metaphoric dimensions of meaning. By analyzing these elements, we can come to a better understanding of how this is so.

The dramatic dimension of a film, in turn, is made up of features such as setting, character development and interaction, storyline, and structural patterns such as crux, climax, and time reference. Although these elements are more readily "seen" in the film, a study of the factors by which they are mediated can greatly enhance one's understanding of how they function and even of what actually happens at the dramatic level. Here we see Polanyi's analysis of wholes and parts once again, as well as his insights into the dynamics between subsidiary and focal awareness. And the whole dynamic roles forward on itself when we turn our attention to the richer, more comprehensive metaphoric dimension. Now it is both the perceptual and the dramatic dimensions that mediate the significance of the larger whole, and we may focus our awareness on either of the former two or on the latter by means of the former. In either case, we attend *to* the one in terms of or *from* the other(s).

When he moves on to address the concept of 'validity' in art, Polanyi both compares and contrasts art to science. He insists that these two disciplines are alike in that they (1) both arise out of the creative imagination, (2) both involve integrative cognitive activity at the tacit level, and (3) both require that their practitioners submit to standards of excellence and criticism. However, within this latter similarity there is a crucial difference in Polanyi's view.

> Art has no tests external to art. Its making and acceptance must therefore be grounded *on the decision of its maker,* interacting, it is true, with both traditions and the public's present inclinations, but nevertheless interacting by and through the maker's own judgments. The fact that the artist must labor to meet his self-set standards is sufficient warrant that he submits to these as being universal standards, not of his own arbitrary or willful making. He may be the first ever to recognize them, yet he feels himself bound by them, not superior to them; for to him his innovation of standards appears to be a discovery, just as the innovative creation of a statistical understanding of nature appeared to modern physicists to be a discovery.
>
> That these grounds of artistic creation are ultimate does not mean, however, that they are infallible; they may be contested by other artists . . . They may eventually be abandoned. But this would be a change (made by artists themselves) to other self-set standards, the adoption of which would then be the ultimate justification for all work done under their guidance. (*Meaning,* p. 103)

This account of the relation between the artist and the work of art applies equally well, according to Polanyi, to the relation between the work and its public. The role played by traditional criteria and current public taste in the evaluation of works of art is real, but it is mediated by and through the individual and collective efforts of the artists themselves. Thus, innovations in art, when successful, constitute a fresh comprehensive unit of meaning toward which the characteristics of previous efforts point. The evolution of the various artistic media can be seen as a forward spiralling circle in which each new cycle both encompasses and surpasses its predecessors. The criteria of evaluation also evolve in this cyclical fashion, albeit in a tacit manner, according to Polanyi:

> But it is the public that must learn its criteria from the artists, not the artists from the public. Whenever we are faced with the necessity of deciding on a judgment, we cannot avoid relying on ultimate criteria. Even a failure to judge demands that we rely on some ultimate criteria for our refusal to judge. The point is, however, that we are often unaware of what these criteria are until after we have relied on them as subsidiary clues in a focal integration. (*Meaning,* p. 104)

It is this understanding of the emerging character of the criteria relevant to the evaluation of artistic efforts in any given age that Polanyi employs when reflecting on the history of art in the West. Inevitably, there is both a destructive and a constructive side or edge inherent within all innovating movements in any field of art. In Polanyi's view, even the nihilistic aspects of what is generally called "modern art" were balanced out by the fresh positive perspective inextricably, and inadvertently, contained within it. The artists of this movement "triumphed over their destruction of meaning in our social life by evoking in this rubbish meaningful images never witnessed before" (*Meaning,* p. 116). Nevertheless, Polanyi still sees modern art as a variation of the "moral inversion" so characteristic of our time, since it may be accused "of having contributed to the very destruction of coherence which formed the grounds for its discovery of novel realms of the imagination (*Meaning,* p. 116).

The visionary art of the modernist movement rejected the sentimentalist rendering of traditional values offered by romanticism, on the one hand, and the empty philistinism of Russian "socialist realism" on the other hand. In this sense it was, ironically enough, a forerunner of postmodernism. Polanyi expresses this paradoxical point thus:

> Modern art has clearly been influential in discrediting all affirmations of noble sentiments, and we may regret this; but this baleful influence does not efface its achievements. It accentuated the decomposition of meaning by crying out against it, but its power to transcend this decomposition by new ranges of visionary experience has revealed to us new worlds of the imagination. On balance, therefore, it would seem to have achieved more meaning, in spite of itself, than it has destroyed. (*Meaning,* pp. 116-117)

Even on this more abstract, sociohistorical level we can see the operation of Polanyi's overall emphasis on the tacit character and dynamic of human cognition and valuation. At the deepest level or dimension of our existence, we are but subsidiarily aware of the factors that constitute the context within which we live and develop. Nevertheless, we interact with these factors, both individually and as communities, by means of our bodily and imaginative indwelling, and are able to form meaningful wholes out of what at first seem like quite disparate particulars. These wholes in turn give rise to and give way to yet further units of significance, becoming themselves the parts thereof.

This concludes our efforts to trace the pattern of Polanyi's interpretation of tacit knowing, as the axis of all cognitive activity, within the aesthetic dimension of human experience. At the very least, this exploration serves to establish the wide range of application to which Polanyi's philosophy can be put. Moreover, it is to be hoped that the foregoing discussion makes a substantive contribution to our understanding of artistic activity and appreciationas well. However, it is time, however, to move on to the consideration of yet another dimension of experience wherein Polanyi's insights can be shown to have highly significant ramifications, namely that of religion.

RELIGIOUS EXPERIENCE AND KNOWLEDGE

Polanyi's understanding of religion, at both the individual and social levels, revolves around his critique of the modernist evaluation of the archaic approach to truth. The dilemma confronting anthropologists and psychologists alike centers in the question of whether archaic, nonscientific peoples operate according to the same cognitive dynamics as we Westerners, and do so in an inferior manner, or whether they operate according to a quite different cognitive pattern, in which case our thought processes must be judged to be incommensurable with theirs. The first horn of this dilemma leads to a position of cultural arrogance on our part, and the second horn seems to entail the impossibility of cross-cultural understanding.

Polanyi argues that this dilemma is based on our own erroneous account of the nature of scientific knowledge. The modernist effort to conceive of science, indeed, of all cognitive activity, as entirely "objective" and devoid of any value judgments and commitments, as based exclusively on inductive inferences which can be verified quite apart from any theoretic interpretation, is in his view entirely false. Part 1 of the present study was devoted to a presentation of Polanyi's rationale for this conclusion, so there should be no reason to repeat it here. Suffice it to say that the role of tacit knowledge in the scientific enterprise must not be overlooked when comparing Western science with archaic "mythology."

Since all knowing, according to Polanyi, arises out of a tacit matrix, which itself is a function of the interaction between subsidiary awareness and bodily participation, the archaic and scientific understandings of reality are necessarily on equal footing epistemologically speaking. The shortcomings of the former involve a tendency to exaggerate the inner coherence of its traditional theoretic or mythological framework, to systematically refuse to be self-critical of accepted beliefs. The shortcomings of the latter involve the pretense that science proceeds without any such commitments and assumptions; the mythology of modernism is that we have transcended the need for myths. As Polanyi argues:

> All empirical observation rests ultimately on the integration of subsidiaries to a focal center. All such integrations—from perception to creative discoveries—are impelled by the imagination and controlled by plausibility, which in turn depends upon our general view of the nature of things. Over a wide range of day-to-day affairs the archaic mind thinks and acts as sensibly as we do . . . In evaluating the differences between the archaic and the modern approaches, we have to maintain that the archaic mind is better in many ways . . . it is closer to the truth than the modern view, which has no place for the quality and depth of these coherences nor, therefore, for the full extent of the subsidiaries that are necessary to their composition. The difference becomes essential in the observation of those comprehensive entities that can be observed only by indwelling. The archaic mind recognizes indwelling as the proper means of understanding living things. (*Meaning,* p. 144)

It frequently has been observed that in the archaic mind the Western division between religion and everyday life has no place. The mythologies of archaic or tribal cultures embody their views of the nature of the cosmos and the human place in it, and these world views are both spiritual and mundane simultaneously. Moreover, the symbols and rituals by means of which these world views are expressed and maintained constitute the religious belief system of these peoples. Such symbolic formulations and practices are epistemologically parallel to the poetic metaphors and artistic creations of the West, which embody the values and aspirations of our own cultural heritage. In each case, these mythological or theoretic frameworks must be understood and evaluated in terms of their overall ability to preserve, guide, and challenge to growth their respective cultures. As Polanyi states:

> The fact is that all empirical knowledge is rooted in subsidiaries that are to some extent unspecifiable. We may add to this as its corollary that the range of meaning covered by verbal statements is unlimited. We have seen how richly poetic meaning can serve to clarify our own experiences and to express them effectively. The myths of archaic people

should be regarded in this light. They are clearly works of imagination; and their truth, like the truths of works of art, can consist only in their power to evoke in us an experience which we hold to be genuine. (Meaning, p. 145)

Polanyi goes on to suggest that the religious beliefs of the West, as well as those of the East, must be treated in precisely the same manner, namely in terms of their ability to sustain and stimulate meaningful and fruitful cultural life. Presumably, this would be the case for individuals as well, and the degree of breakdown of religious belief, within nearly all cultures, would seem to indicate a crisis of worldwide proportions in the religious dimension of human experience.

Because of its commitment to so-called objectivity, the scientific mythology of modernism has rendered it difficult, if not impossible, for the contemporary Western person to entertain any religious beliefs and/or activities in a genuine fashion. In short, we have become so suspicious of putting belief before knowledge, lest we overstep the evidence, that we find ourselves incapable of making any affirmations about ultimate reality and values. This final separation between knowledge and "faith" has become the credo of the modern sensibility. In contrast to this, Polanyi insists that belief must come before knowledge, since there can be no knowledge apart from some initial affirmations as to the possibility and value of knowledge, together with an accrediting of our cognitive powers to achieve it.

This then is our liberation from objectivism: to realize that we can voice our ultimate convictions only from within our convictions, from within the whole system of acceptances that are logically prior to any particular assertion of our own, prior to the holding of any particular piece of knowledge. (*Personal Knowledge,* p. 267)

Polanyi agrees with Augustine that it is necessary to believe in order to understand.

At the cognitive level of experience, what the above discussion entails is that faith lies deeper than mere assent to a set of theological propositions, although it may well include such, to incorporate a full-bodied participation or indwelling by the believer in the ritual and social practice of the religious community. These activities constitute the symbolic expression and embodiment of the fiduciary framework that gives life and substance to the religious world view of a given culture. Although such interaction with and commitment to this framework has been declared inappropriate epistemological behavior by our modern culture, it is in fact precisely the same sort of behavior required for the achieving of scientific knowledge; it is necessary to all cognitive activity. Polanyi offers the following summation of religious experience:

> It is therefore only through participation in acts of worship—through dwelling in these—that we see God. God is thus not a being whose existence can be established in some logical, scientific, or rational way before we engage in our worship of him. God is a commitment involved in our rites and myths. Through our integrative and imaginative efforts we see him as the focal point that fuses into meaning all the incompatibles involved in the practice of religion. But, as in art—only in a more whole and complete way—God also becomes the integration of all the incompatibles in our own lives. (*Meanings,* p. 156)

Perhaps it should be noted that not everyone within the religious community of Christianity, let alone those who worship in other traditions, whether theologian or lay-person, is in agreement with Polanyi's interpretation of religious faith. There is a decided absence of any reference to the historical dimension of religious belief, a dimension that traditionally has played an important role within all the religions of the West. The historical grounding and character of the Jewish, Christian, and Muslim scriptures is every bit as fundamental as are the mythological aspects. Polanyi's focus is on the creation stories and Paul's mytho-poetic theology when he interprets Christian belief. It is surely unclear how his remarks in the following passage can be said to apply to the Gospel accounts of Jesus's life and teaching.

> That is, their possibility cannot lie in our conceiving the events as they represent them as actually having occurred in secular time—at least not *as* such events as these would occur in secular time—because their very detachment rests upon their events being understood as having occurred rather in that "Great Time". . . If the events in a sacred myth must lack this sort of day-to-day possibility—the possibility that events represented in representational art must have—then, whatever their possibility may be, it must be of a different sort. (*Meaning,* p. 159)

In any case, one can clearly see in the foregoing discussion that Polanyi has sought to integrate his critique of the modern view of science and cognitivity with contemporary understandings of mythic and poetic expressions of belief. This integration is of a piece with his overall development of what I have called the "tacit mode" within his philosophy.

Over the years, I have developed my own rendition of Polanyi's postcritical philosophy as it applies to the understanding of religious experience, knowledge, and language. The remaining pages of this chapter will be devoted to a presentation of these extrapolations in terms of these three categories.

One of the chief characteristics of the modern worldview has been the division of reality into levels or realms. This division may well go back as far as Plato, but it became absolutely central to modern thought with the advent of the philosophy of Immanuel Kant. His dichotomy between pure and practical reason, together with that between the knowable, phenomenal world and the unknowable, noumenal world, was meant to "save" religion from rational criticism by placing it in a realm of its own, grounded in morality alone. Thus, Kant "set reason aside in order to make room for faith." This dualism has come to dominate nearly all thinking about religious issues in our contemporary culture.

The standard way to express this realmism is in terms of the customary distinction between the natural and supernatural worlds. Science is said to apply to the former, while religion is thought to apply to the latter, and neither is supposed to interfere with the other's questions, theories, or development. Thus, as Polanyi has pointed out, science is claimed to be completely free from personal and valuational components, and religion is viewed as having nothing whatever to do with empirical issues. Even Polanyi himself, as I said a bit earlier, seems to come very close to embracing this noncognitivist interpretation of religious belief and practice.

To my way of thinking, however, the ramifications of Polanyi's understanding of the relation between boundary conditions and emergent levels of existence for religion would seem to suggest something quite different from this traditional dualism or realism. The mediational character of tacit knowing requires the construal of the world according to a dimensional model of reality in which the richer, more comprehensive dimensions are mediated *in and through* the less rich and comprehensive. Thus, while the boundary conditions put in place by the latter set the parameters within which the former can operate, they cannot determine their nature and dynamics. In short, we attend *from* the physical dimension of existence *to* the social, conceptual, moral, aesthetic, and religious dimensions. Likewise, we attend from the first three to the fourth since the religious dimension is by definition the richest and most comprehensive.

Take a simple example. A statement written on a piece of paper is experienced differently by a person who has never seen writing from the way it is by one who recognizes what writing is, but cannot read, and from the person who can read but who does not know the appropriate language, to say nothing of the one who knows the language yet fails to grasp the fact that this statement is actually a call for help. The physical markings are in each case the same, but the meaning is richer and more comprehensive as each dimension emerges. Each successive dimension mediates but does not exhaust the significance of those that arise in and through it. We attend from the one to the others in discerning their enhanced meaning.

Thus, it is more fruitful to view the relation between religion and science, as well as that between religion and a variety of other aspects of life, as one of interpenetrating dimensions that are arranged according to a hierarchy of richness and comprehensiveness. While the patterns that govern the physical dimension are relevant to but do not determine the meaning of the social and moral dimensions. In like manner, the patterns of these latter dimensions are relevant to, but do not exhaust religious meaning. In other words, in the view that I am here proposing religious belief and practice cannot be separated off from the other dimensions through which they are mediated, while at the same time they cannot be construed as dictating the principles of these either. This mediational understanding of experienced reality enables us to avoid the intellectual controversies and stalemates so characteristic of modern philosophy of religion without falling victim to cultural "schizophrenia."

Another way to put this proposal is to say that it will help us get beyond the traditional naturalism versus supernaturalism debate, as well as the famous faith versus reason dilemma, by viewing the dimensions of experienced reality as interpenetrating and mediating one another along a continuum of increasing richness and comprehensiveness. This continuum is thus arranged according to a *vector* that corresponds to that in Polanyi's account of the interaction between subsidiary awareness and bodily indwelling. In each case, one comes to encounter the mediated reality in question through participatory interaction with the particulars of the dimension that mediates it and by integrating these into holistic units of meaning.

The point here is simply that this model enables us to see the so-called supernatural in the natural and faith and reason as symbiotic aspects of a common cognitive process. The sort of knowledge that arises within religious life and community can be seen as a direct implementation of Polanyi's understanding of tacit knowing. On the one hand, religious awareness can be said to arise as one seeks to integrate the array of subsidiary factors within which one is immersed by both the natural and social worlds. Religious faith may be said to be the result of such integrative acts emerging from bodily and imaginative indwelling at the subsidiary level. On the other hand, these integrations yield a tacit understanding and a commitment that includes faith as trust but includes cognitive activity as well. The religious person "reads" the significance of his or her context as having ultimate meaning in relation to divine realityand asserts this as true.

Thus, while there is no straight line between one's faith and scientific and historical factors, it is neither necessary nor useful to conclude that this means that faith has nothing to do with reason. The tacit discernments that believers make in forming their axial commitments are nonetheless cognitive for being unarticulatable in an exhaustive manner. They form the matrix out of which flows the life of faith, even as those discernments of nonbelievers form the basis for their way of life. All explicit knowing derives from tacit knowing, and together the two function as the symbiotic poles of the cognitive dimension of human life.

The question of the confirmation of knowledge claims is always of special interest in relation to religious belief. If religious affirmations are taken to be claims to tacit knowing, arising from integrative acts that are formed by indwelling subsidiary factors, then the most appropriate way to confirm or disconfirm them is in terms of the quality of the life to which they lead. "By their fruits you shall know them." If a person claims to have integrated the particulars involved in riding a bicycle so as to know how to ride it, then the way to test this claim is to ask the person to ride the bicycle. Likewise, if a person claims to know what love or peace is, then we look to their lives to see if this is in fact the case. The same might well be said of an affirmation such as "God was in Christ reconciling the world"; we must look to see if reconciliation is indeed a characteristic of Christ and of the person making the affirmation.

There are, to be sure, many difficulties with how to go about such evaluation, what counts for and against, and what the facts really are in a given person's or community's life. But this is always the case, whether in scientific inquiry or in everyday life. Is light continuous or discontinuous, wave or particle? How far does one have to ride a bicycle in order to be able to say "I know how to ride it"? Sixty feet or around the block? The point is that we settle these questions; we do not say they are unanswerable and therefore noncognitive. Of course, not all claims to tacit knowing turn out to be true; but neither do all claims to explicit knowing. It is to be expected that in the highly mediated, rich, and comprehensive dimensions of life, confirmation will be more difficult.

According to Polanyi's theory of universal intent, even the affirmations of religious believers must be construed as aiming at the truth, as making a cognitive claim. Clearly, such claims are far more complex and mediated in character than are more straightforward empirical assertions, but they are by nature qualitatively the same. It is this aspect of universal intent that makes Polanyi's account of religious commitment, presented a few pages back, seem somewhat out of harmony with his more general treatment of knowledge claims. For even fiduciary frameworks, which admittedly are based in tacit integrations and commitments, are cognitive in character, according to Polanyi.

This interpretation of religious knowledge claims fits quite nicely with the dimensional analysis of religious experience offered previously. The notion of 'reality as mediated dimensions' and that of 'tacit knowing' go hand-in-hand with one another, for one would expect a mediated dimension of reality to be discerned only tacitly, and, conversely, that which is known tacitly or subsidiarily must be mediated in and through other dimensions. Religious believers claim to discern the transcendent within the natural, not beyond it. Perhaps, this is the real significance of the phrase *Now we see through a glass, darkly.* More specifically, within the Christian faith, the meaning of the Incarnation is to be found in the idea that divine reality revealed itself in the form of a human person amidst historical and social reality. "The Word became flesh and dwelt among us . . . full of grace and truth."

Finally, the suggestion being made here is that the sort of linguistic activity most appropriate to speaking about a highly mediated dimension of reality, one discerned by means of tacit understanding, is the *metaphoric*. On the diagram of the dynamics between tacit and explicit knowing introduced in chapter 2, metaphoric speech would seem especially fitting as the proper mode of discourse for communicating about that which can be known but not wholly explicated. As such, it stands midway between absolute silence at the most extreme tacit pole of the cognitivity continuum and full articulation at the extreme explicit pole. Thus, while religious utterances must never be taken as straightforward empirical claims, neither should they be interpreted as "mere" symbols or myths. Here again, Polanyi's own analysis of religious language and belief, as discussed earlier on, would seem to have oversimplified the issues involved.

Indeed, metaphoric speech can be described as mediating characteristics or insights belonging to one dimension of experienced reality by means of yet another different dimension. As Polanyi's account itself indicated, in metaphor we attend from the particulars of that with which we are familiar toward that which constitutes the meaning of that with which we are unfamiliar. If the metaphor is successful, we may come to know something about that specific aspect of reality that we will never be able to express more effectively in any other way. When we say "Los Angeles is a zoo," we in fact see both the city and zoos in a new way, a way that cannot be reduced to any list of qualities thereof. In like manner, when Jesus said he was the bread of life, he communicated something about his own nature and about the nature of bread as sustenance that cannot be exhausted by explicit discourse.

Metaphoric speech, then, operates at the interface between full articulation and tacit discernment. That of which we are aware subsidiarily and know tacitly we seek to express indirectly by means of the various facets of the metaphoric mode, such as analogy, paradox, story, and metaphor. This is especially true for religious discernments, which are extremely mediated and tacit in character. But, as Polanyi has made abundantly clear, this sort of indirect discourse is equally common in both science and everyday life. At the axis of scientific theorizing there stand such key concepts as mass, energy, and simultaneity, along with unarticulated commitments to truth and the search for knowledge, none of which can be given full explication. In everyday life as well, we commonly speak in metaphors when we are unable to express in direct fashion what we feel or think. This is not a weakness but is, rather, both necessary and appropriate since much of what really matters in life has to do with its more highly mediated dimensions. To say "I love you because you are you" says nothing and everything at one and the same time. To call Michael Jordan "Air Jordan" is, to be sure, rather inarticulate at best, empirically speaking, but it says a great deal about both the player and the game of basketball. Similarly, to speak of God as a "loving parent" is less than explicit, but nonetheless communicative.

One further point needs to be made before bringing this chapter to a close. Although it is true that metaphoric speech goes beyond the subsidiary particulars that make it up, beyond the specific meanings of the ordinary language used in creating it, it is equally true that this does not render these specific meanings irrelevant to the meaning of the metaphor. It matters a great deal which locutions one chooses to use when creating a metaphor. There is a big difference between saying that Los Angeles is a zoo and saying that it is a park, a circus, or an experiment. In the same way, much would be different had Jesus called himself the "centurion of God," the "heavenly emperor," or the "rosebed of life." While the focal meaning of a metaphor is more than the subsidiary meaning of the particulars of which it is composed, it still must operate within the boundary conditions set by them, even when one is speaking of the divine.

Thus, the choice of words and notions used in the formulation of the metaphoric mode involves cognitive activity and discernment. Since it is clear that some terms are more appropriate for expressing a given feature of a mediated dimension of experienced reality than are others, certain criteria must be employed in deciding which is which. Therefore, it is clear that religious language as well will necessarily entail cognitive judgment, at least at the tacit level. To speak of the transcendent as mediated in and through the natural dimension and as known tacitly does not relieve one of the responsibility to speak judiciously.*

There are, as well, other thinkers who have explored the implications of Polanyi's work for various aspects of religious belief and practice. Harry

---

*For more of my own adaptations of Polanyi's thought in relation to the notions of religious experience, knowledge, and expression see, for example, *Mediated Transcendence.* (1989); *On Knowing God* (1981); "Reasons of the Heart," in *Religious Studies* (Fall 1974); "Tacit Knowing and Religious Belief," in *International Journal for Philosophy of Religion* (Summer 1975).

Prosch discusses his examination of religion as a cultural phenomenon, in his *Michael Polanyi: A Critical Exposition* (1986). Likewise, Richard Gelwick provides a general treatment of Polanyi's interpretation of religion in his book *The Way of Discovery: An Introduction to the Thought of Michael Polanyi* (1977). Neither of these accounts takes up the dynamics of tacit knowing as they relate to questions of cognitivity and epistemic validation, however.

A quite different treatment of the implications of Polanyi's philosophy for religious belief and thought is given by J. V. Apczynski in his *Doers of the Word: Toward a Foundational Theology Based on the Thought of Michael Polanyi* (1977). While Apczynski offers many interesting and valuable explorations of Polanyi's thought, the overall aim of constructing a "foundational theology" from the latter's epistemology strikes this writer as wrong-headed from the outset. Given the fact that the very heart of the modern or critical approach to philosophy, which it is Polanyi's express purpose to overcome, lies in the search for an ultimate foundation for knowledge, it should be clear that an attempt to use Polanyi's work as a basis for a foundationalist theology is doomed from the start.

In chapters 2 and 3, I sought to establish a nonfoundationalist interpretation of Polanyi's epistemological thought by introducing the concept of an 'axis' as the center of the cognitive enterprise in replacement for the notion of a 'foundation.' While it is true that for Polanyi all human cognition must begin by accrediting our abilities and judgement-making capacities without first providing a rational justification for so doing, it does not follow from this that these abilities and capacities function as a foundation for our cognitive activity in the sense sought by those seeking to justify religious belief and practice. As Wittgenstein put it, such faculties and commitments neither can be nor need to be "justified" in the rationalist sense, but neither are they arbitrary in the sense of expressing "blind faith." Thus, Apczynski's efforts in this direction get off on the wrong foot at the beginning.

The same can and must be said for the efforts of Alvin Plantinga, and to a lesser extent Nicholas Wolterstorff, which attempt to absolve religious commitment of all need for rational responsibility by calling on the insights of Thomas Ried concerning the epistemic viability of common sense (see Plantinga, "Is Belief in God Rational?" in *Rationality and Religious Belief,* (1979). The notion of 'properly basic beliefs' is not at all the same sort of thing as what Polanyi affirms as tacit knowing, since they are primarily intellectual rather than embodied.

By far the most thorough and enlightening treatment of the ramifications of Polanyi's thought for religious belief and practice is to be found in Andy Sanders, *Michael Polanyi's Post-Critical Epistemology* (1988). Sanders begins by focusing the psychological aspects of tacit knowing in relation to religious faith and then moves on to deal with Polanyi's account of religion as a cultural phenomenon in relation to the hierarchical structure of reality. In these respects, his treatment is quite similar to those of Prosch and Gelwick. It is when he moves on to a discussion of the epistemological aspects of Polanyi's theory of cognition that Sanders has much to offer in a consideration of the postmodern direction of the former's philosophy. Sanders discusses the interaction between analytic philosophy and religious thinkers such as Basil Mitchell and Ian Ramsey and thereby steers a middle course between falliblism and fideism.

The particular move by which he accomplishes this middle way is to follow the insights of J. M. Soskice in her book *Metaphor and Religious Language* (1985). Here he connects up with Polanyi's treatment of metaphor as presented in *Meaning* and discussed earlier on in this chapter. Sanders concludes that with respect to the nature of metaphorical expression, Soskice, like Polanyi, "appears to reject the emotive-cognitive dichotomy, but, unlike him, she sees the emotional function as, in some unexplained sense, derivative. Polanyi clearly stresses the priority of the emotional function over the cognitive one" (p. 263). However, Sanders also concludes that had Polanyi invoked his ontology, "he might have made a case for the referring character of religious language"(p. 263).

Additional aspects of both Prosch's and Sanders's views on the implications of Polanyi's thought for religion will be taken up in the next chapter, which considers other interpretive accounts of Polanyi's philosophy. In particular, Prosch's analysis and critique of Thomas Torrance's exposition of Polanyi's views on religion provides valuable insight into the use and misuse of the latter's postcritical epistemology. The same can be said for Sanders's examination of several other interpreters of Polanyi's approach to philosophy in general and to religion in particular.

8

OTHER INTERPRETIVE INSIGHTS

Having made our way through the main themes of Polanyi's reconstructive postmodern philosophy, it will now prove profitable to consider the interpretive insights that have been offered by other thinkers interested in various aspects of his thought. I shall organize this chapter around the general topics that have been presented in the previous chapters, beginning with the epistemological implications of the logic of tacit knowledge, particularly as they bear on the dominant emphases of modern or critical philosophy, as taken up in part 1. Then I shall move to a consideration of the topics explored in part 2, namely, the patterns of the tacit mode as they work themselves out in fields such as science, political theory, language, education, art, and religion.

Perhaps the single most valuable resource for exploring additional interpretive insights into Polanyi's philosophy is the book *Intellect and Hope: Essays in the Thought of Michael Polanyi,* edited by Thomas Langford and William Poteat (1968). This volume consists of fifteen examinations of different aspects of Polanyi's thought by a number of first-rate thinkers in a variety of disciplines. In addition, there are a half-dozen other books that provide more intensive treatment or overall summaries of Polanyi's thought. While I cannot do justice to each of these contributions, I shall attempt to deal with those that seem to be the most helpful in coming to a fair and productive understanding of Polanyi's reconstructive postmodern philosophy. Also, I shall make an effort to clarify where my own interpretation differs from or agrees with those under discussion.

Knowledge and Modern Philosophy

In her essay "Tacit Knowing and the Pre-reflective Cogito" Marjorie Grene seeks to show how the dilemma created by modern philosophy, as focused in the thought of Descartes, is displayed in the philosophy of Jean-Paul Sartre, especially in his magnum opus *Being and Nothingness.* On the basis of this analysis, Grene goes on to argue that this dilemma is resolved by the substitution of Polanyi's concept of 'tacit knowing' for the more traditional notion of 'explicit knowing' as the axis of cognitive activity. She specifically stresses the importance of the role of embodied indwelling in overcoming the dichotomy between the knowing subject and the known object, Sartre's being-for-itself and being-in-itself.

After having indicated how Sartre, as representative of the impasse of modern thought, was never able to bridge the gap between the body as "known" and the consciousness as "the knower," Grene shows how Polanyi's point of departure resolves this proverbial riddle:

> With the Polanyian starting point, however, the situation is fundamentally, even paradoxically, altered. For in from-to knowledge it is in the first instance the *bodily* awareness that is *my own* and the intellectual—focal—pole of my attention that is *outside* . . . to comprehend is to rely on myself as *bodily* in order to envisage a coherent, intelligible spectacle *beyond* myself . . . The dichotomy, or, more truly, the complimentarity of self and world, inner and outer, is not that between a secret, inner significance-conferring consciousness and a public, outer, meaningless "reality." It is the polarity of a bodily self and an intelligible world. (Langford and Poteat, *Intellect and Hope,* pp. 42–43)

It should be more than clear that Grene's account of how Polanyi's notion of tacit knowing through embodiment co-ordinates nicely with the analysis given of this aspect of Polanyi's epistemology in chapters 2 and 3 of the present book. In approaching this issue by way of Sartre's philosophy, Grene extends the significance and application of the tacit mode into the existentialist version of modernism and thereby performs an important service to a wider and deeper understanding of its importance. In an interesting footnote, Grene mentions the lived-body theme within the thought of both Merleau-Ponty and Gabriel Marcel and then says: "Suffice it to remark in passing that Polanyi's way out though in my view in essential agreement with theirs, is more precisely articulated in epistemological terms and therefore also in its ontological consequences" (p. 42).

While in general agreement with Polanyi's overall effort to reorient our understanding of both scientific and commonsense knowledge, Edward Pols, in his essay "Polanyi and the Problem of Metaphysical Knowledge," is concerned to show that the notion of tacit knowing is not developed sufficiently to allow for metaphysical knowledge. Pols argues that Polanyi does not in the final analysis provide a satisfactory notion of some sort of self-authenticating foundation for a knowledge of a reality beyond what physical science can obtain. He suggests that a reason for this lack may well be that Polanyi equated any such notion with some form of explicit knowing and thus could not allow it to supplant tacit knowing as the axis of all cognition. Pols insists that the notion of self-evidence need not depend on the dynamics of explicit knowing.

> Failing some sort of self-evidence at the foundations, one is left only with a pragmatic consolation that our tacit knowing works—works indeed in the very fundamental sense that we cannot get along without it . . . But such pragmatic considerations do not carry us beyond what we knew we already had: a viable common sense and a viable science. They do not persuade us that the levels of reality we think we see have any more than a common-sense significance. (Langford and Poteat, *Intellect and Hope,* p. 83)

Pols goes on to argue that an adjustment in Polanyi's concept of tacit knowing, such that it would be taken as a foundation for metaphysical knowledge as well, would not do violence to his overall philosophy.

It seems to this writer that Pols has misunderstood the very purpose and meaning of Polanyi's epistemology and that in three ways. First, even though there is some point to thinking of tacit knowing as a kind of "self-evident" point of departure for cognitive activity, the traditional rationalistic connotations of this terminology render this way of speaking inadvisable. The same job Pols wants accomplished is done by the concept of 'integrative act,' which clearly contrasts with inferential processes and thus is not dependent on further reasoning, and so on.

Second, the whole point of the concept of tacit knowing is to do away with the need for the "foundation" of cognition, which Western philosophy, especially in its modernist forms, has been continually and unsuccessfully seeking. This was the central point established in chapters 2 and 3. There it was suggested that the notion of an 'axis' does a much better job expressing the role fulfilled by the dynamics of tacit knowing than does that of a 'foundation.' Indeed, in many respects, it is the assumption that a foundation is necessary as an anchor for cognition, whether of the physical world or any other, that has led modern philosophy into the blind alleys in which it presently finds itself.

Third, the suggestion by Pols that a special sort of guarantee is required in order to render metaphysical knowledge viable seems to buy into an understanding of reality as composed of distinct and independent realms seems uncalled for. On the one hand, Polanyi's view of the world essentially does away with the need to separate the different dimensions of reality from one another since the stratification he speaks of are "emergent" rather than hierarchically independent. On the other hand, what Pols calls the "pragmatic" character of tacit knowing as developed by Polanyi is rich and flexible enough to be able to treat any and all forms of reality however they may be encountered. I have explored the ramifications of this dimensional and pragmatic aspect of Polanyi's thought for what Pols calls "metaphysical knowledge" in my book *Mediated Transcendence* (1989).

A slightly different interpretive slant on Polanyi's work is offered by Helmut Kuhn in his chapter "Personal Knowledge and the Crisis of the Philosophical Tradition." While agreeing that Polanyi's insights do speak directly and convincingly to the dilemmas and dichotomies that plague modern philosophy, especially as found in the subjectivism and relativism of the "historicism" generated by recent Germanic philosophy, Kuhn claims that these insights are in harmony with those of classical Greek and medieval thought.

Facing in the opposite historical direction, Kuhn argues that Polanyi overcomes the short-comings of the British Empiricists, Kant, positivism, phenomenology, pragmatism, and Bergsonian vitalism

> by inserting the cognitive process into nature without jeopardizing the transnatural significance of knowledge . . . Similarly, Plato and Aristotle, the founders of classical philosophy, followed up the clue suggested to them by Socrates in choosing art (techne) as their point of departure and as an analytic scheme—the art of the shoemaker, the physician, or the farmer. Thereby they created a philosophical language modeled throughout on the procedures of craftsmanship . . . In doing so they used their heuristic model, art, in a way which is strictly paralleled by the use to which Polanyi puts his model, which is science. (Langford and Poteat, *Intellect and Hope*, p. 124)

While it must be admitted that Kuhn's attempt to connect Polanyi's thought up with the classical concern with art as a form of knowing is insightful and interesting, it must be noted as well that this did not become the dominant model for cognitive activity for Plato nor for the Western tradition that issued from his philosophy. However, Socrates and Aristotle did tend to make art the pivotal notion in their respective epistemologies. Unfortunately, the *modus operandi* characteristic of these two Greek thinkers did not become that of the makers of the modern mind. They, by contrast, picked up on Plato's visual model of knowing as it is propounded in his famous allegory of the cave, for instance, and proceeded to define knowing as an encounter of subject and object across an epistemic gap that turns out to be unbridgeable.

One other essay in the book *Intellect and Hope* speaks directly to the epistemological problems confronting modern philosophy, and it does so by addressing the supposed difference between the physical and social sciences in relation to Polanyi's thought. In "Max Weber and Michael Polanyi," Raymond Aron analyzes the theories of cognition offered by both Weber and Polanyi in connection with the accepted separation between the natural and social sciences that characterizes the modern or critical approach to knowledge. He begins by acknowledging that it is unclear just how one ought to construe Weber's epistemological posture, whether as that of an objectivist or as that of a subjectivist. This question becomes the foil by means of which he seeks to clarify the relationship between Weber's thought and that of Polanyi.

Although Weber began by distinguishing between the domains of the natural sciences and the social on the basis of the different roles they assign to the personal.

> But social science seemed to him not to be scientific, precisely to the extent that it was personal. Thus he forced himself to separate, within knowledge, the universally valid parts from the subjective and historical elements, in which, indeed, he did not deny the inevitable intervention of the knower, but which seemed to him contrary to the essence of scientific research. In other words, the epistemology of Max Weber represents a supreme effort to take account of the social sciences, and to establish and limit their objectivity, within the framework of a critical philosophy. Starting from the difficulties to which this philosophy was driven, I shall ask what contribution the post-critical philosophy might make to the theory of sociological knowledge. (Langford and Poteat, *Intellect and Hope,* p. 342)

At the conclusion of his account of Weber's stance with respect to the nature of the relationship between the natural and social sciences, Aron draws several specific contrasts between the cognitive theories of Weber and Polanyi. Over against Weber's claim that the social sciences seek explanations of a different sort of reality and thus must involve a different sort of understanding from that of the natural sciences, Aron rightly insists that Polanyi construes all types of understanding as being anchored in tacit knowing and thus as essentially similar. "Without denying the peculiar traits of historical understanding, he sees in the latter a species of a genus, the ultimate term of an ascending series, rather than a break with the developments of the earlier sciences" (Langford and Poteat, *Intellect and Hope,* p. 360).

Second, whereas Weber maintained that the social scientist, despite being reflexively involved and committed with respect to knowledge of social reality, must and does seek rigorously "objective" facts that are independent of the particulars of contextual values and commitments, Aron states that

> Polanyi denies the antithesis between the arbitrary choice of values or interpretive systems and the scientific establishment of facts or relations. On the contrary, understanding is in its very nature the grasp of facts in a context; if the contexts are arbitrarily composed and only the facts are universally valid, science will be arbitrary, like the contexts, and not universally valid like the facts. (Langford and Poteat, *Intellect and Hope,* p. 361)

Finally, in contrast to Weber's insistence that facts and values must be kept entirely separate, Aron points out that for Polanyi

> the understanding of works or persons involves appraisal. History or sociology does not cease to be scientific for including praise or blame . . . the sociologist's understanding of the statement or the judge must refer to the morality of his act or the equity of his verdict. (Langford and Poteat, *Intellect and Hope,* p. 361)

Aron concludes his essay by drawing one last contrast between Weber and Polanyi, a contrast between their basic postures toward both human understanding and human existence. Weber feared the arrogant authoritarianism of those who would seek to dictate values and morals in the social realm, so he found it necessary to restrict social knowledge to what can be established objectively. However, Polanyi saw the way around authoritarianism as lying within a proper view of understanding itself.

> The commitment of faith, he believes, is present from the first stage of knowledge and the hierarchy of spiritual worlds is ordered towards an ultimate goal . . . The science of Polanyi leads without a break to faith; the science of Weber keeps a space for the faith which condemns it and which denies it. (Langford and Poteat, *Intellect and Hope,* pp. 362–63)

This concludes our analysis of those essays in this collection of essays that deal directly with epistemological issues arising from the presuppositions of modern philosophy. There are, to be sure, other interpreters of Polanyi's works who also treat this aspect of his thought, and it will prove helpful to turn our attention to some of these at this time.

One important interpreter of Polanyi's thought is Andy Sanders, author of *Michael Polanyi's Post-Critical Epistemology* (1988). As the title suggests, this book focuses on Polanyi's theory of cognitivity almost exclusively, though the last chapter branches out into the religious implications of Polanyi's thought. Sanders indicates that he approaches his topic from an "analytical" perspective, and indeed the primary distinctiveness of his treatment is its concern with the more or less scientific understanding of knowledge. Thus, the emphasis of my brief summary of Sanders's work will be on the contrast he draws between Polanyi's approach and that of Karl Popper in chapters 5 and 6. I shall return to his exploration of Polanyi's treatment of religion later on in this chapter.

Before turning to Sanders's contrast between the approaches of Polanyi and Popper, note should be taken of his discussion of the contrast between Polanyi's account of the criteria of scientific knowledge and that of Imre Lakatos, as it appears in his fourth chapter. Lakatos is well known for his development of an account (1976) of the vindication of theory of Copernicus that claims to establish it on "objective" rather than on "pragmatic" grounds. Lakatos was particularly disdainful of any attempt to treat Copernicus's theory as only a fresh "paradigm," ala Thomas Kuhn, Stephen Toulmin, and others, including Polanyi. He accused Polanyi of dragging psychological and sociological elements into epistemological considerations by introducing the notion of tacit knowing. Sanders makes it clear that in his opinion Polanyi can and should be interpreted as being more "objectivist" than Lakatos without sliding into "subjectivism" since although Polanyi insists on the crucial role of personal and social factors in the discovery and validation of knowledge, he still may be seen as a "realist" in the broad, critical sense of the term (pp. 128–58).

The attack of Karl Popper on the epistemological theory of Polanyi is even stronger than that of Lakatos, especially as it is expressed in the reasonings of Alan Musgrave, *Impersonal Knowledge: A Criticism of Subjectivism in Epistemology*. This unpublished work is a doctoral dissertation written under the direction of Popper and runs quite parallel to the latter's famous essay "Epistemology without a Knowing Subject" (included in *Philosophy Today*, no. 2, 1969). The overarching theme of this Popperian point of view is that knowledge must be objective and stand independently from any of the processes involved in the dynamics of discovery, such as intuition and insight. Thus, the charge leveled against Polanyi by these thinkers is that his theory is both subjectivist and relativist.

Sanders characterizes this objectivist posture as one in which a "God's eye view" is assumed to be both possible and necessary for real knowledge to obtain. It is reminiscent of the claim made by Laplace that if one could know the exact position, direction, and velocity of all entities comprised by the universe at any given time, then one would be able to give an account of the entire history of the universe, both past and future. Such knowledge is of course generally said to be available only to God, and thus the "God's eye view" designation. It is the view of Popper and Musgrave.

Sanders engages in detailed and extensive analysis of the Popperian critique of Polanyi's epistemology, and in so doing he covers much of the same ground as do chapters 2 and 3 of the present investigation. His overall conclusions are summarized in the following lengthy quotation:

> The upshot, then, of our discussions in the last two chapters is that the Popperians are mistaken in their criticisms of Polanyi. First, Polanyi advocated neither psychologism nor dogmatism in the justificationist sense. Second, their frantic attempts to remove the knowing person from the realm of (applied) epistemology can be shown to be unsuccessful and even inconsistent . . . It is Polanyi's merit to have been one of the first to stress this point at a time when nearly all professional philosophers of science still hoped to save the objectivist ideal of knowledge without a knower . . . Polanyi, in his turn, paid too little attention to the logical side of epistemology. However, his crime is the lesser, because he never denied the important or the relevance of logic. The existence and use of rigorous rules, criteria and procedures is, in fact, simply presupposed. Finally Polanyi has to be credited for his attempt to broaden the scope of epistemology by elaborating the idea that the veracious inquirer is desperately dependent on his culture, its language, practices, and traditions. No God's eye point of view being available, the only thing is to start from where we are i.e. our own modern, pluralist Western intellectual and moral tradition . . .
> Polanyi reminded us of the moral and socio-psychological requirements which must be fulfilled . . . in the on-going search for what is true, good, and just. (P. 225)

Yet another summary and explication of Polanyi's epistemology is offered by Jeffrey Kane in his *Beyond Empiricism: Michael Polanyi Reconsidered* (1984). Kane's account parallels that given in chapter 2 and 3 of the present work, although it focuses more directly on the scientific understanding of cognitivity, whereas my own account is directed more pointedly at the concept of 'knowledge' as defined by modern philosophy. In his final chapter, Kane addresses the educational implications of Polanyi's view of cognition, which were discussed briefly in chapter 7.

Perhaps the most thorough-going presentation and analysis of Polanyi's overall philosophy is to be found in Harry Prosch, *Michael Polanyi: A Criti-*

cal Exposition (1986). Working from within an intimate friendship with Polanyi, Prosch actually collaborated with him on his final volume, *Meaning*. Drawing on the fact that initially Polanyi was a physician, Prosch structures the first three parts of his book in terms of a diagnosis, prescription, and treatment for the ills of modernity as it has taken shape with respect to scientific theory in general and cognitive theory in particular. The chapters constituting parts 1 and 2 cover pretty much the same basic aspects of Polanyi's thought as do those in part 1 of my own explorations, except that they focus more heavily on the cultural dimensions and implications, while my own focus was more strictly on the definition of cognitivity in relation to the modernist tradition in epistemology. In part 3 of his book, Prosch carries his analysis into the arts, religion, and politics. We have touched on his contribution in these areas already.

Part 4 of Prosch's book is devoted to the evaluation of Polanyi's major contributions to epistemology and cultural analysis. After indicating that he himself finds Polanyi's main insights and emphases "plausible," Prosch proceeds to focus two areas of difficulty and/or disagreement among those thinkers who seek to interpret and appropriate Polanyi's way of approaching epistemology and the structure of reality. The difficulties and disagreements he has in mind result in somewhat different assessments of the overall worth of Polanyi's philosophy.

Prosch first focuses the generally admitted key point concerning the crucial distinction between the subsidiary and the focal being present in any perceptual or conceptual cognitive activity.

> This is the key point, because, if his contention is true, then our recognition of this distinction will undoubtedly put a different cast upon our views of what is going on in perception, science, art, religion, and political and moral philosophy . . . Furthermore, the ideals of explicit analysis and detached objectivity will be seen to be false ideals that will not only mislead us, but also destroy our confidence in the work of our minds, and even, at last, in our fundamental humanity. (p. 208)

The strongest criticisms of what Prosch calls the "ubiquitous" or "universal" character of the "from-to" structure of awareness comes from the highly influential philosopher of science, Rom Harré "who maintains that Polanyi is correct in his basic contention insofar as perception is concerned, but incorrect with regard to conceptual knowledge" (p. 208). Thus, Prosch devotes a chapter (15) to examining Harré's critique. The core of Harré's criticism is his contention that all conceptual or propositional reasoning can and indeed must be made explicit. He admits the function of tacit knowing in the psychological dynamics of scientific knowing, in both science and perception, but insists that theoretic reasoning depends on explicit inferential processes.

Prosch does not attempt to resolve this issue on his own but simply juxtaposes Harré's contention to that of Polanyi, namely, that "we always know more than we can tell." Here is how Prosch explains it:

> Polanyi insisted that . . . our judgments do have a logic, since the function of logic is to correctly assess what is really implied by something else. We can, in tacit inference, however, only acquire a tacit awareness of the rules . . . an awareness which becomes implicitly more right as we become connoisseurs, in contrast to the explicit rules of inference that we arrive at in formal logical inference . . . Actually, of course, as Polanyi showed, our proper application of even these hard rules . . . also rests upon many indeterminant, subsidiary elements in which we simply dwell. (p. 216)

Prosch's second critical focus pertains to the question of the necessity of the hierarchical pattern that Polanyi attributes to the structure of reality. Specifically, the charge is leveled, once again, by one of Polanyi's strongest supporters, Marjorie Grene, against Polanyi's notion of a 'stratified universe' encompassing increasingly complex entities that successively emerge from one another. Grene is especially concerned to avoid what she takes to be the dualist view of the mind/body relation implicit in Polanyi's view. Prosch provides an extensive, chapter-long treatment of Grene's argument against this aspect of Polanyi's philosophy (p. 16).

Whereas Polanyi held that a stratified universe is both required by and congenial to the logic of tacit knowing, Grene maintains that not only does the latter not entail the former but that it clutters up and clouds our understanding of it. She is particularly worried that Polanyi holds out for the mind being essentially independent of the body and/or brain. In short, Grene thinks that Polanyi's epistemology can and should be separated from his metaphysics. After showing that Polanyi's view does not entail any form of Cartesian dualism, Prosch concludes that it is pretty much a matter of individual decision as to whether or not one finds Polanyi's metaphysics reasonable. He himself concludes that Polanyi's "basic ontological foundations are as sound as his epistemology" (p. 233).

The final few chapters of Prosch's book take up several additional contrasts between Polanyi's philosophy and some of his erstwhile supporters, but these pertain primarily to the broader issues of cultural application and more properly belong within the concerns of the next section of this chapter. And so it is time to turn to a consideration of these concerns.

ADDITIONAL TRACINGS OF THE PATTERN

In the space that remains, a brief account of various other interpreters' treatment of the application of Polanyi's insights to the areas of science, politics, education, art, and religion will be provided. It should go without saying that such accounts will in no wise do justice to the ideas and suggestions these interpreters offer, but hopefully they will serve as jumping off points for the reader's own further investigations. Here again, it will prove both necessary and wise to limit our considerations to those interpretive contributions available in book form.

In the collection of essays entitled *Intellect and Hope,* there are several pieces that deal with the scientific application of Polanyi's philosophy. In "Polanyi's Interpretation of Scientific Inquiry," Chaim Perelman expresses his general agreement with Polanyi's epistemological understanding of the logic of tacit knowing, but he disagrees with his tendency to reduce scientific truth to the consensus of the members of the "society of explorers." Perelman puts it this way:

> Even if, like Polanyi, I am a partisan of personal knowledge integrated with a cultural tradition, I should like to stress the particular place of science in our culture. For, in science, the techniques of proof and verification make it possible to bring about agreement in essentials, an accord inaccessible in other domains. (Langford and Poteat, *Intellect and Hope,* p. 241)

It can only be said that in this writer's opinion the above remarks clearly indicate that Perelman has failed to digest the real meaning and implications of Polanyi's epistemology as outlined in the preceding chapters of this volume.

In "The Gentle Rain: A Search for Understanding," William Scott acknowledges his debt to Polanyi's interpretation of the scientific enterprise by demonstrating the applicability of his insights to physics in general and to cloud physics in particular. Specifically, Scott focuses on six aspects of Polanyi's thought that were proven especially helpful in his initial efforts to "formulate the underlying assumptions and principles of research in the physics of precipitation" (Langford and Poteat, *Intellect and Hope,* p. 243). The six aspects are (1) "Scales of Organization" in dealing with the levels of reality, (2) "Unspecifiable Arts" involved in making judgments in cloud physics, (3) the inadequacies of the "Laplacian Ideal" in relation to scientific method, (4) the need to incorporate personal judgment into the answer to the question "What is a good Theory?" (5) the role of the notion of the society of explorers in the activities of "Cloud Physicists and Their Colleagues," and (6) the importance of "Commitment and Faith" in any investigative endeavor.

In "Personal Knowledge and Concepts in the Biological Sciences," Sir Francis Walshe begins by tracing the strongly reductionist assumptions that currently dominate biological sciences from neurology through physiology to brain theory. He then moves to a Polanyian critique of this tendency, drawing on the insights of Whitehead along the way. Walshe concludes:

> The path that neurobiology now follows, dominated by mechanistic and reductionist ideas, must surely lead to its disintegration into the tail of the bloodless dance of action potentials and shuttlings at synapses, divorced from the general body of biology, offering its explanations of life and mind in terms of atomic—and presumably in due time of subatomic particles, and stating its generalizations in terms so remote from human experience as to have no explanatory value. (Langford and Poteat, *Intellect and Hope,* pp. 313–14)

Harold McCurdy's essay, "Personal Knowing and Making," seeks to place Polanyi within the development of contemporary psychology. He says:

> What is so remarkable about Michael Polanyi is not that he takes up a third sovereign position, establishes a "third force" as some rebels in psychology like to call their little protest against the two major establishments, but that quietly, soberly, diligently he has developed a way of moving forward out of any established territory, whether affluent or barren, into new dimensions of reality. (Langford and Poteat, *Intellect and Hope,* p. 315)

McCurdy goes on to mention that Abraham Maslow, himself a dominant force across warring factions in psychology, said upon discovering Polanyi's *Personal Knowledge:* "This profound work, which is certainly required reading for our generation, does much of what I had planned to do, and solves many of the problems which had concerned me" (p. 316). McCurdy further says that Polanyi makes it possible to transform the 'or' in the famous debate between Carl Rogers and B. F. Skinner "Persons or Science?" into an 'and'. "Science grows out of personal experience and is shaped by personal acts, even if it threatens destruction to persons. No matter how alien to ourselves it appears, it is something we and our human comrades have devised" (p. 216).

Turning now to the general theme of Polanyi's political theories, there are two essays in *Intellect and Hope* that address topics that fall under this heading. The first, "Man the Measure: Personal Knowledge and the Quest for Natural Law," by Carl Friedrich, and the second, " 'Moral Inversion'—or Moral Revaluation?" by Zdzislaw Najder, are both worthy of our consideration at this juncture.

Friedrich begins with the statement: "The achievement of Michael Polanyi makes possible a new discussion of natural law" (p. 91). He then goes on to explain how this is the case.

> For those to whom natural law is repugnant or meaningless either by reason of its presumed inhuman inflexibility and remoteness or the implausibility of a transcendent justice inscribed eternally upon the "nature of things," Polanyi shows that the values upon which natural law rests are on the contrary disclosures to our human powers of discernment; that natural law, in short, has in common with all structures of meaning that it is manifest to *men* in the convivial exercise of their unique human powers. Against those who fear that if justice has no more substantial ground than the judgments of men, then it will simply be identical with the law, his argument shows that these judgments have universal intent and therefore bear upon a reality which though never exhaustively disclosed is nevertheless truly manifest. (p. 92)

Friedrich concludes his application of Polanyi's view of values thus:

> A return to the old natural law consisting of eternally valid principles is excluded . . . The criterion for determining whether particular law is right are very general rules of procedure, and such rules . . . including the references to the findings of the social sciences as central, claim for themselves general validity in the sense of the old natural law. (pp. 109–10)

Whether or not one fully agrees with Friedrich's positive conclusion on this matter, it is clear that his analysis casts a good deal of light on the notion of natural law, as well as on the significance of Polanyi's thought.

Over against this general positive tone, which characterizes the large majority of the essays in this collection, stands Zdzislaw Najder's forceful critique of Polanyi's key concept of moral inversion in particular and his overall political posture in general. Najder's complaint about what is meant by 'moral inversion' focuses on the tension between it being employed as a description of a *social* phenomenon but described strictly in terms of *individual* qualities in the works of Polanyi. Najder wants to know what, according to Polanyi, social dynamics have contributed to this inversion.

> We shall not find any clear answers to these questions in Polanyi's work. When he describes, very vividly and persuasively, the disintegration of traditional moral values and the resulting consciousness of "living in a spiritual desert" he does it in purely individualistic terms . . .

Polanyi does not ever mention social or group interests giving rise to genuine moral standards or even moral dilemmas. All moral rules, of which he approves, are individual-oriented . . . But it is almost a commonplace that ethics and morals are a product of communal life. It seems strange that Polanyi, who pays so much attention to the role of man's environment and upbringing in shaping his beliefs, disregards the social determinants of morality. (p. 369)

The second half of Najder's critique focuses on Polanyi's failure to provide documentation and textual analysis in support of his general and derogatory evaluation of Marxism and communism. Not only, according to Najder, does Polanyi consistently lump communism and nazism together, but he fails as well to distinguish between Marx, Lenin, and Stalin (p. 375). Najder thoroughly documents Polanyi's ethnocentric naivete concerning the processes that have shaped and twisted recent cultural history. The triumphs of Western imperialism and capitalism are portrayed by Polanyi as the result of ideational transformations exclusively, while their darker side goes unmentioned, and the positive side of revolutionary activities in other parts of the world are passed over as well (pp. 378–83). Najder brings his two criticisms together in the following remarks: "In spite of all appearances and all talk about 'social lore,' 'conviviality,' 'fellowship,' and 'environment' Polanyi's conceptual framework remains thoroughly individualistic, or rather, to be more precise, rests on a sort of individualistic-intellectualist syndrome" (p. 383).

While not all of Najder's points may turn out to be on the mark, I must confess that for the most part they strike me as very much to the point. In my own discussion of the social and political dimensions of Polanyi's philosophy in chapter 5, I sought to call attention to what strikes me as a fundamental disjunction between his epistemological insights and his understanding of human sociopolitical reality. The sorts of complaints raised by Najder render these more abstract criticisms thoroughly concrete. In point of fact, it seems quite clear that when it comes to political and cultural analysis Polanyi frequently reaches beyond his expertise and relies too heavily on his own personal tragedy in the interpretation of what he called "our destruction of Europe." His idealization of the Western tradition, especially in its modern, Euro-American manifestation, may serve well in calling attention to important conceptual values, but it will not do as an account of historical and/or political reality.

Finally, let us turn our attention to the general topic of religion in light of Polanyi's reconstructive philosophy. Andy Sanders, in his *Michael Polanyi's Post-Critical Epistemology,* takes up the question of the implications of Polanyi's fiduciary framework for our understanding of the meaning and truth of religious utterances. Perhaps the chief focal point of this issue is whether or not the religious use of language can be understood and/or evaluated by persons who do not already stand within, or "indwell" religious faith. Sanders indicates that some

> have been very quick to interpret Polanyi here as advocating an extreme form of fideism. According to R. C. Prust Polanyi advocates the thesis that "religious language cannot be understood by anyone outside of faith." This occasions Prust to draw the triumphant conclusion: "This makes religious language invulnerable to criticism from anyone outside of faith." (p. 245)

Sanders thinks this reading of Polanyi, as well as this general view of religious belief, is seriously mistaken. He claims that this interpretation of things religious exaggerates the meaning of the notions of faith and indwelling. He finally concludes that Polanyi is

> saying that "outsiders" cannot understand the results of theology in that they cannot dwell in, or rely on, these results in the same way as the worshipper. Precisely the fact that they cannot do that is what makes them non-believers, rather than worshippers; they fail to see the specifically *religious* point or purposes of religious rituals, symbolic actions, myths and metaphor. But this does not in the least imply that non-believers cannot understand sympathetically what worshippers are about, as regards other points or purposes. (p. 245)

Over against those who would interpret Polanyi in such a way as to imply that religious knowledge is essentially "subjective" in nature, Sanders maintains that tacit knowing does not run contrary to the standard epistemic virtues of consistency, coherence, fruitfulness, simplicity, lucidity, and so forth, even though the reality of God cannot be proven by means of rational argument (p. 249). As one who has spent a good deal of time and published ink dealing with this very issue, I must say that I think Sanders is clearly correct in his reading of Polanyi at this point. My own particular use of Polanyi's insights, as suggested in chapter 7, involve viewing religious experience as mediated in and through the other, ordinary dimensions of human life, including rationality, viewing religious knowing as essentially tacit in character, and religious language as centering in metaphoric expression. Thus, there are, in my understanding of Polanyi's philosophy, "reasons of the heart" that are nonetheless reasons for not being fully explicit; faith first, but not without reason.

Harry Prosch's examination of Polanyi's understanding of religion follows a different tack from that of Sanders. Prosch devotes at least two chapters

(17 and 18) to discussing the similarities and differences between Polanyi's approach and that of Thomas Torrance, a Barthian theologian who sought to appropriate Polanyi's insights in his interpretation of the Christian faith. After having presented a basic outline of Torrance's overall position regarding the connection between Polanyi's notions of tacit knowing and the stratified character of reality, Prosch moves on to focusing what he takes to be the crucial difference between Torrance's interpretation of Polanyi as essentially wrong-headed.

Prosch quotes extensively from Torrance's major work *Theological Science* by way of demonstrating how the latter seeks to incorporate Polanyi's perspective into his Reformed theological posture. He rightly sees Torrance as maintaining that Christian theology attempts to understand and systematize the "facts" of historical revelation, especially in the person of Jesus Christ, in essentially the same manner that science seeks to understand and systematize the facts of nature. Thus, Torrance conceives of theology as a "science" quite parallel to the natural sciences (pp. 239–47).

Here is how Prosch characterizes the crucial difference between Polanyi and Torrance:

> Both Torrance and Polanyi make a distinction between the kinds of realities that natural science deals with and the kind that religion or theology deals with. But their distinctions are quite different ones. Torrance's is between a transcendent reality (a supernatural Being), over and beyond the realm of natural events, and those nearly natural entities interacting with each other in space-time . . . For Polanyi, on the other hand . . . there is one subset of realities which exists independently of our knowledge of them and which science seeks to uncover or disclose, as well as another subset of realities, those of the noosphere, brought into being, in a sense, by our creative efforts through them to achieve meaning in our own lives. These realities are real in that we may expect to see more of what they mean as time goes on—as in great works of art and religion . . . But it would be an illusion to think that they existed before we discovered them . . . in addition to being immanent, not transcendent, the existence of such a gradient of meaning is highly speculative. It is also not identical to the God of any religion. (p. 249)

Prosch concludes that there is no evidence in any of Polanyi's writings for Torrance's conflation of his own ideas with those of Polanyi. In essence, Torrance's position, like that of Karl Barth, represents a "foundationalist" approach to theology, one that insists on the necessity of beginning with the acceptance of divine revelation, "the Word of God," as found in the Christian tradition and Scriptures (p. 254). The attempt to parallel religious faith as the acceptance of certain beliefs and doctrines to Polanyi's understanding of tacit knowing is, in Prosch's view, actually contrary to and not harmonious with Polanyi's overall epistemology (p. 255). I can only add that in my own opinion Prosch's analysis of Torrance's theology, together with his negative evaluation of the latter's use of Polanyi's insights, is very much on the mark.

In the next to last chapter of his book, Prosch turns to a consideration of the question of the dualism in Polanyi's philosophy between science, on the one hand, and the arts and religion, on the other. He mentions two interpreters who have sought to develop Polanyi's thought in such a way as to overcome this dualism, the one by extending the analysis of tacit knowing to include the arts and religion as well, and the other to fold Polanyi's way of treating the latter back into the analysis of science itself. The first interpretive effort is that offered by Sheldon Richmond, while the second is that of Ronald Hall.

According to Prosch, Richmond sees the separation between science and the arts and religion as setting up a dichotomy that undermines the unifying and synthetic power of Polanyi's overall approach (pp. 258–61). Prosch thinks that if these two highly significant dimensions of human experience are not kept separate, the insights and claims of the humanities will need to be subjected to the same sort of evaluative criteria as scientific claims and thus will be set aside as meaningless and/or false. My own reading of Polanyi would suggest that this difficulty can be avoided by viewing the realities that the arts and religion disclose as every bit as real as those of science, but ever so much richer and more comprehensive. Thus, the same general criteria will apply to them, but since these dimensions of reality are experienced as increasingly mediated, they will apply with less rigor and will leave more room for interpretive alternatives. In this way, I would agree with Richmond that the real genius of Polanyi's insights lies in their ability to unify human experience.

The dualism under discussion here is largely the result of a felt contrast on the part of these interpreters between the axis and emphases on Polanyi's earlier works, especially *Personal Knowledge* and his final work, *Meaning*, on which Prosch himself collaborated with Polanyi. Ronald Hall focuses this dualistic development, according to Prosch, in the following manner:

> Hall says that he believes Polanyi's account of art is basically sound and illuminating. But problems arise for Hall when he finds Polanyi, in *Meaning*, contrasting art and science. In Polanyi's earlier works, Hall claims Polanyi held that art and science were grounded in the same structure of inquiry, and the imaginative, creative person was the central feature of this structure. The scientist was not a cool, aloof robot. He was, like the artist, passionately and personally involved in making novel and creative and imaginative integrations. Not only science, but

art as well, made claims to universal intent. The grounds of both science and art were neither objective nor subjective, but personal. (p. 262)

Prosch answers Hall's criticism by pointing out that not only did Polanyi stress the dichotomy between science and the humanities as strongly in *Personal Knowledge* as he did in *Meaning,* but that it is crucial to understand that the difference between them is a function of the difference between the kinds of realities with which they have to do. Prosch says

> In one case there is the intention to try to get at the "reals" of which the situation is actually composed independent of our thought, and which therefore requires observation and verification of the meaningful integrations we have achieved. The other case is the intention to create these meanings that depend for their validity, not upon verification but upon our acceptance, only accomplished when they do in fact carry us away literally into themselves and integrate our lives along with their own integrations. They are also "realities" in that they are truly meaningful in their own terms and by their own standards. (pp. 264–65)

Here again I must side with Hall against Prosch, and possibly Polanyi himself, in objecting to this dichotomy between scientific knowledge and reality, on the one hand, and the arts and religion, on the other hand. Not only does the logic of tacit knowing extend across this division, as Prosch himself admits, but the realities being known in both cases do not need to be construed as fundamentally distinct. This is where the notion of mediated, dimensional realities becomes so useful. The realities of the arts and religion are richer and more comprehensive than those of science and are thus more mediated in character in relation to our experience of them. Thus, they are neither the same or nor wholly other from those of science, but they are more complex and diffuse.

As indicated above, it is not clear to me whether Polanyi himself actually advocates such a strong separation, or if it is the result of Prosch's interpretive efforts, especially in the writing of *Meaning.* The above quotation from Prosch surely seems to imply a view of science that is at odds with the main insights of *Personal Knowledge.* These insights would clearly open the way for a complete revision not only of the dynamics of knowing but of the character of reality as well.

Let me bring this chapter to a close by mentioning yet one more book in which the main themes of Polanyi's thought are presented, namely Drusilla Scott's *Everyman Revived* (1985). Scott sets Polanyi's ideas within the context of the medieval mystery or morality play *Everyman.* Following a narrative not unlike that of *Pilgrim's Progress,* this play traces the path of Everyman from ignorance to knowledge, and Scott casts Polanyi's philosophy in the role of the guide, which can lead the ordinary thoughtful person to the truth. She outlines Polanyi's main emphases from the dynamics of discovery through the logic of tacit knowing; the stratified structure of reality; the basis of the free society, moral inversion, mind-body relationships; and the concepts of selfhood and art, all the way to religion.

Along the way in this highly readable account of Polanyi's overall approach to philosophy and life, Scott takes up many of the interpretive discussions with which we have been concerned in this chapter. Aside from the fact that this somewhat self-conscious literary technique often seems rather forced and stilted, the basic points of Polanyi's work do get presented and explored in a helpful and responsible way. Scott makes it clear that she understands Polanyi and is familiar with the major interpretive issues and interpreters of his work. The particular format of Scott's book renders it difficult to treat in a chapter such as this one. Fortunately, many if not most of the issues and thinkers she mentions have already been treated on the previous pages.

CONCLUSION
RECONSTRUCTIVE POSTMODERNISM

We began this study of Michael Polanyi's philosophy by contrasting it to both modernism, as *con*structed by Western culture, and postmodernism, as the *de*construction of modern thought. My overall claim was and is that it is most helpful to view Polanyi's philosophy as one that seeks to *re*construct modernism while acknowledging its contributions. This is why Polanyi himself entitled his main work *Personal Knowledge: Toward a Post-Critical Philosophy*. He makes no attempt to return to a precritical or premodern approach to epistemological issues, but neither does he deny the positive values garnered by the modern perspective in relation to the limitations of classical and medieval thought.

A Polanyian critique of deconstructionist postmodern would center, as we have seen, around its self-stultifying circularity. To pretend that one can somehow stand outside of the Western tradition and reevaluate it while all the while drawing on its critical tools and methods is embarrassing at best. To claim that any given utterance or text can yield an infinite number of meanings not only renders this claim itself quite problematic, since according to it we cannot be sure what it means, but if carried to its logical conclusion, this claim would undercut the very possibility of linguistic communication. Language presupposes *universal intent* with respect to both meaning and truth, even for deconstructionists since they expect their own utterances to be taken seriously.

A Polanyian critique of modern or critical philosophy focuses on the notion of 'objectivity.' This notion or ideal is what enabled modern thinkers to free Western thought from authoritarian and/or subjectivist approaches to knowledge, but Polanyi maintained that such thinkers, especially those seeking to define and develop scientific methodology, either took this concept too far or misconstrued it from the outset. To define knowledge in such a way as to separate it from its unarticulatable and personal value commitments, from its tacit dynamics, is not only to give a false picture of the cognitive process, but it leads to many epistemological dilemmas and stalemates as well.

The pivot point of Polanyi's reconstruction of the concept of objectivity is, of course, his notion of tacit knowing. By extending the cognitivity dimension of human experience to include the tacit pole as well as the explicit pole, he has made it possible to understand the matrix out of which knowledge is actually generated, namely, the interaction between subsidiary awareness and somatic and/or imaginative participation. This not only allows us to see the crucial role played by personal commitment and aspiration in all knowing, but it acknowledges the cognitive significance of bodily activity as well. Tacit knowing then comes to function as the *axis* rather than the *foundation* of knowledge. An axis serves to anchor or tether that which revolves around it without itself having to be supported by yet another layer underneath it, *ad infinitum.* As Wittgenstein said, the key is to be willing to begin at the beginning, without trying to go further back.

In chapter 1 I outlined the need for a reconstruction of the modern view of knowledge by tracing its development in the thought of Descartes, Hume, and Kant. In each case, it was pointed out how these thinkers, as great as they were, failed to see that they were presupposing the very notions and commitments that they either denied or proved. Each in his own way completely overlooked the significance of the body in cognitive activity, and each tried to define knowledge without any reference to the personal values of the knowing subject. Moreover, none of these thinkers made any acknowledgment of the social or intersubjective character of the knowing process. For these reasons the thinkers of the nineteenth and twentieth centuries for the most part, in one way or another, either rejected or mimicked the founders of "modernism."

Against the backdrop of this epistemological confusion, Polanyi sought to reexamine the actual dynamics of cognitive experience. We traced this reexamination in chapter 2 in terms of the interaction between subsidiary awareness and bodily activity, on the one hand, and focal awareness and conceptual activity, on the other hand. The former interaction involves participatory indwelling among the particulars comprised by a more comprehensive whole on the part of the knowing agent, through either bodily or imaginative action. The latter interaction draws upon the former in focusing these more comprehensive units of meaning, thereby creating a vectorial thrust to the entire cognitive process. The role of the body in this process is clearly crucial.

We completed our effort to properly locate this fresh axis affirmed by Polanyi in chapter 3. There the implications of extending the cognitivity dimension of human experience so as to understand its bipolar character with respect to both tacit and explicit knowing were presented. A good deal of attention was paid to the ins and outs of tacit knowing in particular since it is the reality least familiar to those of us operating within the modern mind-set. Specifically, we discussed various examples of tacit knowing, from simple skills through complex perceptual processes to the mystery of language. Last, the issue of verification, as it applies to claims to tacit knowing, was taken up.

Finally, in chapter 4 it was concluded that Polanyi has done a convincing job of establishing the case for tacit knowledge as a reconstructivist answer to the ills of modernism, in contrast to that of deconstructionists such as Derrida and Foucault.

In part 2 the goal was to trace the patterns of this fresh axis, of what might be termed the "tacit mode," in the various disciplines to which Polanyi himself applied it. We began, in chapter 5, with science and political theory. The main concern there was to redefine the concept of 'objectivity,' in regard to both physical and social science, so as to include the personal components of commitment and value, as well as the crucial role of the body in all knowing. The notion of 'moral inversion' was introduced in connection with Marxist political theory in order to pinpoint the self-contradiciton involved in proclaiming scientific objectivity for one's views with serious ideological fervor.

In chapter 6 the effort was made to explore the ramifications of the tacit mode of cognitivity for language and educational theory. With respect to the former topic, special attention was paid to the dynamics of language acquisition. Here Polanyi's analysis of the interaction between subsidiary awareness and bodily and/or imaginative indwelling was found to be most helpful in taking us beyond simplistic behaviorist accounts, on the one hand, and question-begging rationalist treatments, on the other hand. Also, the concept of 'meaning,' especially as conveyed through metaphor, was clarified by means of Polanyi's discussion of the symbiotic interaction between tacit and explicit knowing. Although Polanyi himself never actually applied his insights into tacit knowing to learning theory, I myself offered such an application, along with a comparison to the views of Whitehead, Dewey, and Carl Rogers. The issues of multiculturalism and vocationalism in education in relation to Polanyi's thought were briefly explored as well.

Polanyi himself did offer an application of the tacit mode to both art and religion, and chapter 7 was devoted to a consideration thereof. Once again, the dynamics of tacit knowing were seen to cast a good deal of light on aesthetic awareness, as well as on the history of artistic periods and movements. At both the individual and social levels, we attend *from* the particulars comprising a work of art or cultural context *to* a more comprehensive meaning that encompasses it. While acknowledging that Polanyi's treatment of religion contains real insight, it was suggested that it could be taken a good deal further, especially in relation to the role of historical and empirical factors in determining the nature and value of any religious belief system. Part 2 concluded with a brief summary of other interpretive insights into Polanyi's philosophy.

The foregoing brief summary of the overall development of this study of Polanyi's postcritical philosophy should make it clear that his approach to epistemological issues is *re*constructive in character rather than *de*structive. Polanyi sought to redirect the modern understanding of cognitivity by revealing how its conclusions contradict its initial and necessary presuppositions concerning the personal dimension of the human search for knowledge. His approach is quite different from and more helpful than that of most other postmodern thinkers, many of which actually extend the errors of modernism to their logical limits rather than correcting them.

I shall bring this conclusion, along with the entire study, to a close by offering an especially timely and vivid illustration of the thrust and significance of Polanyi's work. In February 1996 a six-game chess match took place between world champion Garry Kasparov and an IBM computer called "Deep Blue." Although there have been many such matches before, which were always won rather handily by the various human champions, this match was special because Deep Blue was by far the most sophisticated chess-playing machine ever invented. It is capable of scanning about 200 million positions and moves per second, or in other words, seeing everything that could happen over the next ten to fifteen possible moves. For the first time ever, in the very first game, the machine beat the human champ. Kasparov himself was stunned by this turn of events, while both the chess world and the computer designers were astounded. The media immediately focused on the question of whether or not this signals the beginning of the end for the idea of human uniqueness by virtue of superior cognitive ability (*Time Magazine,* Feb. 26, 1996).

In point of fact, Kasparov went on to win the second game and the final two, drawing games three and four, and thus was victorious in the overall match. He himself said that Deep Blue's overwhelming capacity enables it to combine speed and scope in such a way as to transform sheer quantity into higher quality. He admitted that he had underestimated the power of this computer: "I was lucky to lose Game One; otherwise disaster could have struck later. I got an early warning" (Associated Press, Feb. 18, 1996). The sponsors of Deep Blue were confident that it would not be very long before its future counterparts will beat human champions. Indeed, in 1997 Deep Blue did best Kasparov in a rematch, but the key issue involved here is not *who* wins but *how*; the computer and Kasparov operate on different cognitive bases from the start.

The clue to the crucial flaw in this reductionist type logic can be found in the statement of the Deep Blue team leader that the reason the computer lost to Kasparov is that its engineers "don't have the chess experience and knowledge that Mr. Kasparov has" (Associated Press, Feb. 18, 1996). This is clearly a case of circular reasoning since the point in question is precisely whether machines can, *in principle,* ever have "experience" and "knowledge." To assume that all that is necessary for the machine to acquire these cognitive powers is more fire-power and greater speed is naive at best. The computer's lack of emotion may appear to be an advantage, but it may in the final analysis actually be its undoing.

The idea that sheer numbers can be transformed into the capacity for cognitive *judgment* completely overlooks the simple fact that the human brain is an *organic* phenomenon, while the computer is an electronic device. The evolution and operation of the brain involves biochemical processes that cannot be duplicated by electronic chips, bits, and bytes. These processes are qualitatively far more complex than mere scanning devices and memory banks can ever be made to replicate. What the computer lacks, and will in principle always lack, is the ability to make judgments as to what a given move or position means in relation to a specific context and for the long run. As Hubert Dreyfus makes clear in his profound book, *What Computers Can't Do,* the making of judgments is an ability that arises out of actual participation, by means of embodiment and imagination, in the social world common to human beings. Computers by nature cannot do this for the simple reason that they do not have human bodies.

As one journalist put the matter, very good chess players, what in the trade are termed "masters," such as Kasparov, can still beat computers "because he can intuit—God knows how—what the general shape of things will be 20 moves from now" (*Time Magazine,* Feb. 26, 1996). Although it seems that this writer did not grasp the significance of this remark, it should be clear that the judgments that a chess master makes about the "general shape of things" are not based in articulatable formulae, but in intuitive, Gestaltlike discernments that cannot in principle be captured in devised software programs. If Kasparov, or any other chess master, is unable to articulate their basis, how can a computer program? Whoever wins, the bases on which they do so are fundamentally distinct.

The problem here is a logical one, not an empirical one. The newsworthy thing in this story is not that the machine, after thirty years of trying and millions of dollars, finally manages to win more games than the grand chess master. What is newsworthy is that people still think and write as if machines are or will be capable of cognitive judgment, which is based on grasping wholes *prior* to being able to analyze parts, rather than on mere exposure to ever more data. The issue is not whether computers have "consciousness," it is whether they can formulate expert judgments without being specifically programmed to do so.

Here is how another international chess master expressed the nature of the difficulty involved:

> The disadvantage of computers is that they are mechanical and therefore must make material judgments. A computer can count points, weaknesses, development and other things, but it still must make its judgments on some sort of formula. A human has intuition and can evaluate the initiative and structural aspects of the game more accurately. (Tal Shaked in the *Arizona Daily Star*, Feb. 20, 1996)

He goes on to point out that in game 6 of the first match, Deep Blue made very bad positional decisions, making moves that good human players consistently avoid. "The computer played without a plan, while Kasparov methodically improved his position. The final position, in which Deep Blue resigned, is a total disaster that any human would avoid at all costs."

Kasparov actually began one game by inverting a traditional opening move, a ploy which had no strategic significance. But Deep Blue treated this move like any other, running through the full gamut of options as if all possibilities counted equally. By contrast, any human player, even one without master standing, would have ascertained immediately that Kasparov's move was merely a "cosmetic" maneuver and would have ignored it altogether. Here we can see that quantitative force is no substitute for qualitative discernment, that rote performance, no matter how speedy, is not the same thing as cognitive judgment.

As the saying has it, it does not take a rocket scientist to see the relevance of Polanyi's interpretation of our cognitive powers to this event and discussion. His overall theme, that we always know more than we can tell, provides a fresh angle for comprehending the reasons why computers cannot, and will not, play chess in the same way as human chess masters. Since all knowing is grounded in or tethered to tacit knowing, it follows both that the chess master will be unable to specify the principles upon which he or she makes judgments and that, therefore, those who program computers will be unable to structure them in a manner that parallels the mind of the master player. These judgments are not and cannot be made to be the result of explicit knowledge, and thus they cannot be duplicated or anticipated. This is a *logical* "cannot," not an empirical one, since these judgments are inaccessible.

Polanyi's detailed analysis of the dynamics of tacit knowing, in terms of the interaction between subsidiary awareness and embodied and imaginative indwelling, which in turn yield integrative acts and a grasp of meaningful wholes, goes a long way toward explaining the difference between chess-playing machines and human players. In the final analysis, the matrix out of which tacit knowing emerges remains a profound mystery. The only real clue we have to this mystery is that *bodily* capacities and activities are crucial to it, that cognition is as much a function of embodiment as it is a function of mental processes. Moreover, since computers do not and cannot participate in bodily interaction, they are and will be unable to engage in cognitive activity.

It would seem that human chess players so immerse themselves in the innumerable particulars making up the activity of playing chess, particulars of which they are but subsidiarily aware, that they are able to attend from and through them to the meaningful wholes of which they are the part. The resulting integrations are formed tacitly and serve as the basis or framework for subsequent explicit cognitive judgments. Since a computer has no such subsidiary input, it must base all of its conclusions on explicit programming from the outset. Thus, its so-called knowledge is really parasitic, being borrowed from the articulated reasoning of human beings.

This concluding illustration of the richness and applicability of Polanyi's epistemological insights would seem to be especially appropriate with respect to the larger issue of postmodern philosophy. For there is perhaps no more widely accepted image of modernity than the computer. It some ways the main force behind much of the work in artificial intelligence is precisely the desire to understand human cognition as an analog of electronic devices. Clearly, Polanyi's notion of tacit knowledge takes us past such erroneous endeavors without falling into the opposite error of deconstructionism.

BIBLIOGRAPHY

Apczynski, J. V. *Doers of the Word.* Missoula, Mont.: Scholar's Press, 1977.

Bloom, P. (ed.) *Language Acquisition.* Cambridge, Mass.: MIT Press 1994.

Camus, A. *The Rebel.* New York: Random House, 1956.

Chisholm, R. *Theory of Knowledge.* Englewood Cliffs, N.J.: Prentice-Hall, 1976.

de Grazia, A. *The Velikovsky Affair.* New Hyde Park, N.Y.: University Books, 1966.

Derrida, J. "Deconstruction and the Other." In *Dialogues with Contemporary Continental Thinkers,* edited by R. Kearney. Manchester, England: Manchester University Press, 1984.

———. *Writing and Difference.* Chicago: University of Chicago Press, 1978.

Dewey, J. *Experience and Education.* New York: Macmillan, 1975.

Dreyfus, H. *What Computers Can't Do.* New York: Harper and Ros, 1979.

Foucault, M. *Discourse on Language.* New York: Harper and Row 1976.

———. *Language, Counter-Memory, Practice.* Edited by D. F. Bouchard. Ithaca, N.Y.: Cornell University Press, 1977.

———. *Power/Knowledge.* New York: Pantheon Books, 1980.

Gelwick, R. *The Way of Discovery.* Oxford University Press, 1977.

Gill, J. H. *If a Chimpazee Could Talk.* Tucson: University of Arizona Press, 1997.

———. *Learning to Learn.* Humanities Press, 1993.

———. *Mediated Transcendence.* Macon, Ga.: Mercer University Press, 1989.

James, William. *Pragmatism.* New York: Longmans and Green, 1925.

Kane, J. *Beyond Empiricism: Michael Polanyi Reconsidered.* The Hague: Peter Lang, 1984.

Kant, I. *Critique of Pure Reason.* New York: St. Martin's Press, 1929.

Kearney, R. (ed.). *Dialogues with Contemporary Continental Thinkers.* Manchester, Eng.: Manchester University Press, 1984.

Langford, T., and Poteat, William (eds.). *Intellect and Hope.* Durham, N.C.: Duke University Press, 1968.

Lyotard, F. *Libidinal Economy.* Bloomington: Indiana University Press, 1993.

———. *Peregriuations: Law, Form, Event.* Columbia University Press, 1988.

Merleau-Ponty, M. *Phenomenology of Perception.* Humanities Press, 1961.

———. *Signs.* Evanston, Ill.: Northwestern University Press, 1964.

Pazant, Geoffrey. "Subsidiary Musical Awareness," unpublished manuscript.

Pinker, S. *The Language Instinct.* New York: Harper Collins, 1994.

Plantinga, A. "Is Belief in God Rational?" In *Rationality and Relgious Belief,* edited by C. F. Delaney. Notre Dame, Ind.: University of Notre Dame Press, 1979.

Polanyi, M. *Knowing and Being.* Edited by Marjorie Grene. Chicago: University of Chicago Press, 1969.

———. *The Logic of Liberty.* Chicago: University of Chicago Press, 1951.

———. *Meaning,* with Harry Prosch. Chicago: University of Chicago Press, 1975.

———. *Personal Knowledge.* New York: Harper and Row, 1964.

———. *Science, Faith, and Society.* Chicago: University of Chicago Press, 1964.

———. *Society, Economics, and Philosophy: Selected Papers.* Edited by R. T. Allen. New Brunswick, N.J.: Transaction Publishers, 1997.

———. *The Study of Man.* Chicago: University of Chicago Press, 1959.

———. *The Tacit Dimension.* Garden City, N.Y.: Doubleday, 1966.

Popper, K. "Epistemology without a Knowing Subject." Reprinted in *Philosophy Today* 2. Edited by J. H. Gill. New York: Macmillan, 1970.

Prosch, H. *Michael Polanyi: A Critical Exposition.* Albany: State University of New York Press, 1986.

Rogers, C. *Freedom to Learn for the Eighties.* Columbus, Oh.: Charles Merrill, 1983.

Sanders, A. *Michael Polanyi's Post-Critical Epistemology.* Amsterdam: Rodopi, 1988.

Scott, D. *Everyman Revived.* London: Book Guild Limited, 1985.

Skinner, B. F. *The Technology of Teaching.* Englewood Cliffs, N.J.: Prentice-Hall, 1968.

———. *Beyond Freedom and Dignity,* New York: Harper, 1971.

Soskice, J. M. *Metaphor and Religious Language.* Oxford: Clarendon Press, 1985.

Whitehead, A. N. *The Aims of Education.* New York: Macmillan, 1929.

Winch, P. *The Idea of a Social Science.* London: Routledge and Keegan Paul, 1958.

Wittgenstein, L. *On Certainty.* Oxford: Blackwell, 1969.

———. *Philosophical Investigations.* New York: Macmillan 1953.

———. *Tractatus Logico-Philosophicus.* London: Routledge and Keegan Paul, 1961.

NOTE ON SUPPORTING CENTER

This series is published under the auspices of the Center for Process Studies, a research organization affiliated with the Claremont School of Theology and Claremont Graduate University. It was founded in 1973 by John B. Cobb, Jr., Founding Director, and David Ray Griffin, Executive Director; Mary Elizabeth Moore and Marjorie Suchocki are now also Co-Directors. It encourages research and reflection on the process philosophy of Alfred North Whitehead, Charles Hartshorne, and related thinkers, and on the application and testing of this viewpoint in all areas of thought and practice. The center sponsors conferences, welcomes visiting scholars to use its library, and publishes a scholarly journal, *Process Studies,* and a newsletter, *Process Perspectives.* Located at 1325 North College, Claremont, California 91711, it gratefully accepts (tax-deductible) contributions to support its work.

Index